THINGS THAT
MUST NOT BE
FORGOTTEN

憶童年

THINGS THAT MUST NOT BE FORGOTTEN

A Childhood in Wartime China

MICHAEL DAVID KWAN

First published in Canada in 2000
by Macfarlane Walter & Ross

First published in the United States in 2001
by Soho Press, Inc.
853 Broadway
New York, NY 10003

Library of Congress Cataloging-in-Publication Data

Kwan, Michael David, 1934–
Things that must not be forgotten : a childhood in wartime China /
Michael David Kwan.
p. cm.
Originally published: Toronto : Macfarlane Walter & Ross, 2000.
ISBN 1-56947-248-3 (alk. paper)
1. Kwan, Michael David, 1934—Childhood and youth.
2. China—History—1937–1945—Biography.
3. Sino-Japanese Conflict, 1937–1945—China—Beijing.
I. Title: Page facing t.p.: Yi tong nian. II. Title.

DS777.5195.K9 A3 2001   00-066193

Calligraphy by Michael David Kwan
Book design by Gordon Robertson

10 9 8 7 6 5 4 3 2 1

This book is for those who went before me, and those who will come afterward. It is also for Julian, who encouraged me to write it but did not live to see it in print.

I am indebted to my agent, Robert Mackwood, for his unwavering confidence in my work, and to my editor, Gary Ross, for his perceptive advice.

Contents

前言

Introduction

THIS IS A BOOK OF MEMORIES.
China from the mid-1930s to the late 1940s was a tangle of contradictions. The joy and pain of those years shaped me into what I am. Some people and events from my early life remain as vibrant as yesterday, while the mind, for unfathomable reasons of its own, hides others behind a protective scrim, keeping them tantalizingly out of reach.

My father's several careers, spanning the years I've written about, kept him in the public eye. But he was also an extremely private man, particularly reticent about exactly what he did during those troubled times. Afterwards he never volunteered information. Though he would answer precisely when asked to expand on a particular incident I remembered from my childhood, it was always with unmistakable reluctance. Only towards the end of his life, with a little prodding, did he talk about the past less unwillingly.

I once asked him whether he would write a memoir. His answer was a resounding no. A man is born, strives to lead a decent, useful life, and dies. He saw nothing remarkable about that and preferred to leave the way he is remembered to those who knew him. He cast an uncommon ambiance around my early years, when charm and elegance often existed a mere breath away from squalor and despair.

Flashes of real beauty and grace sometimes came from unlikely sources, while pain and humiliation were inflicted by those from whom one could reasonably expect better. Therein lies my tale.

Shortly after my father died, Mother sent me a box of Father's papers. As they were all in Chinese, which she did not read, she asked me to examine and dispose of them as I saw fit. Among other things I found the journal he had written between the autumn of 1945 and early 1946, a testament of his efforts on behalf of his country in time of war. The journal furnished background material for this book. It also stirred the embers of memory.

When I returned to China in 1987, after four decades' absence, it was strangely as though I'd never left. My late cousin Julian, who had been Father's confidant and whom I had not seen since childhood, became my mentor. He and his wife, Rebecca, helped fill some of the gaps when memory or understanding failed in my search for roots. They also helped interpret events that a child observed but did not grasp.

This is a story I feel compelled to tell, and I have approached it with as much care, respect, understanding, and objectivity as I can muster. The people, places, and events are as I saw them. I apologize to those whom my words might offend.

A Note About Place Names

The events recounted in this book took place mainly in Beijing and Qingdao. In recent years the Giles-Wade system of romanizing Chinese names has been replaced by the current, more accurate-sounding pin-yin. I have used this latter system. Beijing used to be romanized as Peking and is still referred to as Peking in many parts of Europe. During my early childhood, the city was renamed Peiping for a time. I refer to it as Beijing throughout. In the same way, Tienjin was Tiantsin, Beidaihe was Peitaho, Qingdao was Tsingtao. Other Chinese cities have acquired new names: Mukden is now Shenyang, Hankow is Wuhan, Canton is Guanzhou. I have settled on the old romanization for Nanking and Chungking, because these spellings are still used in modern references and are more recognizable.

— M. D. K., Vancouver, January 2000

第 一 章

M A R I A N N E

L IFE WAS NEW THEN. Day was gold and green. Night was black and terrifying. Warmth was a narrow brown face, black sombre eyes, a generous mouth that crooned or scolded, and full round breasts. Shu Ma, my nanny.

Another face loomed large, round, and jolly under a shiny bald dome. Zhang was major-domo in my father's house. No matter how busy he was, Zhang always made time for me, if only for a moment, jabbering in a silly voice to make me laugh. His big calloused hands were surprisingly gentle when he picked me up. I loved to rub his polished head, tweak his nose, wring those jug-handle ears. I could wind Zhang round my little finger, but when the laugh lines smoothed out and his eyes became two black buttons, I knew my wiles would not work. Time to mind my p's and q's.

We lived in a large, three-storey house built in the nineteenth-century-German style. Cold draughts wandered the hallways, shadows crouched menacingly in corners. Disembodied voices and footsteps floated up and down the stairs. It was a spacious, melancholy place that came alive from time to time and buzzed like a hornet's nest. The excitement affected everyone. Footsteps quickened. Usually subdued voices became shrill. At such times Zhang's shiny dome would be seen only briefly. He would gaze down at me from a great height, exchange a few hurried words with Shu Ma, and then disappear, ignoring my demands to be carried. My parents were entertaining.

The top floor of the house was my domain now that my older half-brothers, Albert and Tim, were away at school. Across the hall from my bedroom was a room full of toys. Electric train tracks ran all the way around it, complete with switching signals, water towers, stations, and tunnels. But my favourite toy was a rocking horse with a real mane and tail, more beautiful than any horse that ladies and gentlemen rode on the bridle paths in the park. Hour after hour I sat astride it, rocking, rocking. The rocking horse carried me through the air, far from the four walls that contained me. My squeals of delight would cause Shu Ma to wag a finger.

"Hush! They will hear!"

"They" were my parents, whom I seldom saw. Once in a while I was taken down the stairs to my father. He was the sort of man whose presence is felt even in a crowded room, always impeccably dressed and groomed, always preoccupied. To this day, the smell of a fine cigar evokes memories of my father, for he was seldom without one. Sometimes he gingerly dandled me on his knee, careful not to spoil the perfect crease of his trousers, holding me at arm's length in case my diapers leaked. When he was in a particularly good mood, he took out the pocket watch he wore on a gold chain, holding it close to my ear and making it chime. My father was forty-five when I was born, and I think I was as much a surprise to him as he was to me. Neither of us relished our visits. Yet when they were over, I felt an indescribable loss and buried my head in Shu Ma's ample bosom until she rocked and crooned the pain away.

I was not allowed to venture downstairs alone. Once, when I was two, I crawled down backwards, a step at a time. The floor below mine had many rooms. All the doors were shut except one. It was a gleaming white room. All the furniture, the carpets, and the walls were white. A lady dressed in white was seated on the bed, dabbing at her toenails with a tiny brush, making them the same vibrant red as her mouth and fingernails. She looked at me without interest or surprise. I was fascinated by what she was doing and crept closer to watch. She did not seem to mind. As she bent over to blow on the gleaming nails, I did too. She laughed and extended a languid foot for me, and I blew on her wet nails. She reached over to a tiny bowl of coloured squares on the bedside table and popped one in her mouth. When she picked up her tiny brush again to do the other foot, I too grabbed a square and popped it in my mouth. She whirled on me, shrieking, "Spit it out! Spit it out!" She seized me by the shoulders and shook me. "If you swallow it, you'll die!" She struck me hard across the face. My mouth flew open and the little square, now a sticky lump, dropped onto the carpet.

My screams brought Shu Ma, who swept me up in her arms. An angry tirade followed us up the stairs: "Why did you let the brat come down here?" I have hated chewing gum ever since.

Marianne's terrible joys and sudden rages frightened me. Her face has always been a blur, like a faded photograph, except for the vivid red mouth. She was the daughter of a Swiss railway engineer. My maternal grandfather had been one of the "foreign experts" that flooded China between the two world wars. Disillusioned with Europe, lured by tales of easy fortunes to be made, André Lavelle moved his wife and little girl to China. He soon found himself marooned in the limbo between worlds that was the northeastern city of Harbin.

Harbin is a curious blend of east and west. The Russians settled there in large numbers in the late 1890s, when negotiations were begun to push a rail line through it to Vladivostok. The settlers attempted to create a city reminiscent of St. Petersburg. Wide boulevards lined with shade trees flow into cobbled squares and circuses dominated by statues and fountains. Today monolithic steel and glass towers dwarf the spires and onion-shaped domes that Marianne knew when she was growing up. The mansions of the rich and powerful have been turned into offices of this or that ministry. Some have been restored, but most are tumbled down. Today the city is trapped in a time warp where past and present have been carelessly fused. Dusty chandeliers glimpsed through tall French windows, reminders of a gracious past, hang behind plucked chickens left on the sill.

Marianne walked those streets, peered through those windows. She probably lived in one of the drab granite apartment buildings that line the street facing the station square. These ugly buildings with their curious blend of *fin de siècle* European architecture and Chinoiserie reflect all the dashed hopes of their inhabitants. Marianne aspired to the tantalizing world she glimpsed through the windows of the great houses, a world beyond her reach.

My father was in his forties and she barely twenty when they married. He was administrator of one of China's major railways, the Bei-Ning, linking Beijing with Liaoning province in the northeast, and he led the Chinese delegation to the International Railway Conference of the League of Nations in Paris. He had been around the world twice; was fluent in a dozen languages; hobnobbed with world leaders, statesmen, scientists, artists, writers, and musicians. He was also a friend of the underprivileged.

Marianne moved into what she thought would be a dream world. Instead she found herself all at sea. She was ill-equipped to manage a household that included two sons from a previous marriage, teenagers not much younger than herself, plus a staff of cooks and maids, chauffeurs and gardeners. Nor did she fit in with the xenophobic Chinese society or the caste-bound expatriate community. In time, even the giddy round of parties, receptions, and balls that was my father's hectic social life came to pall. It was a lonely life, for my father's work frequently took him far from home.

By 1934, the year I was born, China was torn by internal strife and Japanese occupation. In 1928, the Kuomintang Central Government of Chiang Kai-shek had moved its capital from Beijing south to Nanking. It could not have done otherwise, for the rest of the country was in the hands of either the party's splinter groups or local militarists who remained loyal to the central government as long as their personal interests were not affected. Communism was the other burgeoning force to be reckoned with. China was in a state of latent civil war, with hostilities breaking out from time to time. When Japan, whose expansionist schemes for eastern Asia had long been known, attacked Muckden in the resource-rich Liaoning province, Chiang Kai-shek's forces did not resist. Nor did he declare war on Japan. Chiang preferred to complain to the League of Nations in Geneva. Japan quickly occupied the whole of the northeast. In 1932 it created Manchukuo, a puppet kingdom, and placed Pu Yi, China's last emperor, on its throne. Japanese influence began spreading insidiously across northern China like ink on a blotter.

The stout granite walls of the legation quarter of Beijing, where we lived, enclosed an oasis of safety. For foreigners and the few privileged Chinese who lived there, China's sporadic wars and civil unrest were unpleasant rumours to be ignored. Marianne's existence in this artificial environment was further complicated by her unexpected pregnancy. She threw herself down a flight of stairs trying to miscarry, but I was stubborn even then.

A grandfather clock stood in an alcove at the foot of the main stairs. Its musical chimes could be heard throughout the house. Once a month a Swiss clockmaker came from his shop to clean and wind it. One day he sent his young nephew in his place. Marianne started a harmless flirtation which developed into a love affair. When my father found out, he had the young man fired. That made the lovers desperate. The next time my father left Beijing on business, Marianne gathered up her jewels and all the money she could lay her hands on and ran off to Shanghai. My father divorced her.

For a time Marianne and her lover were happy. When the money and jewels were gone, love soured. Her lover could not find a job, as no one would employ a man who had run off with a prominent official's wife. Marianne wrote piteous letters to my father, begging for help, which went unanswered. As a last resort she threatened to kidnap me. My father bought a huge Great Dane called Rex, who became my companion day and night.

Rex was my only playmate. We must have been a curious sight on our daily excursions to the park. Shu Ma, with my wrist firmly clasped in her big strong hand, took the lead. Zhang followed with Rex's leash in one hand and a bucket in the other, for the dog consumed prodigious amounts of water, especially in warm weather. Sometimes I climbed on Rex's back and rode him, my feet barely touching the ground. Rex grumbled, but he was good-natured and tolerated his little rider.

Children played in an open area at the centre of the park where a statue of Joan of Arc stood, put there by the French. Rex and I romped on the grass, chasing each other and wrestling, always under the watchful eye of the two servants. Other children stayed away, put off by the huge dog.

One cold, blustery winter's day, when the park was almost deserted, we found a woman sitting alone on a bench by the statue. Zhang hurried towards her. Shu Ma clutched me, muttering under her breath. Zhang and the woman spoke in low voices. Finally they both approached. The woman squatted down so our eyes were level. Her face was muffled by a white veil, and the collar of her coat was turned up against the wind. All I could make out was a bright red mouth and the scent of lilacs.

"Do you remember Mummy?"

I shook my head. She brushed aside the fringe of hair that fell into my eyes.

"Will you give Mummy a kiss?"

I shook my head again. When she tried to take me in her arms, I backed away, shrieking for Shu Ma.

"I'll buy you a present," she said. "Anything you like!"

A fire engine roared by, bells clanging. I pointed. "I want that!"

She looked dismayed. "I'll get you one. Tomorrow. Please, can I have my kiss?"

I shook my head. The two servants drew me away. That is the last memory I have of my mother. She didn't come back to the park again, nor did I get a toy fire engine, but the elusive scent of lilacs has never left me.

2

第二章

R E S I S T A N C E

MARIANNE'S DEPARTURE did not leave a void in my life, for I hardly knew her. But she took with her my father's pride, and he retaliated by removing all traces of her from his life. He went away for an extended period, leaving the house – and me – in the care of Zhang and Shu Ma.

Plasterers and painters transformed the place, especially the second floor where my parents had lived. Marianne's white rooms were redone in warm tones of soft brown and beige. The gold-trimmed white furniture she loved was replaced by red wood pieces with stark straight lines. The innumerable photographs of her, and an oil portrait that had been commissioned by my father, were removed. The grandfather clock disappeared. Marianne had a passion for flowers; the house had once been a riot of lilies and roses and ornate scented bouquets in huge crystal vases. Now there were flowers only on the main floor, and only when guests were expected. In weeks, a house once plush and sumptuous had become spartan, almost severe. Not a hint of Marianne remained, and nobody ever spoke her name.

With Marianne gone and my father away, I was suddenly free to roam. His study fascinated me. A huge mahogany desk caught the light streaming through French windows. Deep leather armchairs and a coffee table were arranged around a wood-burning fireplace, complementing walls lined floor to ceiling with books in a dozen languages which my father read voraciously. On one end of a long mahogany table with curved legs and huge clawed feet Zhang arranged newspapers and magazines. Mail went on the other end. Framed photographs of statesmen, artists, writers, and celebrities crowded the space between. There were also silver-framed pictures of the family. My paternal grandfather, from whom all of us inherited the inverted V-shaped eyebrows, resplendent in Qing dynasty court regalia. His equally regal wife, my father's mother, seated in her high-backed chair, her features carefully composed. My elder half-brother, fair-skinned, sad-eyed Albert, looking studious in his school blazer. My other half-brother, Timothy, darker-skinned, craggy-faced, belligerent in his boxing shorts and gloves. And me, in Shu Ma's protective arms, gazing startled at the world.

I was precocious, silent but inquiring. Toys never lasted long. I dismantled them to see how they worked but could not put them together again. I pulled wings off flies out of curiosity, poked pins into caterpillars, marvelling at the green slime that oozed out instead of red blood. I seldom spoke, but when I did I spoke clearly and could switch from Chinese to English without effort, though my Chinese vocabulary was broader. I grew used to having my own way. I had no playmates, nor do I remember craving any. I watched and listened.

I liked the big house in the Legation Quarter better after its transformation, though it certainly held no charm for my father. Perhaps my mop of light brown hair — which did not darken to black until my teens — reminded him too much of Marianne. In any case, he had other pressing reasons for his long absences.

Since the 1890s, forward-looking Chinese, including some of the nobility such as my grandfather, had advocated the building of railways. They saw this infrastructure as an integral part of modernization, arguing that, aside from expediting communication and benefiting commerce, railways would bind a huge and unwieldy country into a nation. To secure the necessary funds, the Chinese signed treaties giving foreign lenders rights of way through vast tracts of land. Once built, the railways were operated jointly by the Chinese and their foreign partners.

In the 1930s there were effectively two governments in China, not counting provincial governments under the control of local militarists. The urban areas, with a mercantile middle class, took their cues from Chiang Kai-shek and the Kuomintang. The country's huge rural population, on the other hand, turned increasingly to Mao Zedong and the Communists, who were carrying out radical land reforms. Mao's great strengths were his understanding of the peasantry and his ability to galvanize it into an effective guerrilla force. The railway was the lifeline of both these factions, and of the Japanese. Troops and supplies, as well as communication and commerce, used the same lines, albeit on different days and in different parts of the country. Conditions were chaotic.

After 1937, most of China's major ports and railway lines were in Japanese hands, forcing Chiang to move his capital a second time, from Nanking to Chungking in the mountain fastness of Sichuan. However, the Japanese were finding it difficult to police the area they controlled. In the long run, sporadic guerrilla attacks, which the Japanese compared to mosquito bites, became a serious drain on morale and material.

Chiang's nationalist government depended on foreign loans to stay afloat, but aid from Britain was drying up as war with Germany changed from a possibility to an inevitability. America, meanwhile, though uneasy about Japanese expansionism in Asia, adopted a wait-and-see attitude where China was concerned.

Countries with high stakes in China accepted the Kuomintang as the legitimate government. In spite of her myriad problems, China was a huge untapped market for their products. The trick was to keep Japan from gobbling up these foreign interests as she swallowed China. Thus, Germany surreptitiously fed Chiang military intelligence to help keep Japan at bay. He was more interested in destroying Mao's burgeoning Communists than in fighting the Japanese.

The administrator of the railway was a Kuomintang appointee, seconded by its foreign partners. My father, as administrator first of the Beijing-Liaoning line, and later of the Tienjin-Pukao line as well, walked a tightrope of diplomacy. Keeping the trains running required most of his time and all of his sagacity.

It was during one of my father's absences that my Swiss grandmother, whom I had seen only in photographs, arrived unannounced. She was even larger than her pictures had led me to believe. She had masses of straw-coloured hair caught in a knot on the nape of her neck, ruddy cheeks bulging with fat, beady blue eyes, and a pinched red mouth like a doll's.

I was small for my age, sickly, prone to colds. Her big square hands were quick to pinch and prod. She pulled off my clothes and examined me fore and aft. Then she forced open my mouth to count my teeth. I bit her. She boxed my ears.

Gran'mère spoke French. Though our servants managed pidgin English, only Zhang, whom Father had lured away from the French Embassy, could communicate with her. Gran'mère's voice boomed through the house. She was determined to fatten me up and to make me speak French. Zhang's bald pate glowed with fury. He had been left in charge of his master's house and son and no one was going to usurp his authority.

Finally my father returned. He was happy to see me, and brought armloads of gifts, but Gran'mère's presence dampened his spirits. Meals were conducted in silence, or in strained politeness. Intense conversations were abandoned mid-sentence when I appeared. Behind the closed doors of the study, they shrieked at each other in French. I was both frightened and exhilarated, for I guessed they were arguing about me. Zhang stood outside with his ear to the jamb while Shu Ma and I cowered in the shadows.

"She wants to take the boy," Zhang translated, "but the master won't . . ."

"Not now!" Shu Ma hissed, clutching me tighter to her bosom.

One day not long afterwards Gran'mère donned her little black hat with a bit of veil in front and a bunch of gaudy flowers at the back. She adjusted the dead animal that European women wore around their necks in the 1930s and left with more baggage than she had come with. She did not say goodbye. From my third-floor window, I watched her being driven off in my father's black Rolls-Royce. Shu Ma was grinning for the first time in weeks.

Whenever my father was home, the house quickly filled with guests. He could not bear to be alone. I was not quite four years old when he decided it was time to introduce me to society. I was driven to a barber shop, where the unruly mop of hair that fell across my forehead and stuck out over my ears was cut like an adult's, complete with a part on one side. Then we went to a tailor. Children those days wore tailored shorts with long knee-high stockings till they were at least six. Then they graduated to long pants. My father accelerated the process. I was measured for a proper suit in navy blue serge. The last stop was the shoemaker's, where my father ordered me a pair of black oxfords like his own.

Under my father's careful tutelage, I was groomed to enter society. He showed me how to enter and leave a room, unhurriedly, head held high, shoulders squared, back straight. He taught me how to greet his guests, when to shake hands and when to bow and when to combine the two, modifying the bow to a slight inclination of the head. He taught me to answer the questions I would be asked. He turned it into a game that was challenging but fun.

He was giving a party. Temporary staff were added to serve the guests. Zhang bustled from room to room in his new white gown. Wonderful aromas wafted up to the third floor through the shaft of the dumb waiter from the kitchen, along with much clatter.

I brimmed with excitement all afternoon. By the time guests started arriving it was all Shu Ma could do to keep me from galloping down the stairs prematurely. Finally, Zhang came for me. He straightened my tie and gave the toes of my black shoes a quick swipe. He and I both knew the true measure of a gentleman was his shoes. They must be spotlessly shined, and the heels must not be worn.

We went slowly down the stairs. Through the closed doors of the living room came a hubbub of voices. Across the hall, the servants were preparing to serve dinner. Beyond the huge rectangular room where there would be dancing later, the musicians were tuning their instruments. As Zhang flung open the door, laughter and voices spilled into the hallway. I stood stock-still, as rehearsed. My father disengaged himself and came to greet me. We bowed to one another, and I was immensely proud as we threaded our way through the throng.

My father seemed to know the whole world – doctors, lawyers, captains of industry, diplomats from distant lands, artists, and writers. There were eccentric characters such as the Chinese actor whose frightening glass eye kept falling out of the socket, and a silver-maned poet who always spoke in rhyme.

I met George and Hester Findlay-Wu at one of my father's parties. Although I called them aunt and uncle, we were not related. The Findlay-Wus and my father were great friends. Uncle George was "Anglo-Chinese," his father scion of a wealthy Scottish family of distillers, his mother the daughter of a Chinese merchant. Uncle George's parents never wed. Though the father eventually returned to Scotland and married, he provided handsomely for his Chinese family. Uncle George and my father became close at Cambridge.

The Findlay-Wus lived in the British Concession of Tienjin, the nearest port city to Beijing, where Uncle George had business interests. They came up to Beijing frequently. My father looked forward to their visits, for they brought laughter into the house. In middle age, Uncle George was tall, elegant, and strikingly handsome, with eyes like a cat's that changed colour according to the light. Hester was small, dark-haired, neither pretty nor plain, and exuded a serenity and warmth that sets apart Englishwomen of a certain class. She came from a family that included as many daughters as a Jane Austen novel. A gentle soul, Hester took an immediate liking to me. The feeling was eagerly reciprocated.

At about this time, the invading Japanese clashed with the poorly equipped Chinese army at a place near Beijing called Lugoqiao, also known as Marco Polo Bridge. For the Chinese, the struggle was heroic but futile. The Japanese seized the advantage to swarm through north and central China. The Lugoqiao incident finally united the contentious Chinese factions. Chiang and Mao became unlikely allies in the struggle to rid their country of Japanese domination. Resistance against the invaders went underground.

I never understood exactly how my father became involved in the resistance, but I got the impression it had something to do with Uncle George. During the Findlay-Wus' visits, Chinese men with broad-brimmed hats pulled low over their eyes crept into the house and huddled with Uncle George and my father for hours. Zhang carried trays of sandwiches and drinks into the study, then stood outside the door, keeping everyone away. Especially me.

"Your father is busy," he explained. "Children are not supposed to interrupt when grown-ups have work to do."

Auntie Hester echoed these sentiments, gently but firmly leading me upstairs whenever I sought to satisfy my curiosity. She was visibly relieved when we heard the study door open upon a murmur of voices, followed by footsteps down the hall.

After one such evening I awoke to find only a single place set for breakfast. My father had gone off during the night.

"Did he go away with those men?" I asked Zhang.

"What men?"

"With the hats."

"I haven't seen any men with hats," Zhang said, placing a piping hot bowl of porridge before me, to which Shu Ma had added a generous amount of milk and a tiny spoonful of sugar.

"They were in the study!" I cried, fiddling with my food. I hated porridge.

The look in Zhang's eyes could have stopped a truck.

"Well, I saw them," I faltered.

"There was nobody in the study," Zhang said in a low voice. Before I could protest again he added, "But your father left a present." He grinned, and I hurried through my porridge. I knew the present would not be forthcoming until I finished every mouthful. Such was our little game, for both Zhang and I knew I had not dreamed the men in the broad-brimmed hats.

When I was four, my father returned from an extended absence dreadfully ill. Zhang and Lao Zhao, the chauffeur, carried him straight to his room. I clamoured to see him, anxious for the gifts he had surely brought me. But there were no presents this time.

I started to cry. Zhang took my head between his hands, and his black button eyes stopped my tears. "Your father is very ill," he said seriously. "He will need lots of rest, and you can help him get better by being good."

My world shrank again to the top floor of the house. Zhang said, "There will be no running up and down the stairs, or talking and laughing in the corridors." Two young women in starched white uniforms and little caps with a red cross in front were installed in a guest room. The entire second floor reeked of disinfectant. The nurses tried to hide from me the bloody bandages they carried out of the sickroom. Zhang became haggard. The servants, ordinarily happy and garrulous, went about their business in silence. Even Shu Ma developed dark bags under her eyes.

In the park one day, I overheard Shu Ma say to another nanny, "They're doing what they can, but he should be in hospital." She held up her thumb and forefinger. I had seen children making that same sign, playing. One child would point at another, shouting "Bang, bang, bang!" and the other child would flop on the ground. I did not understand what they were doing, but it frightened me.

Not long afterwards, Auntie Hester arrived alone and went straight to the sickroom. I waited impatiently on the landing. When she finally emerged, looking ashen, I flew into her arms before she was halfway up the stairs. She clutched me to her breast. I could tell she had been crying. I began to cry too without knowing why. She laid a finger against my lips and led me up the stairs.

She talked to Shu Ma softly, in pidgin English. My nanny understood more than she could say, nodding solemnly. The two women packed my things, Auntie Hester holding up clothes against my body to see which I had outgrown.

"We're going on a train," she explained cheerfully. "You're coming to live in my house for a while."

"And my toys?" I asked doubtfully. I loved Auntie Hester, but children have priorities.

Having three of her own, Auntie Hester knew how to talk to children. She said I could take a few, but the rocking horse had to stay because it wasn't allowed on trains.

"Shu Ma?"

"Shu Ma will come with us. Zhang will stay to look after your father."

"Rex?"

"Rex will stay to help Zhang."

Before we left, I was taken to my father's room to say goodbye. A young woman in a stiff white dress opened the door just a crack. All I could see was a mound of bedclothes. I waved, and the young woman quietly shut the door. Auntie Hester, teary-eyed, ushered me down the stairs.

We were going on an adventure. I couldn't wait to board the train for Tienjin.

3

第三章

HALF-CASTE

T HE FINDLAY-WUS lived in a Tudor-style house in Tienjin. The house was surrounded by a high wall with shards of broken glass embedded in the top to discourage intruders. A wrought-iron gate opened onto a scrap of lawn bordered by flower beds, a riot of colour. The backyard was covered with flagstones. On one side were the servants' quarters and on the other a garage that housed the family Studebaker. The house was not as big as my father's. The overstuffed furniture and clutter of ugly bric-a-brac made the rooms seem smaller than they were. I felt suddenly in danger of smothering.

My room was the front part of the attic; its windows looked out on the garden and the street beyond and its side walls angled up to the centre of the ceiling. It felt bigger than the rooms downstairs because it was sparsely furnished, containing a narrow bed, a chest of drawers, and a large cupboard for clothes and toys. Shu Ma was relegated to the servants' quarters, and there was no night light.

The Findlay-Wus had two daughters and a son, all in their early twenties. Irene, the oldest, with big, luminous eyes and long curved lashes set in a heart-shaped face, modelled herself after the actress Loretta Young, whose autographed picture, in a silver frame, stood on her dresser. Irene was vain but good hearted. Eddy, the son, was the only one in the family who spoke Chinese without a foreign accent. He was tall, big boned like his father, but more Chinese-looking. Auntie Hester doted on him. Barbara, the youngest, took after her mother. Bright, bubbling with energy, she was a young woman in a hurry.

Also part of the household was Auntie Hester's younger sister, Ellen. The siblings could not have been more unalike. Ellen, with reddish hair and hazel eyes, was grave and kind but shy. She read copiously, played the piano, and loved animals. She was not much older than her nieces. On one of the family's trips "home," Hester had invited Ellen to China mainly to help with three unruly children on the long voyage back. Ellen became mired in her sister's life and had been in China ever since.

All three children worked for their father. For the two daughters it was just as well, for there were few things young women from respectable families were permitted to do in the 1930s. It was Ellen, surprisingly, who had broken away from the family business, striking out on her own to work as a stenographer in a law firm. Although all four younger people fended for themselves, they lived at home. Moving out was simply not done, particularly if you were a young, unmarried lady.

Eddy was not happy with the arrangement. Uncle George expected his son to take over the business one day, but Eddy had other plans. A state of undeclared war existed between China and Japan, and ever since the Marco Polo Bridge incident, anti-Japanese feelings had become widespread. Eddy, the happy-go-lucky daredevil, chafed to fight the invader. In the meantime he was having a good time, but not with the staid young Britons of his mother's choosing.

I was a fish out of water in this jolly, boisterous, but often contentious household. The energy that hummed through the place exhilarated but also confused me. When I tried to join in, Auntie Hester's crisp clear "Children are seen but not heard" put a damper on my fun.

I got to know my half-brothers in the house of the Findlay-Wus. Albert and Timothy were at college in Tienjin. With a flat of their own, they led a freewheeling life that must have been the envy of their "fast" young friends, as Auntie Hester called the group that clustered around Eddy. I particularly liked Tim. He was bright, energetic, and full of fun. He had no patience for book learning, preferring to do things with his hands. He fixed the toys I dismantled. He and Eddy Findlay-Wu raced about town on motorcycles without a care in the world.

Albert, by contrast, was brooding and quiet and hovered on the fringe of the group. After my father's first marriage ended, he had plunged into work and travel, leaving the two boys in the care of servants. When Albert, then in his teens, fell ill with a high fever, everyone assumed it was a bout of flu. A doctor was summoned when he became delirious, but too late. Albert had meningitis, eventually emerging from the illness completely deaf. My father sent him to the best specialists but his hearing could not be restored. He learned to lip-read in both English and Chinese. His handicap made the diplomatic career he hankered after impossible, so he studied art, intending to go into the new field of advertising. But it was not what he really wanted out of life and he grew bitter and unpredictable. A careless word or gesture set off volcanic rages. Time and again the Findlay-Wus vowed to have no further truck with him, despite their close friendship with my father. Each time Ellen served as mediator, making peace for him, until the next blow-up.

As I settled in, I became like one of the stray puppies Ellen kept bringing into the house, treated with kindness but a firm hand. I learned to bathe and to dress myself. Shu Ma supervised but was forbidden to help; surreptitiously, she tied my shoelaces. I ate with the grown-ups, sitting at the end of the table next to Auntie Hester. Shu Ma kept an eye on me. Auntie Hester considered it the over-protective fussing of a nanny who did not know her place, and the two women were soon at loggerheads. Shu Ma, however, had reason to be concerned. Large chunks of meat and potatoes disagreed with me. It took a few embarrassing emergency exits from the table to convince Auntie Hester that my nanny knew a few things about me she did not.

Gradually, I was being distanced from my beloved Shu Ma. For the first time I was alone at night. Shu Ma was told to leave my room as soon as I was tucked in. In my father's house I had always had a night light, a little gnome dozing under a glowing mushroom that I found comforting. Here it was pitch dark. One night I awoke and heard the house creak. I called for Shu Ma but she had been banished to the servants' quarters. I screamed and screamed until finally I fell asleep. Next morning I had a fever. When I whined about the dark, Auntie Hester said firmly, "Grown-ups don't sleep with the light on."

We lived a charmed life in 1938. While the Japanese overran much of north China, the Concessions under foreign protection were out of their reach. Until the late 1920s there had even been a constabulary of locals maintaining law and order, dressed in British bobby uniforms, commanded by British officers, looking for all the world like something out of a shoestring production of *The Pirates of Penzance*.

Outside the enclave the Japanese held sway. Tienjin had a bustling commercial centre lined with shops, restaurants, cafés, bars, cabarets, brothels, and grandiose art deco cinemas. A rest and recreation centre for the Japanese forces, the place teemed with off-duty soldiers bent on a good time. A good time often meant violence. Aside from public executions, which were routine, random killings also took place almost daily. Out with Auntie Hester one morning, I saw a beggar decapitated for no reason at all. The head bounced into the gutter, spraying blood, as pedestrians squealed and dodged out of the way. I recoiled in horror as the body lay on the ground, twitching. The perpetrator stood over it, laughing and jabbering. Though these things happened only a few streets away from the house, none of it really concerned us.

Auntie Hester ran an English household, permitting neither atrocities in the streets nor cultural differences within its walls to disturb its placid routine. She pretended the Chinese men in broad-brimmed hats who came to see Uncle George simply did not exist. There was not a vestige of China in the house. The language was banned. Even the servants had to speak pidgin English. I spoke Chinese with Shu Ma when no one else was within earshot. On the surface all was sweetness and light, but the tension could be felt. There were frequent, restrained quarrels, particularly between mother and son, mostly about his chumming around with young Chinese.

To this day, Chinese of mixed blood exist in limbo. They fit neither the Chinese mould nor the western. In my childhood, Eurasians were divided into categories according to their westernness. The crème de la crème were the products of a western man married to a Chinese woman. These children had western surnames, adopted western customs and beliefs, and saw themselves as being a cut or two above the natives. (Westerners, of course, did not consider them equals.) The next category were the offspring of unwed Chinese women and western men. Since they had no legal right to western surnames, they became hyphens, like George Findlay-Wu. In their eagerness to play down their Chinese side, they often adopted exaggerated western attitudes and became the worst snobs and bigots. Their stiff nineteenth-century social etiquette and prejudices, such as choosing their children's friends and marriage partners, sometimes led to devastating consequences. The lowest rung on this social ladder were the progeny of Chinese men married to western women. People of mixed blood with Chinese surnames were considered Chinese by everyone except other Chinese. Regardless of how the Eurasian saw himself, however, both sides saw him as the result of moral degeneracy and, therefore, as a lesser human being. As a child I was blissfully unaware of the differences between one human being and another. I would learn the meaning of the expression "half-caste" in all its variations soon enough.

The spring after I went to live with the Findlay-Wus, the Hai River rose drastically and the household mobilized, building foot-high brick-and-concrete thresholds onto outside doors and gates against the possibility of flooding. After several days of rain I looked out the window one morning and saw that the street was filled with swirling brown water. I flew downstairs, bursting with excitement. The family, already seated at breakfast, did not share my enthusiasm. I wanted to know what was going on. Auntie Hester shot me a look I knew only too well.

"Children are seen but not heard!"

I wolfed my food and asked to be excused. At Uncle George's nod I raced upstairs and found Shu Ma tidying my room. I went round and round, pestering her with questions. She ignored me till she was done, then drew me over to the window and, as we looked out, explained in her simple way about the flood. Shu Ma had a way of saying things that was very graphic. I could picture everything she told me, the heartbreak and devastation and sickness. "Poor people will suffer again," she sighed. Ellen had made almost the same remark at breakfast.

"Are we poor people?"

Shu Ma ruffled my hair with her big rough hand. "I am," she said.

I leaned hard against her, but there was no way to bridge the gulf between us.

The flood waters kept rising. Soon the garden was submerged, and water seeped into the basement. The furnace went out. The electricity failed. The days were bearable but the nights were dark and miserable. After dinner everybody dispersed to their rooms to huddle in bed. From my window, for hours at a time, I watched people go by in rowboats amid the bloated bodies of dead dogs, cats, even humans. The harried English doctor came and injected us against cholera and typhoid. In the city, starving people were breaking into stores, looking for food. Uncle George took down the hunting rifle hanging over the mantle in his study.

"Just in case," he said, oiling it carefully. "One must be prepared."

The three young women had stopped going to their offices. Instead they donned hip waders and white tunics with red crosses on the front and back and set off to help at soup kitchens, hospitals, wherever they were needed. Eddy quietly provided them with tiny pistols that fit into their purses.

Eventually the flood subsided, the dankness left the house, and the saturated garden was coaxed back to life. In the meantime, Eddy joined the outlawed Students' Union, a group that openly lobbied for resistance against the Japanese. In a particularly ugly exchange growing out of her son's Chinese sympathies, Auntie Hester lost her temper. "So the Japanese are killing the Chinese," she cried. "Somebody has to whip sense into them! There are too many as it is!"

Eddy, furious, stormed out of the house. He never came back.

Nobody mentioned Eddy after that. There was simply one empty place at the table. Now and then I caught a wistful look on Auntie Hester's face as she glanced at the vacant chair, but her pride kept her from raising the subject of her lost son. Later we heard he had gone to Chungking and joined the air force.

Life soon returned to its placid routine in the house on Lambeth Road, except that the shadowy Chinese men came more frequently and the dinner conversation more often centred on "home," meaning England. Chungking was sometimes mentioned, but always in a whisper. Because Eddy was there, it was not a word that Auntie Hester cared to hear.

Eddy's empty chair eventually came to be filled by another young man, Robert Wong, one of his friends. He had seen Barbara at a party and followed her home. Flowers began arriving daily. "The place is beginning to look like a funeral parlour!" quipped Uncle George. The next time Robert delivered flowers, Uncle George and Auntie Hester scrutinized him from the drawing-room window.

"Half-caste," she muttered under her breath.

That unfortunate expression sent Uncle George into a rage. To Auntie Hester's chagrin, he invited Robert to dinner, and, a few days later, Robert's parents as well. Robert's father, a professor of English literature, had been a contemporary of Uncle George and my father at Cambridge. Wong had married the daughter of an

English merchant. The young couple came back to China to oversee Mrs. Wong's family's business interests. But Wong had no head for commerce. At a time when women were expected to live in their husband's shadow, it was his big, bluff, and somewhat vulgar wife who took charge. No doubt it was also Mrs. Wong's irresistible personality that got her husband a professorship at the university.

From the start Auntie Hester set her mind against Robert. To begin with he was from the wrong caste – not even a hyphen. Besides, courting Barbara was out of the question as long as Irene, the oldest, had no suitor.

Or so Auntie Hester believed. In truth, Irene had a secret beau. On her free afternoons she often took me shopping, or to the park in the French Concession. Some days we went instead to a café run by Russian émigrés. Wherever we went, we seemed always to bump into a big, athletic Russian fellow with a shock of stiff blond hair, sky-coloured eyes, and a strong square jaw. Yuri was a great sport; we played tag or hide and seek, and when I got tired he hoisted me onto his broad shoulders and galloped like a horse. Anyone seeing us together would have thought we were a family. For me it was all fun and laughter. I was too young to understand the sighs and deep looks that passed between Irene and Yuri. In those days young men and women did not even hold hands in public.

"You like Yuri, don't you?" Irene asked after our first excursion.
I nodded.
"I do too. That's why we have to keep him a secret."
"What's a secret?"
"Something special you don't tell anyone."
"Not even Shu Ma?"
Irene gripped my shoulder and looked deep in my eyes.
"Not anyone! Promise?"
"I promise."

Around this time Uncle George fell ill. Doctors with worried faces came and went. Everyone tiptoed around the house. Auntie Hester,

preoccupied with "George's trouble," as she called it, ceased noticing anything else. Irene and Barbara had more freedom.

Irene became reckless. Now and then she, Yuri, and I went to
the cinema. We usually went to one of the dingy second-run houses,
where Irene was less likely to meet people who knew her or her
parents. As an extra precaution we arrived just as the house lights
dimmed. The air was foul with cigarette smoke and garlic breath.
The noisy audience cheered the hero, hissed the villain, and chattered loudly through the dull bits, quieting for the gaudy production numbers if it happened to be a musical. The flickering images
usually put me to sleep until "The End" flashed on the screen and
we dashed for the exit. *Snow White and the Seven Dwarfs*, however,
fired my imagination, and I refused to budge till the house lights
came up.

Irene stifled a gasp. Her sister and Robert were sitting a few
rows behind us.

"Well, look who's here!" crowed Robert, tweaking my nose, then
turned to Irene to say impishly, "I don't seem to have met your friend."

Irene, turning quite red, made the introductions.

"Won't Mater be surprised," Barbara remarked, showing a row
of small white teeth. "Let's all go for tea at the Russian Tearoom.
Robert, be a dear and call Mater to join us. There must be a phone
booth nearby." Robert looked uncertainly from Barbara to her
grim-faced sister, unsure what to do.

"We have other plans," Yuri said. He tipped his hat and steered
us out of the theatre.

Headstrong, used to having her way, Barbara blurted Irene's
secret to their mother. The cat was out of the bag. In that family,
serious confrontations took place in whispers behind closed doors.
Mother and daughters hissed at each other. There were tears and
recriminations, and I was forbidden outings with Irene thereafter.

Had Yuri been British, Auntie Hester would have welcomed
him with open arms. Instead, he was one of the few Russians who
did not claim some connection to the Romanovs. Because he was a

railway engineer working as a ticket clerk, Auntie Hester assumed he was either shiftless or not too bright. In short, Yuri was not suitable.

Uncle George, meanwhile, after being confined to his sickroom for many weeks, emerged a changed man. He looked wan, and his face was covered with great patches of pinkish new skin. He had aged. He moved more deliberately. His voice had lost its resonance. The doctor came almost daily, and there was even more talk of "home," or perhaps Hong Kong, where better treatment was possible.

It was during Uncle George's long convalescence that Yuri was finally invited to the house on Lambeth Road. In one of his light-hearted moments, Uncle George remarked, "The Seven Dwarfs brought us Yuri Tulinkof!" The big Russian was charming, as wholesome as buttermilk, but he lacked money and prospects, insurmountable obstacles.

Since Yuri worked for the railway, and my father ran it, Ellen took it upon herself to ask Father if something could be done. As it turned out, there was no work for a mechanical engineer in Tienjin, but my father got Yuri a job with the railway in Mukden, a cold, forbidding place in Japan's iron grip. It had a strong Russian presence and my father thought that, with Yuri's skill and background, a job there would be his chance to prove himself to Irene's parents. Irene, however, let it be known she thought Father was pandering to George and Hester's prejudices. Perhaps he was, unwittingly.

"It's your fault," Irene shouted at Ellen. "You did it to keep us apart!"

They fought like badgers. It was the only time I had ever seen Irene in a temper.

"You want us to be old maids like you!" Barbara chimed in, siding with her sister.

The sisters soon reduced Ellen to tears. Auntie Hester sat calmly knitting in a corner while all this uncharacteristic noise swirled about her, a peculiar little smile creasing her lips.

Yuri's departure, like most occasions in those days, was an excuse for a party. Everyone wore evening clothes except the guest of honour. Yuri, exuding an air of solid dependability, wore his usual rumpled tweeds. After dinner – a long, increasingly boisterous meal – the living-room carpet was rolled up for dancing. A new radio-gramophone in a heavy baroque cabinet filled the room with the sounds of Fats Waller, Benny Goodman, Artie Shaw, and Russ Columbo crooning, "And then she holds my hand . . . Bah-bah-bah-boo . . ."

Nobody noticed me watching from beneath the grand piano. My vantage point gave me a curious perspective. My eyes widened as a pair of carefully polished oxfords glided by. It wasn't the shoes but the way the wearer moved that identified my father. I recognized the bottom of Ellen's pale blue gown, too. I started out of my hiding place, intending to leap at my father, excited by the presents that were bound to be in the next room; but something about the way they danced, gazing at each other without speaking, moving as one, made me slide deeper into the shadows instead. My chest was suddenly so tight I could hardly breathe. I crept up to bed, listened to the music seeping in under my door, and cried myself to sleep.

My father began coming down from Beijing regularly. In the Findlay-Wu household, only Ellen seemed serenely happy. Irene grew morose without Yuri, and Barbara became openly rebellious. Uncle George had a relapse that kept him in bed for weeks, and then, soon after he got back on his feet, another relapse. Auntie Hester was edgy and short tempered.

I noticed that my father's visits often coincided with the visits of the Chinese men in broad-brimmed hats who came and went like shadows in the night. While they talked in the study, Uncle George sat morosely sipping scotch in the living room and Ellen played the piano for him. Sometimes I crawled out of bed to listen at the top of the stairs, usually falling asleep before the music stopped and having to be carted back to bed.

Beyond the Concession life grew ever more grim. The Japanese occupation was making life in Tienjin difficult, and the chaos in the Chinese city was beginning to seep through. Shortages of flour, rice, and especially coal penetrated the Concessions. Uncle George thought it time to divest himself of his business interests and leave, and he set about doing so; but he was frail, and everything took time.

Tim's fierce temper, meanwhile, got him into trouble. One afternoon he and Robert rode their motorcycles downtown. On a busy street they were stopped by a crowd watching a drunken Japanese gendarme beating a rickshaw puller who had dared to demand payment. Such beatings were common, and nobody tried to intervene. Tim saw red, however, and waded in. Several other gendarmes leaped into the fray. It was a short but furious fight. Tim, outnumbered, was beaten and hauled away to the gendarmerie while Robert raced back to Lambeth Road with the news.

An urgent telegram brought Father from Beijing on the next train. Through the influence of a Japanese nobleman serving with the high command in Beijing, my father got Tim released, slightly the worse for wear. I eavesdropped while Father berated Tim and Robert in Uncle George's study. Father decided his son would sail on the next boat for Hong Kong, before he got into more hot water.

"I'm out of here, squirt!" said Tim, ruffling my hair as he passed me in the hallway. He looked pleased.

Robert, who had been aching to leave ever since Eddy went to Chungking, vowed he was going too, and a few nights later Barbara slipped out of the house. By the time Auntie Hester found her note on the breakfast table, Barbara and Robert were bound for Hong Kong on the same ship as Tim. The ship's captain had married them.

Barbara's elopement infuriated Auntie Hester and devastated Uncle George, for she was the apple of his eye. With her gone, the house on Lambeth Road lost its carefree spirit.

One Sunday afternoon in the spring of 1939, my father arrived in a shiny red Ford convertible. The whole household spilled onto the sidewalk to ogle the vehicle. Though everyone clamoured for a ride, it was Ellen who got the first turn. The rest of us wandered back inside. Auntie Hester and Uncle George talked softly in the living room, but stopped abruptly when I came within earshot. Lately there had been a lot of that, and I wondered what secrets were being discussed.

Finally we heard the car returning. Auntie Hester rang for tea as Father and Ellen came in arm in arm.

"We're going to be married," Ellen announced.

She kissed me gently on the forehead and told me that she loved my father and me too, and that she would make a happy home for the three of us. "I'll be your mummy . . ." she whispered.

My throat went dry. "Mummy" was cold, distant, bad-tempered. "Mummy" was a scent that made my nostrils tingle and my eyes water, a hank of hair and a blood-red mouth without a face to go with it.

"I don't want a mummy," I howled.

Ellen moved away from me; a quivering smile tugged at her lips as she fought back tears. My father moved to intervene but she signalled him no.

Ellen never understood my outburst, nor, I think, ever forgave it. It was the word "mummy" that caught in my throat like a fish-bone. I liked Ellen, but I wanted her to, Auntie Hester's sister and no more. I wanted what any five-year-old wants. I wanted the world to stay just as it was.

4

第四章

PEACEFUL
HAVEN

I N THE UNQUIET SPRING OF 1939, Ellen's engagement to
my father reverberated through the Findlay-Wu household.
Poor Auntie Hester. Following Eddy's quixotic departure and
Barbara's elopement, the engagement of her sister was the last
straw. Friendships faded in the ferocious heat of her disapproval.
She bristled at the prospect of her sister marrying a Chinese, even
one she considered a close friend.

She herself had married a Eurasian, of course, but in her mind
Uncle George was white. He could pass for a white, after all, speaking and carrying himself like a proper English gentleman. Auntie
Hester either lived down or ignored everything his – and her own –
hyphenated surname implied. The Findlay-Wus moved among the
best houses of the foreign community. Their circle inevitably
included some Chinese; but these were prominent men, such as
my father, who could benefit Uncle George's business interests.

"He's fifteen years older and has married – *and divorced* – two
other foreign women," Hester stormed at Ellen. "Worst of all,
there are three half-caste sons. What sort of life is that for an English lady?"

Flushed but determined, Ellen stood her ground. Uncle George remained aloof.

All I knew about marrying was what I gleaned from the last scene of movies, when Irene and Yuri were dragging me towards the exit half asleep. "What happened?" I would ask. "They got married," one of them would answer, "and lived happily ever after." So what was there for Auntie Hester to fuss about?

In the midst of the sisters' stormy exchanges, Ellen found a surprising ally in Irene. Following her sister's and her aunt's examples, Irene announced she was going to Mukden to marry Yuri.

"I absolutely forbid it," cried Auntie Hester, wringing her hands. "It's an impossible place to live. And your weak chest." She clutched her heart theatrically. A few years earlier Irene's chest X-ray had shown a shadow. Tuberculosis was a great killer in those days, and Irene had been confined to a hospital for months before it cleared. Ever since, Auntie Hester had raised the spectre of a relapse as a means of controlling her daughter.

"Believe me, your father and I know what's best," Auntie Hester said, more gently.

"I don't care. I won't be dictated to any longer." Irene's eyes brimmed like those of her favourite movie star. "I've written to Yuri. He will send me a ticket. It's all settled."

Auntie Hester sagged into the nearest chair, sobbing into hands cupped over her face.

Things did not go off quite as Irene planned, however, for Yuri put a stop to her notion of joining him. Though he was finally working in a job he was trained for, he was barely making ends meet. Besides, he too feared the primitive conditions in Manchukuo would be too much for Irene's delicate health. Nor would he accept the rapid promotion my father offered him until he felt he had proven himself. Marriage would have to wait.

"The boy has spunk," Uncle George remarked.

Yuri's honesty and pride deeply impressed Uncle George, but Auntie Hester remained unmoved. Meanwhile, to Auntie Hester's chagrin, Ellen and Father's wedding preparations went ahead. Uncle George's own precarious health provided his wife with a different tack.

"You've been homesick for years," she pleaded with Ellen. "I should have sent you back long ago. Never mind. Now we'll all go together."

But Ellen had made up her mind. "If marrying John means remaining in China the rest of my life," she said with finality, "I am content."

I sensed my life was about to change drastically when Ellen began taking charge of me. Father confirmed my worst fears when he said, "Having a mummy who loves you is better than Shu Ma!" They were getting rid of my Shu Ma just as the Findlay-Wus got rid of servants who had outlived their usefulness.

"I don't want Ellen! I don't want Mummy!" I cried. "I want my Shu Ma!"

Ever kind and patient, Ellen bit her lip and put on a brave face even in my stormiest moments. Father was less understanding. "We'll see about that, young man," he growled ominously.

As the wedding drew near, I was once more turned over to Shu Ma. There were many prenuptial parties, but none at Lambeth Road, for the Findlay-Wus had put the house up for sale. It was with a sense of relief one morning that I returned to my room after breakfast and found Shu Ma packing my things.

"We're going away," she said, sorting my clothes into two piles, one to take, one to be discarded.

"Where?"

"Your father's house by the sea."

"What's the sea?"

"Lots and lots of water." She spread her arms to show me how much. I rushed into them, knocking her to the ground. She righted herself, laughing. Her leathery fingers stroked my cheek tenderly, but her eyes became hooded and remote. "You're getting too big for me."

Next day Zhang arrived in a new blue robe, and a wide-brimmed straw hat, clutching a folding fan and looking like a middle-class Chinese merchant. After paying his respects to the master and mistress of the house, he went straight to the kitchen, where he sat talking to the cook and Shu Ma in a grave, low voice.

Later in the day, a gleaming black car flying the railway's pennant – dark blue, with a yellow winged wheel in the centre – stopped in front of the house. A smartly dressed Chinese gentleman in grey fedora and silver-rimmed glasses alighted. In those days silver-rimmed spectacles with window glass for lenses were a status symbol separating Chinese intellectuals from the hoi polloi. Shortly after this fellow's arrival, I was summoned to the drawing room.

"Here's the boy," Uncle George boomed with forced joviality. Auntie Hester stared fixedly out the window, the way she did when she was upset. I shook the Chinese gentleman's slim, manicured hand. His thick black eyebrows seemed carelessly glued straight across his narrow face; this formed a hairy fringe over the silver-rimmed spectacles. A thin mouth balanced the straight line of the brows. The hair, neatly parted in the centre, was smoothed down with heavily scented pomade. Mr. Ho, my father's secretary, spoke carefully articulated English.

"He is not very old."

"He's five," Uncle George boomed in a voice unnaturally loud, the voice he used on people he disliked. "How old did you think he was?"

"But Midder Kwan's other sons – " Mr. Ho faltered.

I caught the man's inability to pronounce "mister" and it made him less intimidating. From that moment Mr. Ho became Midder.

"Mr. Ho has come to take you away," Auntie Hester announced without turning round.

"Will I come back?"

"You'll live with your father and Ellen," Auntie Hester replied, still gazing out the window. "Soon you'll go to school . . . and play with other children."

"Do you speak Chinese?" Midder cut in suddenly.

"Of course," I piped in Chinese.

"Good. You must speak only Chinese on the train."

"Why?"

Midder glowered at me. "Your father commands it."

Late in the evening, after I'd said my goodbyes to Uncle George and Auntie Hester, Midder and I drove to the station. Standing on the curb waving, Uncle George and Auntie Hester were, I think, a little sorry to see me go. Perhaps it was like giving away the last of a litter of puppies, which happened often enough in that house. In a way, I suppose I was sorry too. For a while the Findlay-Wus were the closest thing I had to a family.

Zhang and Shu Ma had gone ahead with the luggage and picnic hampers. We had two first-class compartments – Midder and Zhang in one, Shu Ma and I in the other.

Auntie Hester had repeated several times I was not to eat or drink anything served on the train – "Goodness knows what Chinese germs you might pick up!" The proof of her phobia was the two hampers containing cold chicken and slices of ham; potato salad and pickles; bread; squares of cheese and butter; cake, cookies, fruit; flasks of tea and hot chocolate – enough food for days. Aside from germs, there was the fear of delays and of being stranded without food or drink if we encountered fighting along the way.

The German-built train was all dark wood, polished brass, crystal lamps, and overstuffed black leather seats. The conductor strutted about, brass buttons and gold braid flashing against his dazzling white uniform. It was all very exciting. The train stopped frequently, and whenever it did mobs swirled around, screaming to be let on.

"Peasants!" Shu Ma sniffed haughtily. "Don't take any notice."

Once or twice, just before the train stopped, a barely audible announcement in Japanese and Chinese crackled over the public address system. The conductor bustled in, pulled down the window

shades, and wagged a meaningful finger at us before he left. Zhang
came into the compartment, exchanging eye signals with Shu Ma,
who quickly gathered me in her arms, forcing me to be still. The
train ground to a stop. Outside, I could hear scuffling sounds,
shouts, and loud pops like firecrackers being set off. It sounded like
festivities and I wanted to witness them, but Shu Ma made me sit
perfectly still, not saying a word, till the train moved again. The
shades remained drawn until the conductor reappeared.

"Everybody all right?" he chirped, and quickly answered his
own question. "Of course everybody's all right! Tea will be served
in half an hour." He opened the blinds and left, the door clicking
shut after him.

When I woke in the morning, we were travelling across a flat
plain bordered on one side by rugged mountains. I had never been
this close to mountains, and the sight took my breath away. Midder
answered my eager questions with great patience. He came from
an old family in central China who lived in genteel poverty, the last
two generations having squandered the fortune their hardworking
forebears had accumulated. Midder was one of a handful of bright
young Chinese men who had gone to MIT in Boston on a national
scholarship. He was perhaps twenty-seven or -eight, a few years
older than Eddy, but not at all like him and his crowd.

When the train pulled into Beidaihe, another car flying the railway pennant was waiting. A gaggle of foreigners spilled onto the
platform, surrounded by baggage, screaming children, pets in
cages, and servants cackling like distracted hens. Japanese soldiers
and Chinese policemen marched up and down the platform bark-
ing at everybody. Outside the station we were besieged by hawkers. Boys with sloe-eyed donkeys offered to transport luggage for
a few coppers. The din was frenetic but good-natured. Zhang bar-
gained with the donkey boys at the top of his lungs, smiting the air
with his folded fan for emphasis. Shu Ma stood guard over the luggage, arms folded across her breasts, the corners of her mouth
turned scornfully down.

Midder and I piled into the car and sped away, through quiet streets lined with the summer "cottages" of members of the foreign community and of a few wealthy Chinese who lived in Beijing or Tienjin. The cottages were really mansions built in styles ranging from Georgian to nineteenth-century French provincial; there were Swiss and German chalets, Spanish haciendas; all were set in extensive gardens. In mid-May Beidaihe was waking from her winter sleep. Some of the houses were already occupied while troops of servants and local craftsmen readied others. The season lasted from the first of June to the end of August.

It was a tight-knit community where everyone knew everyone else. Parties moved from one house to the other all summer. When house parties palled, there was the tennis club or the hotel, where a band played dance music in the afternoons and evenings. The town boasted one tiny cinema, and Keisling's, a bakery run by an affable Austrian émigré that grew into a fashionable café.

One entered my father's villa through a stone moon gate over which were carved the Chinese characters *Ai Lu*, meaning "Peaceful Haven." A wide gravel drive swept past well-tended lawns and flower beds to the house, shaded by massive old ginkgo trees. The house was a square doughnut, its white walls topped with a red tile roof. Wide verandas ran all round, with a flagstoned courtyard in the centre. At the back, a covered walkway connected the main house to the kitchen, the laundry, and the servants' quarters. Beyond was a stable, a pen for goats kept for milk, and a chicken coop. A low stone wall separated the house from farm land beyond.

Father had bought the villa for Ellen and was having it renovated. Workmen were everywhere. The household staff had already arrived from Beijing, together with crates of furniture, books, and the paraphernalia that stuff people's houses. Midder supervised this organized bedlam, a mêlée into which Zhang and Shu Ma were drawn. Midder showed me around the house and garden. The stone wall marked the boundary within which I could wander at will. Beyond that, he emphasized, I had to be accompanied by an adult.

"But the sea is out there!" I protested.

Midder shrugged. "All right. But only for an hour. I have work."

The tide was out, and a ragged line of seaweed and shells marked the water's farthest reach. Wavelets lapped the shore. Little crabs scuttled across the sand to disappear into mysterious burrows. Tiny fish trapped in tide pools swam round and round, waiting for the tide to carry them back to the sea.

Midder shed his stuffiness with his street clothes. In his swim trunks he seemed as eager as I for the sea.

"You watch me from here," he said, drawing a circle in the sand around me, before plunging headlong into the water. He swam with clean strong strokes until I could see only his head bobbing up and down between swells. He tried to teach me to swim, but he did not have the knack of communicating with children and after a few gulps of bitter salt water I refused to continue.

Midder swam every day, even in the wildest seas. One afternoon we put on our swimsuits as a storm was brewing and the tide ran high. Whitecaps, racing towards the shore, reared up, curling into shiny white foam and thundering down, sending electric currents through the sand to the soles of my bare feet, then retreating with a teasing laugh. Midder dived through the breakers, emerging on the other side, waving and shouting at me on the shore. Feeling his excitement, I waded in. The water swirled around my ankles, scooping out the sand under my feet as it receded. Each time the water rushed past me, I sank a little deeper. Suddenly it took hold of my ankles and pulled. I fell backward and a great sucking sound filled my ears as light flashed before my eyes. I felt myself lifted up, tumbled head over heels, and sent plummeting down a smooth black tunnel. With an awful thud I landed face down in the sand. A pair of hands seized my shoulders and dragged me, spewing and gasping, out of reach of the surf.

That experience taught me forever to respect the ocean. It also gave Midder the fright of his life. A trip to Keisling's for ice cream secured my silence. Not even Shu Ma could worm out an explanation for the sand in my hair and in my trunks.

As I had no routine or companions, Zhang thought up chores to occupy me. I was to feed the chickens and collect eggs from the hen house every morning. Next to the hen house was the goat pen. A gangling black kid with a mischievous glint in its eye and a stiff-legged swagger caught my fancy. Billy, I decided, was mine. I went into the pen with a length of rope, determined to take him for a walk. Goats ate everything in sight and therefore were not allowed to wander the garden or farm land. Still, I thought Billy could do little harm if I took him where the grass was tall under the stone wall.

"Come here," I coaxed. "Come here."

Billy backed away suspiciously, pawing the ground. As I came closer, he lowered his head and charged. The hard little lumps that were the beginnings of horns struck me in the pit of my stomach and bowled me over. The gate behind me was open and the goat's nostrils twitched at the smell of cornfields and vegetable gardens beyond. Before I could stop him, he had leaped over the stone wall and disappeared down the neat rows of corn.

"Come back!"

Billy bleated triumphantly somewhere in the green depths of the cornfield. There was nothing to do but go after him. The corn was taller than I. Waxy green leaves arched overhead, cutting off the sun. The goat was somewhere in the green-black shadows, but where? I went in one direction, then another, following shifting shadows. All I could see were green leaves and corn stalks and greyish yellow tassels lazily blowing in the breeze, mocking me. Sweat stung my eyes. I tripped and fell headlong into a ditch of muddy water.

I was now out of the clutching forest of corn. On one side, a vegetable garden bordered a sheltered cove. On the other, a woodland of low trees rose in a series of rocky hillocks towards the mountains. Not far away a young man, brown as the earth, wearing only a loincloth, was weeding a vegetable patch.

"Hey!" I yelled.

He went on working.

I didn't like being ignored by a low-class stranger and yelled again: "I'm the young master!" The words sounded hollow even to me. The man took no notice, not even when I squatted down beside him. He smelled of the earth. His head was shaved except for a tuft of hair at the nape of the neck where a pigtail had been. His high-cheek-boned, square-jawed face was not unpleasant. What he was doing absorbed him completely. He worked swiftly, compactly, the rhythmic movement of his strong fingers making his arm muscles ripple.

"I lost my goat," I said.

He finally glanced at me, eyes crinkling with amusement, and shifted down the row on his haunches. I shifted with him, lost my balance, and sprawled on the ground. He took no notice. I followed the silent man doggedly until, finally, he pointed at a weed, worked his fingertips into the soil around it, and pulled. Then he indicated with his eyes that I should do the same. His silent authority made me obey. He watched out of the corner of his eye, reaching over to help with the more stubborn weeds. We moved crab-fashion towards the foot of a knoll.

I soon discovered weeding was not as simple as it looked. Nor was squatting for someone not born to it. My legs wobbled and I either pitched forward, scraping elbows and knees, or fell back on my rump with such force that stars whirled before my eyes. After several spills, my silent companion showed me, by mime demonstration, the fine art of squatting. Still he did not speak.

"I lost my goat!" I yelled.

He made a face and covered his ears. I started to say it again, but he cut me off by pointing imperiously at a weed. Anger roiled inside. No one had ever treated me like this, but something kept me weeding. Sweat ran down my face, and my shirt stuck to my back. The man scratching the earth seemed oblivious to the heat.

By the time we reached the end of the row, the sun was over-head and I was groggy from the heat. The man turned towards a path that led up the knoll, beckoning me to follow. Though I'd been taught not to go with strangers, I followed without hesitation.

A thatched stone cottage stood on a terrace cut into the hill-side. A stone stove with a wok set into it stood against the outside wall, shaded by a roof of dried sorghum canes as hard as bamboo. On the far side of the cottage was a pen where a huge sow content-edly suckled two piglets. A dappled grey donkey dozed in a scrap of shade. Billy, tied to a hitching post, planted his feet firmly apart and lowered his head, ready to do battle.

"That's my goat!" I exclaimed.

"Know." So he could speak, when he pleased.

"Why didn't you say so?"

"Safe," he said, letting me into the pen. Billy bleated but did not move. I shortened the distance between us, and the goat butted me in the stomach. The man picked me up and dusted me off.

"Hurt." It was both question and statement, and I nodded. My dignity was bruised more than anything else.

"Ride," he said, pointing at the donkey.

"Yes!"

The man lifted me onto the donkey and wound my fingers around a handful of mane. The donkey's ears twitched but he did not complain. The man untied the rope from the hitching post and looped the loose end around my arm. He gave the donkey a gentle slap on the flank, and it headed down the knoll at a steady clip-clop. Billy bucked at the end of the rope, but the donkey's steady pace forced it to follow, bleating indignantly. The man stopped the donkey at the edge of the field and lifted me off. We stood grinning at each other.

"What's your name?" I asked.

"Hu."

"Lao Hu," I said, *Lao* meaning old, for he was older than I.

"*Xiao* Hu," he corrected, Xiao meaning young but also an acknowledgement of caste. "You."

I scuffed the ground with the toe of my shoe. "They call me Hai Zhi, the kid."

He grinned, turned the donkey around, and headed back up the path.

"I'll come again tomorrow! Okay?"

Hu waved without looking back.

From that day, I hurried through my chores and then headed for the fields looking for Hu. He was a silent man; living and working alone had made him thus, I suppose. He spoke in gestures or single words, seldom in sentences. He fashioned a hat out of sorghum leaves for me that was cool and kept the glare out of my eyes, though he never wore a hat.

"Used to it," he explained.

Shucking off shirt, shoes, and socks, I weeded with Hu or gathered tomatoes, cucumbers, beans, lettuce, and cabbage. Hu showed me how to catch crickets and pluck cicadas out of trees with a long stick tipped with a lump of sticky resin. He taught me to weave cages for them out of sorghum leaves, and how to feed them so they would whir and chirp as happily as if they had been free. He showed me tadpoles in ditches, starfish and seahorses in tide pools. He showed me where to look for oysters and clams. He showed me birds, lizards, and snakes, and how to tell which were harmless. On days when the work was light we broke off to catch giant grasshoppers. When we had a dozen or so in the cloth bag Hu carried to keep them in, he killed each one, a single blow with a rock.

"Never hurt them."

Afterwards he prayed, kneeling and touching his forehead to the ground, thanking the Lord of the Earth for providing the grasshoppers and the grasshoppers for giving up their lives to sustain him. I mimicked him. What started as a game turned into something profoundly mysterious that I accepted without question. We made a small fire at the edge of the field and roasted the grasshoppers on a flat stone laid over the flames. When they turned dark brown they were done. In the meantime, we pulled leeks, garlic, and tiny hot chilies shaped like firecrackers from the field. Hu tore up a pancake the size of a wok, rolled the roasted grasshoppers and vegetables smelling of earth into the pieces, and we ate. Those were the most delicious meals of my childhood.

When I returned home Shu Ma smelled garlic and leeks on my breath, and her mouth stretched into a thin disapproving line. "You don't eat proper food. But peasant food!" She rolled her eyes in disgust and grumbled that I was running wild and turning into a peasant, as brown as a nut. "Your father will have a fit!"

My father and Ellen had receded into the far corners of my mind. I'd barely thought of them since I left Tienjin. All the packing cases in the courtyard had disappeared. The rooms had been aired and furnished without my having noticed. Only when Midder announced before going back to Beijing, "Your father and new mummy are arriving soon," did the prospect of their arrival become real. It filled me with dismay.

I sought refuge with Hu. He helped me overcome my fear of the sea, teaching me to float, first on my back, then face down. He found a piece of driftwood for me to hold onto and taught me to kick. Finally he taught me to use my arms and legs like a frog. Hu also taught me to respect the sea's moods; when to go in and when not to; which of its creatures were friendly, and which were not. We hauled kelp out of the sea and spread it to dry in the sun for food and fertilizer. Between bouts of work we swam to cool off. He caught a fish and a crab and cooked them over an open fire for our midday meal. Replete, we lay in the shade of a great rock. Sky and sea blended in seamless perfection above us. I was happier than I had ever been.

"I'll tell my father, 'I know Hu,'" I announced. "Friend" had not yet entered my vocabulary.

Hu sighed. At first his words came haltingly.

"Your father. Good man. Gave me cottage. Gave me donkey. These fields to farm. In the winter I live in the house. I look after the goats and chickens. Keep the place safe from bandits. For all this he only takes a few vegetables and some corn."

I had never heard him say so many words at one time and I waited, fascinated, for him to continue. But he only smiled sadly. Pointing at himself and then at me, he shook his head. An oppressive weight dropped on my narrow chest. Children know nothing of the invisible line separating one human being from another, but they feel it. Between Hu and me, the line came suddenly clear. I picked up my things and ran blindly for the house, the hot earth burning the soles of my feet.

Shu Ma was waiting to scold me and haul me under the shower. "Your father is arriving!" she chastised. She sniffed my breath and went to pick mint leaves in the garden. "Brush your teeth," she ordered on her return. "And chew these. Do as I say."

An hour later, from the veranda, I watched the shiny black car drive up to the house. My father alighted with his new wife, who gazed about in tremulous delight. Ellen reached for Father's hand and brushed her lips against his cheek. She was about to say something when she caught sight of me and opened her arms.

"Come to Mummy!"

5

第五章

THE TOAD

ADJUSTING TO LIFE WITH FATHER, a kindly stranger who lavished me with presents, was not so difficult. But I dreaded the thought of kind, sweet, patient Ellen turning into another shrieking horror. She wasted no time turning me into her ideal of a son. She took me to the barber-shop run by a little watery-eyed Polish gentleman with a bald head and bristly moustaches. The cow-lick that fell across my forehead had to go. "We can't have you looking like a little Hitler," she remarked. The little barber snickered, but something told me he was not amused.

The barber had two children, twins about my age, and before the haircut was done they were invited to tea. Their visit was awkward from the beginning. Eva and Paul spoke Polish and a smattering of Chinese. We had to manage in Chinese.

"What do you want to do?" they asked. Eva and Paul often spoke the same words at the same time.

I had never played with other children and did not know what to do with these two. "Why don't you show Eva and Paul your toys?" Ellen suggested. I took it for granted that everybody had a playroom full of toys. In Beidaihe I had a train set that ran all the way round the room, just as I did in Beijing. The twins, however, were drawn to the many boxes of lead soldiers.

"Let's have a war," crowed Paul.

"Let's have a war," echoed Eva, her close-set eyes, exactly like Paul's, gleaming with mischief.

When the twins left an hour later, the room was a shambles. "There must be other children around," I heard Ellen say to my father, and I could tell by her tone of voice Eva and Paul would not be invited back.

The harder Ellen tried to be mummy, of course, the more I backed away. She had a picture book from which she identified various flowers in the garden for me. I became supremely disinterested in flowers. Instead, I derived a guilty pleasure from putting things I found — slimy fungus, snakes, lizards, frogs — things that I knew horrified her — into her underwear drawer. Her startled shrieks gratified me but infuriated my father.

Father decided I must learn to swim — anything to keep me occupied. I refused to go near the beach. All Ellen's gentle persuasion produced was a sullen shake of the head. "He needs a good spanking," rasped my father, exasperated. "I've had enough of this."

Ellen reminded him they were still on their honeymoon. "Give him time to get used to us," she said in her quiet way. "It must be very strange for him." Father grumbled, eyeing me from under wrinkled brows, but he relented.

I enjoyed tormenting Ellen, but sometimes when she looked at me a wistfulness crossed her face, so poignant that I ducked my head or burst into childish boisterousness to assuage the nameless stab of pain that ran through me. The harder she tried to be a proper mummy, the more actively I resisted, and the more guilty I felt — another reason to reject her.

From the splendid isolation of the low stone wall I watched the other children play. A deep, unplumbed place in me yearned to be a part of their games, yet I couldn't make the first move to join them. Not even the picnic basket Shu Ma took down to Father and Ellen lured me to the beach. I sat and watched, a little spectator viewing the odd emptiness of his own life.

One still, hot afternoon, when a flat sea lapped the shore, cicadas whirred fitfully, and dragonflies hovered lethargically, the shouts of the children on the beach grew shrill. Paul and some other boys sauntered by, bent on mischief. They stopped where I sat on the wall. Paul bowed in the Japanese manner, legs tight together, palms pressed against the knees.

"Oh, young master!" he sing-songed in Chinese, "show us beggars your room full of toys!"

The others jeered, chattering in a curious gibberish of Chinese mixed with that universal language children of different nationalities adopt when they play together.

"He's a dummy," piped Eva. "He doesn't know games or anything!"

"I bet you can't swim," sneered one of the boys.

"I can too," I replied hotly. "Only I don't want to!"

"Can't! Can't! Can't!" chanted the others.

"Can! Can! Can!" I yelled back.

Someone dragged me off the wall. I hit the ground with a thud and there was a great ringing in my ears. Shouts of "Show us! Show us!" penetrated my numbed brain. I was distantly aware of struggling to my feet, my legs seeming very long and detached, moving of their own accord, propelling me towards the thin white line between sea and sand. Then I was in the water, and the shouts stopped. I was a fish heading out to sea. I swam till my chest ached and my arms and legs grew leaden.

Xiao Hu's voice seemed to call to me from a great distance. "Float . . ."

I flipped over on my back, gasping, chest heaving, vaguely aware of the danger I had put myself in but unafraid. I floated there, peaceful and alone, until someone seized me and towed me to shore.

"Don't fuss," I heard my father admonish Ellen. "He's all right. He probably swallowed a bit of water, but the little monkey can swim."

I was pleased with the note of surprise in his voice. Father was terribly proud of Tim's athletic prowess. My bit of foolish bravado impressed him. The next time Midder came, Father complimented him profusely for teaching me to swim and scolded me, half-jokingly, for pretending I could not. Midder took it all in stride. It cost him a few trips to the ice cream parlour to keep me from spilling the truth.

I did not make new friends. With my shock of light brown hair and Chinese features, the other children, all Caucasians, regarded me as a curiosity, to be teased now and then. Most of the time they left me alone.

Whoever said "East is east, and west is west, and never the twain shall meet" did not visit the villa at Beidaihe. My father's many summer house guests began to arrive, and most were westerners. The Chinese provided a dash of colour, with their entourages of servants and hangers-on. Whereas westerners wore summer whites or swimming gear, the Chinese came overdressed and dripping with jewels. The foreigners got sunstroke while the Chinese gossiped in the shade of the veranda, screaming at their servants and sipping endless glasses of iced tea. The ebb and flow of people relegated me to the periphery of my parents' life.

Somnolent mornings preceded boisterous lunches served outdoors on long picnic tables set under the trees. Replete with food and fine burgundies, the ladies drifted off to their rooms, while the gentlemen gathered in my father's study to pore over newspapers that arrived on the noon train.

The news that summer was mostly bad. Europe teetered on the brink of war. In China the fall of Canton and Hankow moved the conflict with Japan into a new phase. The Kuomintang (KMT) was split by internal dissent. The charismatic, eloquent, and ambitious Wang Jingwei had been an early follower of Dr. Sun Yat-Sen, as well as his personal assistant. Upon Sun's death in 1925, Wang had seen himself as the great man's successor. As head of the military, however, Chiang Kai-shek took control of the KMT. Wang tried to form a separate government in south China with the help of the Communists but soon discovered he could not work with them either. Chiang wooed him back with a largely ceremonial post as president of the KMT. Wang remained Chiang's most bitter critic and rival, going so far as to publicly call on the central government to come to a peaceful settlement with Japan. He defected a second time, setting up what he called the Reformed Government of China in Nanking. The Japanese were not averse to the idea of jointly governing the large swath of China, including the major rail lines and seaports they already controlled. Because of Wang's earlier waffling, though, formal recognition of his new regime was slow in coming. Nor did Wang receive the autonomy he had hoped for. He had created nothing more than a puppet government for the Japanese.

Until the summer of 1939, the foreign residents of Beidaihe had been more or less insulated from China's turmoil. Then, one night at dinner, a series of short, sharp pops, like a car backfiring, interrupted the conversation at table. Ellen cocked her head. "It can't be," she murmured, and continued eating. The conversation grew less animated, however, as everyone kept an ear tuned. A few minutes later, after a prolonged barrage, a thud noisily rattled the windows. One of the Chinese ladies began to whimper. Father signalled Zhang to douse the lights and close the wooden shutters.

"There's nothing to worry about." Father's voice was calm, and in the dark the scrape of knife and fork against his plate was oddly reassuring.

The others resumed eating. No one spoke. The only sounds were of breathing, and of silverware on bone china, until several loud explosions erupted amid bursts of gunfire. The noise was coming closer. The fighting could not have lasted more than a few minutes, but it seemed like hours.

Once things had calmed down, Zhang brought in candles, the electricity having gone off. Now everybody talked at once.

Amid the excited chatter something compelled me to unburden myself.

"I caught this big toad," I began, tugging Ellen's wrist to catch her attention. She smiled at me, and turned to the person on her other side. "I put it in Mrs. Soong's bed," I added, raising my voice in a way I'd been told a gentleman did not.

"That's nice." Ellen patted my hand. Turning to her table partner, she inquired pleasantly, "Would you like more dessert?" She touched her linen napkin to her lips and signalled the server. "I think I'll have a bit more too."

It turned out guerrillas had destroyed a Japanese supply dump near the railway yard on the outskirts of Beidaihe that evening. By the time I went to bed, our guests had been coaxed back into good humour. Then pandemonium erupted in one of the guest rooms. Mrs. Soong was screaming at the top of her lungs; her husband, trying to calm her, became more and more agitated, adding to the din. Both spoke shrilly to their servants, who scampered up and down the corridors like chickens with their heads cut off. I buried my head in my pillow, chortling with glee. Through my open window I could hear my father's voice coming from the veranda.

"Something about a toad in Mrs. Soong's bed," he was saying to one of his other guests.

"Or a simple case of Japanese jitters," replied whomever he was talking to.

The Soongs no doubt would have gathered their servants, packed their bags, and left in high dudgeon at once, but the next train did not go till morning. By then martial law had been declared, and trains in and out of Beidhaihe were halted.

For the next few days there was curfew from dusk to dawn. It was said that violators of the curfew were being executed. The Japanese held manoeuvres along the beaches and in the mountains. Nobody ventured beyond the garden, and the village boys with ponies or donkeys for rent no longer clustered outside our gate waiting for customers. Ellen moved with studied calm among the guests, the epitome of the gracious hostess. The Soongs kept haughtily aloof and left in stony silence on the first train out of Beidaihe once rail service was resumed. The house was much quieter without them. In spite of their enormous wealth and influence, nobody much cared for the Soongs.

At about this time I began sleepwalking. My destination on these nocturnal wanderings was my father's study. It was a large nautical room decorated with scale models of historic ships, antique charts, and a polished conch shell displayed on an elegant mahogany stand. That shell drew me like a magnet. I carried it back to bed and slept with it pressed against my ear. In the morning I did not remember a thing.

My father decided it was time to have a talk. Inevitably, my stubborn refusal to call Ellen "Mummy" came up, as did my nocturnal rounds. Father, for all his skills at diplomacy, did not have the knack of talking to children, and all he accomplished in the end was another bout of hysterical tears. I did become aware of my sleepwalking, however, and it frightened me. So I forced myself to stay awake. When I finally fell asleep from sheer exhaustion, my night wandering resumed.

"Put the conch shell in his room for a while," Ellen suggested. "It might help."

One batch of house guests left and another arrived. An English couple from Tienjin who had sent their children back to England the year before – when Britain and America had suggested that all non-essential personnel should leave China – told Ellen in no uncertain terms what was best for me.

"Servants!" said the woman in her fruity English voice. "Give an inch and they take a yard! Leaving a child in a nanny's care" – she gave me a pitying look – "is ruinous! Ruinous! I say get rid of the creature as soon as you can. And send the boy to boarding school, as soon as possible. You can't miss with the Jesuits!"

My father squinted against the smoke of his cigar and said nothing.

Dr. Kietel, a sandy-haired German with piercing blue eyes who had attended my birth, was among the new arrivals. The good doctor was everybody's favourite. He not only sang Schubert lieder in a pleasant baritone, he told stories that had everyone in stitches. He took me swimming and taught me to ride the squat, heavy-limbed Chinese ponies rented from one of the urchins who gathered on the fringes of the beach.

Dr. Kietel was fun to be with. One day we were building a sandcastle on the beach, and Ellen came down with a basket of strawberries and ice cream together with a thermos of coffee.

"You have a very nice mummy," the doctor remarked, sipping his coffee.

"She's Ellen," I snapped.

"I thought she was your mummy." The doctor's voice was warm and soothing.

"She's not my m–mm. . ." The very word choked me. In a panic I dropped my ice cream and strawberries. Everything blurred and a child sobbed, "I don't want Mummy," over and over, as red-lacquered fingernails pinched and poked, and a horrible gaping red mouth engulfed me. The doctor held me until the crying stopped.

I heard my father asking what the matter was, and the doctor replying in German, in the same warm pleasant voice, as he stroked the back of my neck. The two voices mingled with the pounding sea, lulling me. I did not understand what was said except that the name "Marianne" came up several times.

"The sleepwalking probably has something to do with her . . ."

I knew my father was now speaking to Ellen, for there was a special quality to his voice when he spoke to her.

I was put to bed with a fever. The next few days I was kept quiet in my room. Probably because of the high child mortality rate in those days, a fever was treated as potentially life-threatening, and I revelled in the attention: new toys, plenty of fruit jelly, and Shu Ma to look after me.

One day Dr. Keitel asked me out of the blue, "Do you remember what Irene calls Auntie Hester?"

"Mater."

The doctor grunted, and clasped his hands together.

"Anything else?"

"Mother."

"What does it mean?"

"It's her name."

"Right," Dr. Keitel twinkled. "My name is Heinz, and yours is David. That's how we're called. But sometimes grown-ups change their names for a very good reason." He had my attention, and he talked gently about Auntie Hester and Irene and Ellen and Father. "Why don't you think of a new name for Ellen?" he asked.

I felt my scalp tingle.

Dr. Keitel smiled. "Let's go to the ice cream parlour."

My father no longer insisted I call Ellen "Mummy." As that loathsome word faded from my mind, my sleepwalking tapered off. Soon it stopped altogether.

The lazy summer wore on, and a subtle change crept into our days. A dispatch box for my father began arriving nearly every day from Beijing. Sometimes Midder brought it, looking hot and distracted in his stiff-collared shirt, tie, and jacket. He and Father always went straight to the study. Zhang stood outside, jaw set like a steel trap, keeping everyone away, sometimes for hours on end. When the two men emerged, they were chatting about trivialities. Sometimes Midder joined us for afternoon tea, eating wafer-thin cucumber sandwiches and little cakes before catching the evening train back to Beijing.

Nights were long and black after the destruction of the Japanese munitions dump. Japanese gendarmes and their Chinese and Korean collaborators patrolled the streets and the beaches after dark. Gunfire punctuated the dance music from our gramophone nearly every night. The music was simply turned up to drown out the noise. Laughter and voices became shriller. Nobody seemed to care whether it was the Japanese killing the Chinese or the Chinese killing one another.

On one of the last days of summer, Midder arrived unexpectedly. That morning my father and the other grown-ups had ridden down the coast on ponies and donkeys to the port city of Qinghuangdao, where a Dutch freighter with a shipment of cigars, coffee, and brandy had docked the day before. Midder left his briefcase in the study, then went straight out the back gate, walking with sure, quick strides up the path between the corn and sorghum fields. I darted into the cornfield and followed him.

Midder stopped a short distance away. With his back to me he stood talking to someone squatting on the ground. The conversation was friendly but restrained and intense. When the other person stood up, I saw it was Xiao Hu. The two men talked with their heads close together. Once Midder looked up at the mountains, and I thought he pointed at the trail that wound up to the peak. Xiao Hu, looking in the same direction, said something in his peculiar monosyllabic way. Without warning, Midder turned to glance back over his shoulder. He seemed to look straight at me. I shrank into the shadows, sensing I had seen something I shouldn't have. I hurried back through the cornfield, following the stone wall at a trot. Shu Ma was waiting on the veranda, looking grim.

"I saw Midder" – it all came out in a breathless jumble – "out past the cornfield, talking to Xiao Hu."

Shu Ma pressed a finger against her lips.

"Is it a secret?" I whispered.

Shu Ma's fingertip did not move.

The grown-ups were back by dinner, flushed with happiness. It had been a successful shopping spree. In the meantime, Midder had slipped out as silently as he had come. I waited for a lull in the conversation, then said to my father, "Midder was here today."

My father pushed a sliver of meat onto his fork with the end of his knife. "He was here the other day."

"I saw him," I insisted.

"Of course you did, son." My father went on eating. "The other day."

Ellen said something to distract me, someone else engaged my father's attention, and Midder was shuffled into the background.

Next morning I woke early and waited impatiently for the grown-ups to get out of the way. As soon as they set off for the tennis club, I raced across the fields to find Xiao Hu.

Debris was strewn around the stone mill where he had been grinding corn – by the look of it, all night. Now the donkey stood dozing at its hitching post while Xiao Hu sewed up the full gunny sacks with a long iron needle. He shot me a glance and went on with his work.

"I was looking for you," I said.

Xiao Hu grunted.

"You're going up there, aren't you?" I asked, pointing as Midder had.

Xiao Hu gave me a blank look, as if he did not understand.

"I'll tell my father!" I yelled, suddenly annoyed.

Xiao Hu finished sewing the last sack. He swept the debris into a pile and threw it in a large basket, ready to carry back to the cornfield for burning.

"Come," he said, hefting the basket.

I scampered down the knoll after him. He emptied the basket into a large hole at the edge of the field and heaped half-dried stalks and leaves over the debris. Then he took the basket back to the cottage, signalling me to wait. When he returned, he was carrying a pancake rolled in a cloth, together with a handful of little red peppers.

"Catch grasshoppers," he said with a twinkle.

We shared the roasted grasshoppers rolled in pieces of pancake with hot peppers. Something about his manner made me wonder when we would share a meal again. When the food was gone, he told me to go home.

"Can we go crabbing tomorrow?"

He did not answer, merely gazed towards the track leading up the mountain.

"Bandits are up there," I whispered, for by now there was fighting in the mountains every night, rumbling explosions and soaring flares and bursts of machine-gun fire.

"Your father . . ." Xiao Hu began, but changed his mind. After a pause he said simply, "Good man." He smiled and raised a finger to his lips. I did not know whether the secret was that he was going up the mountain with sacks of corn meal, or that my father was a good man. Lately everything seemed to be turning into one big secret.

Summer was at an end. In town many of the shops were already shuttered. So were some of the villas. As our house guests had departed, the staff went back to Beijing, everyone except Zhang, Cook, a maid, and Shu Ma. The house felt strangely unsettled. Father seemed on edge, and Ellen had a preoccupied air.

It was September 2 before we heard on the wireless that Britain had declared war on Germany.

"We must get back to Beijing as soon as possible," said Ellen, as though such a move was conducive to the war effort. My father concurred absentmindedly.

That night, after Ellen tucked me in, Shu Ma tiptoed into my room. She crouched beside the bed, lifted a corner of the mosquito net, and, calling me by an affectionate nickname, whispered, "Haizhi, are you awake?"

I turned to her drowsily. She stroked my hair and face. Her voice sounded so far away, I had to struggle to grasp what she was saying. "You're all grown up and I must leave." Her voice faded into swirling darkness. "You will not see me again."

In the morning Ellen came to wake me.

"Hurry," she chirped, lifting the mosquito net. "You'll be late for breakfast."

I remembered Shu Ma as in a dream. Every word she said rang clear. Ellen whistled a cheery tune as she laid out my clothes.

"Where's Shu Ma?"

When there was no answer something within me exploded. "Where's Shu Ma?" I yelled, and flew at her screaming, "I want Shu Ma! I hate you!"

It took the combined strength of Zhang and Ellen to get me under control. My father rushed in. Through my screams and weeping I heard Ellen asking him to leave the room: "Stay out of it, dear. I'll handle this my way."

Zhang rocked me on his lap, for I would not let Ellen near me. It astonished me to see her cry.

The sun threw long shadows across the platform that evening as we boarded the train. I thought of Xiao Hu in the mountains, but they were out of sight, on the other side of the train. I stood rooted to the window, steeped in misery. The platform began to slip away, but it was really the train moving. I spotted the little grey donkey and a figure beside it, scanning the first-class windows. I could feel Xiao Hu looking straight at me, though he couldn't have been. I started to wave but caught myself and looked up at my father. There was a curious smile on his face. As the train gathered speed, he raised his hand in a gesture that might have been a wave; or perhaps he was merely flicking the ash from the tip of his cigar.

The next moment Beidaihe vanished in a cloud of steam.

6

第六章

THE MAGIC
CIRCLE

To mark his new life with Ellen, my father had bought a new house in the Legation Quarter of Beijing. It was large and airy, French windows filling the rooms with light. The walls were pale grey, eggshell white, or soft blue, and the wood was polished to a warm honey-coloured glow. The main floor had a formal sitting room with French windows that opened onto a narrow terrace and a small garden. A baby grand piano stood near the fireplace. Folding doors separated the sitting room from a long narrow dining room. Farther down the hall was another long room which was my father's study, furnished in much the same way as the one in the German merchant's house my father had rented. Across from the dining room was a rectangular room with many large windows, recesses, and alcoves. A crystal chandelier hung from the centre of the ceiling. Smaller fixtures lit the niches where my father displayed pieces from his extensive collection of Chinese art. The reception room was used for formal gatherings.

Rex and I had the run of the house, except for my father's study, which was out of bounds. Father and Ellen occupied the second floor, where there was a small sitting room and a dining room for the times we ate alone. A sunny room facing south, with a huge fan-shaped window, was Ellen's favourite; here she sewed and did her correspondence on a roll-top desk.

After my father left for the office, Ellen occupied her mornings with correspondence, phone calls, and discussion of the day's menu with Cook. Lao Han spoke pidgin English and had also learned to read. Often the discussions involved the fine points of recipes. Lao Han was a gem and he knew it. From the start he made clear to Ellen that the kitchen was his domain.

"Missy no come kitchen. Missy come kitchen, Cookie quit!"

A gong regulated our lives: eight o'clock, breakfast; one o'clock, tiffin (the Anglo-Chinese word we used for lunch); eight o'clock, dinner. I amused myself until tiffin, after which I was sent off for a nap. At three Zhang roused me. Sometimes Ellen and I had tea at home, other days she took me shopping. En route we stopped at various houses at which the chauffeur, Lao Zhao, who stood well over six feet, impressive in navy blue livery, marched up to the door, rang the bell, and presented cards for Ellen and my father. Everyone had "at homes." Ours were on Wednesday evenings.

Ellen said we lived in a magic circle. The Legation Quarter isolated us from war, disease, poverty, and starvation. The thick stone walls around the quarter, rebuilt at the turn of the century after the Boxer rebellion, were designed to separate the foreign community from the Chinese. A city within a city, the quarter was a hodge-podge of European architecture lining paved, tree-shaded streets. The foreign community, including diplomats, captains of commerce and industry, and soldiers, lived there. The quarter had its own shops that catered to residents, its own banks, a hotel, and two hospitals. Until shortly before I was born it had even had its own electric company, telephone exchange, postal service, and police. Beyond the wall, an open area separated the quarter from the Chinese city. When some of the legations still had their own garrisons, soldiers drilled on it. After they were withdrawn, this open area was used for soccer and polo. Until the 1920s Chinese were not allowed to live in the quarter. Later the rules were relaxed and a few well-connected Chinese, such as my father, took up residence.

Outside the Legation Quarter, China's realities overwhelmed us. Smoke from charcoal fires mixed with the stench of open sewers made the air almost unbreathable. Since the Marco Polo Bridge incident in 1937, the already teeming streets had become even more clogged with refugees. Clinging to ragged bundles of clothing, they eyed us dully, claw-like hands outstretched. Mangy stray dogs vied for scraps of garbage with ancient-faced children whose distended bellies showed they would never reach adulthood. Beggars displayed horribly mangled limbs. Lepers without noses, eyelids, or fingers wailed piteously. Frightened little girls with painted faces hung their heads, while their pimps, often hard-bitten older women, hawked their charms as if they were bits of furniture.

Holding a handkerchief against her nose with one hand, Ellen shepherded me with the other, clutching her purse. "Come along, David. Don't dawdle. Don't look at the beggars!" Big-boned and hard-muscled, Lao Zhao moved like a panther a few paces behind us, his big fists swinging easily. Fiercely protective of my father and his family, he kept beggars, pickpockets, and purse-snatchers away.

Our destination was often Dong An Bazaar on Wangfujing. Chock-full of stalls selling everything from diamonds to toothpaste, the place was a heady mixture of smells: sandalwood, incense, flowers, medicinal herbs. The greasy aroma of roast duck, a Beijing specialty, mingled with the stink of pickled cabbage. The bazaar was an amazing place, half shopping arcade and half amusement park. The throng still pushed you along the treacherously sweaty cobblestone paths, but the mood was lighter, less threatening. Ellen slackened her pace. There was time to watch acrobats and jugglers, and magicians who extracted eggs from my ears. Monkeys in clown costumes did tricks and chattered for coins. Shadow puppets enacted scenes from popular Beijing operas. Artisans fashioned wonderful figurines by blowing lumps of molten molasses candy stuck on the end of long glass tubes, the way glass-blowers do. I was never permitted to stop to listen to storytellers. Ellen did not understand Chinese, but she knew that storytellers were arrested from time to time, for mixing social comment with old folk tales.

"They might be saying the wrong things," she said, pushing me away.

"They're only telling a story!"

"It might be the wrong kind of story, and we'd get into trouble with the authorities."

After Ellen made her purchases, we stopped at the Beijing Hotel for tea served from wonderful silver samovars heated by a spirit lamp underneath. We nibbled thin cucumber-and-water-cress sandwiches, little cakes, and mouth-watering chocolate éclairs. Couples dressed to the nines danced to a string orchestra playing Palm Court music from behind a screen of potted palms.

Each afternoon Ellen and my father had cocktails before dinner. When there were no guests I joined them. We always dressed for dinner. Zhang served me juice in a wine glass and turned the hors d'oeuvre tray so that the things I liked best — stuffed mushroom caps and little crab canapés — pointed at me. Then my father and I played a game. Whoever spoke first chose the language. If Father began in English, I had to carry on in English. When there was a change of topic, I could continue in the same language or switch to Chinese. The rule was to keep the two languages completely separate. Ellen dropped out as soon as we switched to Chinese. Evenings when my parents were not entertaining or being entertained, Ellen read to me. She began with a beautifully illustrated copy of *Robinson Crusoe* from Father's library. A perceptive reader with a gentle voice, she evoked vivid mental images and lulled me into a delicious lassitude.

In the first days after war in Europe had been declared, the international community splintered. In the Legation Quarter, almost everyone gave a wide berth to the compound flying a swastika. At first, when Herr Henschel, the chinless and balding German consular official, came down the street with his large, stately wife on his arm, people crossed to the other side. However, the tension soon evaporated. As Irina, a Russian duchess down on her luck, said expansively, "So Europe is going up in flames. We're on the other side of the world! As long as the Japanese leave *us* alone, who cares!"

In this surreal atmosphere, we three were discovering one another. Ironically, Ellen was the more familiar to me, through our both having lived with the Findlay-Wus. As for my father, he proved to be a complex man, charming and elegant, who enjoyed life but disliked ostentation. He led an extremely public and hectic existence but was also very private. He was reluctant to talk about himself, the places he'd been, the things he'd done, the people he knew. Whether his reticence grew out of his reserved personality or out of the sensitive nature of his work I could not say – perhaps both. Though all three of his sons were baptized Roman Catholics, he did not subscribe to any organized religion. He believed in a supreme being, but was guided by his personal credo: "To thine own self be true."

My father had no idea how to talk to or play with a child and treated me as a miniature adult. He was wonderfully articulate, his knowledge inexhaustible, but he never lectured. Together we visited historic sites in and around Beijing. Occasionally Ellen came with us, but the best times were when Father and I were alone. I had his undivided attention, and I think he enjoyed my wide-eyed enjoyment of the tales he told.

I never tired of the Sunday morning thieves' market at the Temple of Heaven. Every square inch in front of the circular structure was occupied. Father moved through the throng, exchanging greetings with the traders and distributing money to beggars. The market was arranged in sections. On the outer fringes bird sellers sold mynah birds that talked in unearthly voices and parrots that cawed, whistled, and yelled obscenities. The best songbirds were kept in hooded cages to prevent their unique song from being corrupted by imitating others. Farther on were fish mongers with a dazzling array of exotic red and white carp and goldfish with gossamer fins and tails.

Our destination, the antique market, was beyond the gem market, where former palace eunuchs sold jewels from a bygone era and servants peddled small artefacts on behalf of some noble bannerman (a member of one of the Manchurian clans of the last imperial dynasty, each clan having its own distinctive banner) who stood haughtily aloof, giving the lie to a flat purse. There were foreigners, too, selling exotic furs and Russian religious icons. These were desperate times, and people made a few yuen however they could.

Though some of the antique dealers looked suitably sinister, not all were thugs or grave robbers. Father knew many of them, and we seldom went home empty-handed. One day a trader approached my father to say he had an extraordinary artefact to show him. We followed the man to where an object, at least five feet tall, covered with a sheet, stood on the flat deck of a mule cart. Under the sheet was a huge stone Buddha's head, probably hacked off a statue, from a cave temple. My father examined it, asking questions.

"I wouldn't sell it to the devil," the man said, nudging and winking. "This belongs in China."

"Which devil?" my father asked casually.

"He seems to know a lot about Qing dynasty porcelain," the trader said. "Indeed, he's never been interested in anything else. But this piece made him drool!"

My father's eyes narrowed imperceptibly. "A tall Japanese? Bullet head, thick glasses, small moustache?" He spoke softly, as if to himself, eyes fixed on the Buddha's head. "Speaks Chinese like one of us?"

The trader nodded. My father made up his mind at once, and the trader's mule cart followed Father's car into the Legation Quarter. The entire household staff was summoned to carry the great stone head into the house. At the front door, however, they stopped. The entrance was too narrow.

"Take it down," my father ordered.

Even with the door down, the entrance was still a hair's breadth too narrow.

"Remove the door frame," said my father.

Ellen had been watching anxiously, but her protests fell on deaf ears as Zhang and Lao Zhao ripped out the door frame. Finally, the stone head was carried into the house. Fortunately, the inside doors were wider and the head could be installed in the centre of the reception room, where the chandelier lit it to advantage. I wasn't sure whether Father's satisfaction derived from ownership of the piece itself, or from having prevented it from falling into the hands of a Japanese.

Father had introduced the International Lions Club to China, establishing the first club in Tienjin in 1937. He and his fellow Lions did much to alleviate the suffering of the numberless refugees who flooded the city as the Japanese advanced across north and central China. Now he cajoled the foreign community and wealthy Chinese merchants into establishing a club in Beijing as well. The Lions established soup kitchens and shelters for abandoned women and children, where volunteer doctors and nurses offered whatever treatment was possible under primitive conditions.

It was through volunteering at one of these shelters that Ellen fell afoul of the Baptist ladies. When she announced one day that she had invited them to tea, my father groaned.

"They seem perfectly nice," she assured Father.

"I'm sure they are, my dear," he said.

As it turned out, they were a droll lot, boiled and starched till they creaked. Each one clutched a black book. From the top of the stairs I could hear a murmur of voices, but no jollity or rattle of teacups. Presently, I heard the piano; one of them was pounding the keys and thumping the foot pedal. Then they all sang, doleful tunes liberally sprinkled with the words "Jesus" and "lord" and "love." When the racket finally stopped, I crept down the stairs just as the ladies were preparing to leave. A thin rail of a woman in a black hat, who seemed to be the leader, cornered me. Tapping my forehead with the tip of a dry, talon-like finger, she asked in a deep contralto, "Have you been born again, boy?"

Ellen caught my eye and shook her head.

"No, ma'am," I said.

"My dear!" She whirled upon Ellen. "Is that true?"

Ellen drew herself up to her full height. "None of us have been *born* again."

The ladies gasped. The thin one cleared her throat purposefully. "Sisters," she cried, "we must give thanks for being brought here." Jabbing the air with her bony finger as though it were God's lightning rod, she exclaimed, "We'll see you're born again. Never fear!"

When Ellen recounted all this to my father at dinner, he mimicked the thin woman. "Never fear! They'll be back."

And they were, a few afternoons later. The piano was assaulted again, and the house shook with "Rock of Ages" and other God-fearing tunes.

That same morning, on the way home from walking Rex, I had badgered Zhang into buying me a toy mouse from a street vendor. It was fashioned out of grey felt and had a long pink tail. Rubber bands attached to the tail activated tiny wheels under the body; when you pulled the tail, the mouse skittered across the floor. I was playing with my mouse when the singing began. Between songs I heard the skinny woman either speaking in a very stilted manner or reading. When she paused, the others intoned a single word that sounded like "amah," an anglo-Chinese word for maid-servant. Overcome by curiosity, I tiptoed downstairs. The living-room door was ajar and I could see Ellen sitting in the centre of the room, hands folded stiffly on her lap, while the ladies knelt in a circle around her, clutching their black books.

The skinny one again attacked the piano with fingers and foot — thump, thump, thump — and the ladies broke into another song. Ellen spotted me and blinked hard. She wanted me to go away.

Instead I made faces, trying to make her laugh. I could see the corners of her mouth quiver in spite of herself.

I pulled the tail of my toy mouse and it raced across the room, stopping inches from Ellen's foot. One of the ladies shrieked and leaped into a chair. The others scattered noisily to the corners of the room.

Mice were a menace in those days, and the skinny woman shouted for order while the others babbled incoherently. The commotion brought Zhang running as I went to retrieve the mouse.

"It's only a toy," I said, dangling it by the tail.

The woman in the chair fainted. Zhang signalled with his eyes for me to leave the room.

From my window I watched the ladies bustle out of the house, chins jutting with indignation. When Ellen came into my room, I was smearing crayon on a colouring book. Silently she extended her hand; I put the toy mouse in it. I expected her to be different somehow, more like the skinny lady, but she seemed the same.

"Did you get born again?" I asked nervously.

She shook her head and burst into laughter. I threw my arms around her, relieved they hadn't changed her.

Because the husbands of those women were important members of the diplomatic and business communities, my father was put in the awkward position of having to make amends. Life was becoming increasingly complex for him. Sandwiched between Chiang Kai-shek's Kuomintang, still perceived as the legitimate government of China, and the pro-Japanese Wang Jingwei regime in Nanking, my father was expected to keep the railway running and to protect its foreign investors' interests at the same time. His main concern was preserving the railways for China; he was convinced she would need them to unite and modernize as part of the new community of nations that would emerge when the war ended. Meanwhile, maintaining the delicate balance of diplomacy must have been nerve-racking. His endeavours required more and more of his time.

Keeping a precocious child occupied became Ellen's challenge. In one of her forays into the city, she found a book of phonetics. On a cold rainy afternoon, when I was restless and out of sorts, she asked, "How would you like to read by yourself?"

"You mean like grown-ups do?"

I was elated. The lessons began at once. Within days I had learned to sound the entire alphabet, and soon I was sounding words. Before long I was reading *Fun with Dick and Jane*. It was a silly book, but its idealized home and family touched me, and Ellen gradually became the young matron in the book.

One day when there was a lull in the conversation at lunch, I decided to try out a word I had been practising. With a wildly fluttering heart I said evenly, "Mother, can I have more soup, please?"

Ellen looked at me, startled. Father set down his chopsticks.

"Mother, can I have more soup, please?" The second time was easier.

Father passed my bowl and Ellen, eyes shiny and moist, filled it.

I learned to read and write Chinese at about this time. My first tutor was a renowned calligrapher, a bannerman with vague connections to the last imperial house. The prince was a tall, thin man with the lantern jaw, heavy brows, hooded eyes, and fleshy mouth characteristic of the Aisinjoro clan. In flowing Manchu robes, he moved with slow, stately purpose, like a galleon under full sail. Although he behaved as though he was royalty, he actually made a meagre living selling calligraphy and taking a few students, but mostly depending on the generosity of friends.

Three times a week I was driven to the prince's house in the heart of the Chinese city. He lived in an old courtyard house down a tortuous *hutong*, or alley, barely wide enough for the car to pass. He had several wives, dozens of children, and an army of servants.

My lessons began formally. The chief eunuch, a sly, obsequious, dried-up scarecrow with a prune face, met me at the gate. Dressed in faded court robes, he guided me through the house. "The railway administrator's third son has arrived," he announced in a high reedy voice every time we crossed a threshold. Curious faces peered from doorways and cracks between curtains. My brown hair and western clothes stood out among the gaudy Manchu court costumes.

The prince received me in a large room with a small round table in the centre and two straight-backed chairs. A *kang*, or sleeping platform, on which large plump cushions were scattered, ran along one wall. A cup of tea, cigarettes, and matches stood on a small table in its centre.

On entering the room, I bowed with my arms pressed against my sides, a pupil paying homage to his master, reciting at the same time the formal salutation the eunuch had taught me outside. The prince responded by inviting me to sit across from him at the table, and the lesson began.

Written Chinese evolved from pictographs. Each character represents a word; it is a language that can only be memorized. The prince used two-sided cardboard squares with a picture on one side and the corresponding character on the other. He showed me a picture.

"What is this?" he asked in his deep sonorous voice.

"Niao," I replied.

He turned the card over and showed me the character for "bird." By the time he had explained each brush stroke, a highly stylized bird had taken shape in my mind. Then we went on to the next card.

The second half of the lesson was calligraphy. There were two forms to master: small calligraphy, for everyday use, and large calligraphy, a fine art. The selection of brushes was crucial. The prince insisted on the finest pig bristles. Ink was prepared by grinding a stick of compressed carbon in a few drops of water on a flat stone. Fifty turns clockwise, fifty counterclockwise. In the meantime the brush was left to soak in a dish of water. The tip had to be soft, but the hairs must not be extended or the brush would not hold the ink. When writing, one sits bolt upright, the brush held vertically, in line with one's nose. The arm rests firmly on the table, the wrist elevated but relaxed. Fingers and wrist manipulate the brush.

By now I was reading English quite fluently, but my Chinese lagged behind. It occurred to me that at the rate of thirty characters a week it would be a long time before I could read a story book. I was impatient, and before long the prince lost interest. After he had gone through the day's ten characters, he napped on the *kang*, sitting cross-legged in the Manchu fashion. I ground my ink and did my calligraphy sloppily. I preferred small calligraphy because large calligraphy exposed my weaknesses.

"We need grace, and dash," cried the prince, making sweeping gestures in the air, despairing of my mediocrity.

The prince was often "indisposed," though never on the days his fee fell due. He himself never touched money. His plump chief wife took the envelope and counted the bills with the tip of her tongue flicking between painted lips. The lesson could not begin until she finished.

One day when the prince was indisposed, I was taken to play with his son, a boy of nine or ten called Xiao Niu, or Little Bull. Evidently the prince had had several sons, all of whom had died in childhood or infancy except this one, who was named after an animal to ward off evil spirits. To further confound the forces of evil, the boy kept a tuft of hair like the stump of a tail at the back of his shaved head. The ruse seemed to have worked.

Xiao Niu looked me up and down, his arms folded across his chest.

"So you're the half-caste brat," he said arrogantly. "Kow-tow!"

Kow-towing is a particularly distasteful form of salutation left over from feudal times. It's used for greeting one's elders for the first time, on festive occasions such as the Chinese new year, or on meeting so-called royalty. To kow-tow, you kneel in a crouching position, palms pressed flat to the floor. Then you knock your forehead audibly against the floor, thrice, the louder the better.

"I will not!" I shot back.

The eunuch made bleating noises, and Xiao Niu made a fist. The blow lifted me off my feet. The next thing I knew Lao Zhao was wiping blood from my face and bawling at someone. The eunuch laid cold compresses on my forehead to stop the nosebleed, and the prince's chief wife plied me with hot almond tea and cake.

"I'll whip that Xiao Niu!" she kept repeating. "I'll give him the hiding of his life! But you mustn't tell your father."

When we got in the car, Lao Zhao shook his head. "Kid, you have to learn to fight." He jutted his chin towards the windshield and the teeming streets. "This is a hard place."

"Where will I learn?"

"I'll teach you," he said, rubbing his hands together. "But . . ."

"I won't tell!" I said quickly.

And so Lao Zhao taught me the rudiments of Chinese boxing in the garage. First he showed me how to block blows with an arm, sidestep the attacker, and strike back with a chopping motion aimed at the neck or ribs. "That usually takes the wind out of his sails," Lao Zhao grinned, as we practised the moves over and over. "Don't be afraid," he encouraged. "You won't hurt me." Though I gave it my best effort, I was poorly coordinated and clumsy. Lao Zhao pondered a moment, then brightened.

"I'll show you something easier."

This time, when he threw a punch, I was to seize his wrist and pull his arm over my shoulder, grabbing the upper arm with my other hand.

"Now hook one foot around my ankle, bend forward, and heave!"

I did as I was told, and Lao Zhao landed on the floor with a thump.

"I think you've got the idea," he said, rubbing his rump ruefully. "Let's do it again."

Try as I might, however, I could not flip him a second time.

"I let you flip me to show you the effect of what you were doing," he chuckled. I stamped my foot with exasperation. He let me stew a bit before he said, "Now I'll show you why you couldn't do it a second time."

I felt much better after he showed me how he'd prevented me from flipping him over. Gradually my confidence grew.

"I'm not teaching you to be a bully," he cautioned. "This is to protect yourself." His eyes bore into me, reinforcing the idea. "And to teach that little prince a lesson," he added with a wink.

The prince became conscientious again and for a while I made good progress. Then he slacked off. At first he reclined against a mound of cushions on the *kang*, eyes half shut, while the eunuch conducted the reading lesson in a voice neither male nor female. The prince interjected from time to time, correcting mispronunciations like a singing master catching missed notes.

"Watch my lips!"

He wrapped his mouth around the offending word like a tasty morsel, and I repeated it until the prince sighed his approval. In this way I acquired the Beijing accent I have to this day. Then the eunuch resumed in a voice that made my flesh creep.

Once, when the prince failed to appear at the appointed hour, Xiao Niu came into the room. "Is my father in fairyland?" he asked loudly. The eunuch gestured for him to leave. Instead, the boy marched up to the table and swept everything on to the floor.

"You!" he shouted at me. "Foreign Nose!" And a stream of words followed that I had never heard before.

"Show him!" Xiao Niu yelled at the eunuch. The eunuch danced about, flapping his arms, begging the boy to leave. The two weaved about the room, Xiao Niu darting this way and that and the eunuch cackling after him like a hysterical hen. Suddenly, Xiao Niu lost interest and marched out of the room.

I repeated some of the words I'd picked up to Lao Zhao.

"What do they mean?"

"Dirty things." From the way he said it, I knew they were words I should not repeat.

"And keep away from that eunuch."

The next time the prince was absent, Xiao Niu's antics — shouting and turning somersaults — made it impossible for the eunuch to finish my lesson.

"Maybe you two should play together this afternoon," the eunuch suggested, eager to extricate himself.

Xiao Niu's eyes narrowed. "Is this monkey fur?" As he went to pull my hair, I dodged, grabbed his tuft of hair, and yanked his head back, simultaneously kicking his feet from under him. He landed on the tile floor with a yelp. Lao Zhao had taught me well.

The eunuch flew to the boy. "How dare you pull the young prince's life line!" he quavered, shaking a finger at me, eyes wide with alarm. Some powerful superstition was attached to the stub. The eunuch laid his little prince on the *kang*. Xiao Niu groaned.

"Where does it hurt?" inquired the eunuch, massaging the boy's back and limbs, murmuring comfort. Presently, Xiao Niu drifted off to sleep. The eunuch tiptoed from the room, saying he would bring almond tea and cakes. As soon as he was gone, Xiao Niu sat up.

"Who taught you to do that?" he asked in a quiet voice.

"Somebody."

"Will he teach me?"

"No. He doesn't like you."

Xiao Niu flapped his arms dejectedly.

"I think you're all right, when you're not playing the bully," I muttered, feeling a rush of pity.

As the eunuch's bustling footsteps sounded outside, Xiao Niu lay down again and shut his eyes. The eunuch entered and scowled at me. He laid a tray with two covered bowls and a plate of little cakes on the table and went over to shake Xiao Niu, gently crooning endearments until the boy opened his eyes.

"Have a little almond tea," he coaxed. "A mouthful, to comfort your faithful slave."

Xiao Niu allowed himself to be propped up with cushions and the hot, sweet liquid to be spooned into him. Every time he moaned the eunuch went into a flap, plumping cushions, anxiously inquiring where it hurt. Xiao Niu whispered something and the eunuch left the room.

"He's such an idiot," Xiao Niu said. "It's because he hasn't got this –" He grabbed his crotch.

"Why?"

"It got chopped off."

I cringed. Xiao Niu's mean streak resurfaced, and he described in gory detail how a boy becomes a eunuch.

"I bet you've never heard of anything like that, huh?"

I shook my head, sick to my stomach.

"My father is probably in fairyland," Xiao Niu said. "My mother too. That's why the old fool didn't go running to her. There would have been a real circus if he had!" The boy laughed mirthlessly.

"There is no fairyland."

"There is too!" Xiao Niu's voice had risen in pitch. He could see I was not convinced.

"My father and mother go there all the time!" He stuck a thumb in his mouth, folding three fingers into his palm, extending the thumb and the little finger straight out, making sucking sounds. "It's called swallowing clouds and spitting fog." I gaped at him uncomprehendingly. "Foreign kids are so stupid," he cried, exasperated. "I'll show you!"

He swung off the kang, dragged me from the room, and ran across the courtyard into a small garden. I followed, frightened yet curious. We went through a moon gate into a secluded courtyard shaded by an old willow tree. A heavy, sweetish smell drifted through the door of the main room, which stood ajar. Xiao Niu pressed a finger to his lips, dropped on hands and knees, and crept towards the door. I followed suit. Xiao Niu beckoned me to peer through the opening.

In the half-light, I could make out the prince and his chief wife stretched toe to toe on the kang, sucking on long skinny pipes. A maid gently turned the bowls at the end of the pipes over the flame of a tiny lamp. The two languid figures sucked noisily, breathing out great clouds of heavy grey smoke that made me gag.

"Are they swallowing clouds and spitting fog?" I whispered. Xiao Niu made a face at me and nodded.

Later that day when my father asked what I learnt that day, I said, "I saw the prince swallowing clouds and spitting fog."

Father's smile disappeared. He wanted to hear the details, so I prattled on. "He was lying on the *kang* but the little prince insisted his father was in fairyland," I finished. "Can that be possible, Father?"

Father sighed and shook his head. Midder found me another tutor.

After the experience with the prince, my parents decided lessons with Master Chien would took place in my playroom, where a desk and a blackboard had been set up. Master Chien was a classical scholar who had probably been a minor official in the last dynasty. He reminded me of a gnarled old tree, dry and wrinkled but stately. The deep rumbling voice that came out of his spare frame was a surprise, yet in keeping with his solemn demeanour. Master Chien dispensed with reading cards. Instead we plunged into the classics.

"Man is born virtuous. Though resembling one another by nature, each person is ruled by habit." The memorized tenets of Confucius rattled around in my brain with the poems of Li Bai, Wang Wei, and Xu Dongpo, rhyming sounds rather than words with meaning.

Master Chien did not tolerate questions. "Eventually the mind will devise answers," he said loftily. He believed the more one suffered, the more one learned.

Calligraphy was still my cross. The aesthetics of soaking the brush and grinding ink had to be mastered first. I hated these rituals and complained bitterly to my father, but he sided with the tutor: "You must do as you're told."

Master Chien was terrified of dogs. On mornings when he was due, Rex was banished to my bedroom and the door kept shut. At first the dog barked and scratched, demanding to be let out. Master Chien trembled like a leaf until Rex quieted down. In time the dog got used to being banished and did not protest. After Master Chien left, however, Rex sniffed the chair he had used and followed his scent to the door, growling.

One morning everything went wrong. I had not memorized a poem, I spilled the ink, and finally I broke my brush. At his wit's end, Master Chien whacked me across the knuckles with his folded fan. Rubbing my smarting hand, I asked to be excused to go to the bathroom. I left the door ajar, and instead of the bathroom I went into my bedroom. Rex leaped at me, anxious to be set free. I hugged his big head and whispered, "Sick 'em!"

With a low growl the dog charged through the door. Master Chien squealed, picked up a waste basket, and waved it in front of him like a lion tamer. Rex circled, growling. He was more playful than vicious, and if Master Chien had stayed calm the dog would have left him alone. But he panicked, terrified, skipping about and jabbing at the dog with the basket. Rex leaped up, knocking him flat on his back.

Hearing the commotion, Mother hurried upstairs. She discovered the hapless tutor spreadeagled on the carpet, Rex sitting on his chest, me rolling on the floor with laughter. Every time Master Chien moved, the dog growled ominously.

Ignoring Mother's apologies, Master Chien marched out of the house and never set foot in it again.

My parents decided it was time I went to school.

7

第七章

S C H O O L

D A Y S

THE INTERNATIONAL SCHOOL was a one-room school-house tucked away at the back of the American compound in the Legation Quarter. A soft-spoken young teacher, Miss Kramer, presided over six children. Buzzy, a husky blond ten-year-old, was American. Donald, with a head too big for his body and thick glasses that magnified his eyes, was British. The two pretty blond girls were exact opposites: the American was a chatterbox, while the Dutch girl with the deep, grave eyes hardly spoke at all. The dark-haired girl was from Australia, a tomboy with a rowdy laugh.

Miss Kramer divided us into four groups. Donald and I, the youngest, were in one corner. Next to us were the Australian girl and the pretty American, who smiled every time I looked her way. She was the prettiest girl I'd ever seen. Buzzy and the Dutch girl, who wore her braids looped around her ears, had individual programs, he because he was older than the rest, she because she knew little English. Miss Kramer, trailing the scent of lavender and starch, her long dress rustling, moved smiling and calm from one group to the next, keeping us happy and busy.

I did not know how to interact with other children or to play games and had to acquire new skills. One of the first things I learned was the pecking order. Buzzy was the undisputed leader. "Mary Jane is my girl," he told me earnestly. "I get to sit next to her at lunch and carry her books and walk her home after school."

"That's all right," piped Donald. "Gwen and Gretchen and I are going home in David's father's car."

Soon after I started school, the Findlay-Wus finally sold their house in Tienjin and prepared to leave China, first for Hong Kong, then "home." The strained relations between our families had eased, and Uncle George, Auntie Hester, and Irene came up to stay with us before embarking. The two women were just as I remembered them, but Uncle George had deteriorated further. His once handsome face, now splotchy, was awful to look at. He tried to be cheerful, but he tried too hard.

Before leaving for Hong Kong, he wanted to revisit all his favourite places in and around Beijing. Mother and Auntie Hester went along with diminishing enthusiasm. Mother had a household to run, and her regular round of volunteer work and social activities to keep up, which let her off the hook. Auntie Hester was simply not interested in seeing the sights. She told all their friends who came to see them, "You have no idea how glad I am to be leaving. And George is too, I'm sure." Irene spent her days languidly swanning around the house, brightening only when the mail arrived.

One morning Uncle George suggested going to the Forbidden City.

"Can we go, Father?" I chirped. "I want to show Uncle George all the statues of the animals. Birds too! Can we?"

"But George," Auntie Hester cut in, "it's rather warm out, and you don't feel well in the heat."

"Stop telling me how I feel," said Uncle George. "It's definitely the Forbidden City today, David." He tousled my hair. "Think you can be ready in fifteen minutes?"

As Uncle George made for his room, with Auntie Hester trailing after him protesting, Father shot Mother an inquiring look. She shook her head ever so slightly. So the four of us went off – Father and I, Uncle George leaning on his cane and walking rather slowly, Auntie Hester holding a parasol over her head and looking grim and put-upon.

Peddlers thronged the space between Tiananmen and Wu Men (Meridian Gate) selling cooked food, fruits and vegetables, native crafts, and cheap toys. Sheep herders and dusty camel trains camped in the shadows of the vermilion walls. Mongols in bright silk tunics rubbed shoulders with leather-clad Manchus and brown-skinned Tibetan lamas in their scarlet and yellow robes. Everywhere you turned there were beggars; there seemed to be more each time we went. Auntie Hester took my hand forcefully in hers, darting a scandalized look at Father, who seemed unconcerned when I dawdled to look at this or that.

"There's nothing to look at," she said flatly. "They're just silly people!"

Father and Uncle George moved through the milling crowd, greeting traders they knew. Some traders greeted me by name. Auntie Hester was horrified, but her protests fell on deaf ears: the two men had become engrossed in conversation with a Mongol caravan owner just arrived from the northeast. They seemed to be questioning the man intently about what he'd seen.

Father always had a pocketful of loose change for the beggars. "You've got the bandage on the wrong leg," he teased a man with a game leg who lay on the cobblestones whimpering. The man chuckled. "Administrator," he said, grinning roguishly and tugging his forelock as he pocketed the proffered coin, "the other leg needs a rest."

Auntie Hester was fit to be tied. The awful conditions, the mass of humanity, appalled her. When we approached the Meridian Gate, where the crowd thinned, she said to my father, "John, I simply must protest! How can you expose the boy to all this riff-raff?"

Father glanced my way, a twinkle in his eye, but made no reply.

Within Meridian Gate there was hardly a soul, for admissions were steep. Auntie Hester breathed a sigh of relief as she gazed towards the audience hall across the vast square, the majestic marble steps and terrace. The melancholy, decaying beauty of the place never failed to touch me. I took Uncle George's hand, and we walked slowly towards the hall. The only sound was the tap-tapping of his cane on the cobblestones, echoing back and forth from wall to wall. On the terrace was a group of mythical animals and birds depicted in stone and bronze. My favourite was the Chi Lin, a fierce-looking creature with the head of a dragon, body of a deer, and hooves of a horse. It sent shivers down my spine.

"Do you believe in Chi Lin, Uncle George?"

Uncle George glided his hand along the creature's mane. For a moment his eyes gleamed with tears. He gazed at the other statues, then back across the square to where Auntie Hester stood waiting, in the shade of the gateway we had come through. Father was walking towards us, head down, deep in thought.

"I believe in Chi Lin," said Uncle George. He spoke to me the way my father did, as if I were a miniature adult. "They say the Chi Lin appears when a wise man is born, or about to die." He sighed, and his smile was forced. "I wonder if he will do the same for a foolish man."

Father was upon us, and Uncle George put on a bright face. The two men moved off, arm in arm, talking earnestly. Father signalled me to go keep Auntie Hester company. I ran back to where she waited, fanning herself with a handkerchief.

"What have they got to talk about?" she said irritably. "Oh, I shall be so glad to see the last of China!"

While Uncle George and Auntie Hester were staying with us, the Chinese men in broad-brimmed hats who used to visit their house in Tienjin reappeared. Occasionally an unprepossessing fellow with a bald head and eyes like black holes came with them. A silent man, he moved as though fitted with well-oiled wheels. No one ever mentioned his name; he was known simply as "the General."

The men talked for hours on end. Sometimes Buzzy's father, Captain Wood, and Donald's father, Mr. Burton, joined them. While these conversations took place, Zhang stood guard outside the study door, and Lao Zhao stationed himself out of sight around the corner. Mother paced the living room upstairs, while Auntie Hester sat nervously knitting. Now and then the women exchanged a few words in a kind of verbal Morse code. Both brightened noticeably when the Chinese men finally left.

Uncle George and my father remained in the study a while longer, smoking cigars and sipping brandy. When they finally came upstairs both were blank-faced. Uncle George seemed tired, yet relieved. Auntie Hester quickly led him to their room.

"Must you deal with them?" Mother complained. She looked stricken.

"There's a war on," Father replied.

"It's always the war!"

Father tried to put his arm around her, but Mother moved away. Then, seeing me in the doorway, she reached for his hand, a gesture of solidarity or reassurance. They stood like that a long moment, gazing at one another.

"Might as well get used to it," Father said. "It's going to get worse before it gets better."

Being older, Buzzy knew things the rest of us did not. After his mother left them, he had lived with his father on various postings all over the world. When I told him about the Chinese men in hats, he said, "Those are secret agents. So is my old man."

"Your father's a secret agent?"

"So is yours."

"My father's the administrator of the railway!" I objected.

"Aw, he's both," Buzzy said, as if stating the obvious to an idiot. He grabbed me by the collar to make a point. "That's why they're talking to the Headsman."

"We don't know anybody called that," I said, trying to sound as though I knew what I was talking about.

He made a face. "The General. My dad calls him the Headsman because that's his job." Buzzy drew a finger across his throat and let his head loll forward. "He does Chiang Kai-shek's dirty work!"

Donald gasped. Buzzy loved an audience, and now that he had us riveted, he launched into another of his tales, which usually began, "When we lived in the Philippines," or "One time in Hawaii . . ."

It was a curiously lively, edgy time. Though the walls of the quarter stood stoutly between us and the Chinese city, cracks were appearing. Mother and her volunteer ladies who took turns at soup kitchens and refugee shelters brought home stories of the horrible privations of ordinary people who had been uprooted from the land they cultivated, forced to flee their homes or businesses. Countless people were being separated from their families not only by the Japanese but by the equally ferocious fighting among the Chinese themselves.

In spite of the Kuomintang's corruption and ineptitude, the foreign powers still recognized it as China's national government and best chance for freedom and democracy. My father did too. There was no way of knowing, in 1941, that Chiang's pledge of building a true republic once the Communists were eliminated and the Japanese driven from the land was, at best, a pipe dream.

When the post of administrator of the Jin-Pu Railway (linking Tienjin and Pukau with spurs to Beijing in the north and Nanking and Shanghai in the south) fell vacant, the national government in Chungking nominated my father to fill it. Britain, the railway's foreign partner, seconded the nomination. Though she was now fighting for her life in Europe, Britain took the long view, determined to keep a foothold in China after the war. Father was reluctant to accept the post, but pressure was brought to bear. Finally, a representative of the British syndicate, who was stationed in Shanghai, flew to Tienjin. Father went to meet him. When he returned, he was administrator of the Jin-Pu Railway as well.

In the spring of 1941, Father and Midder went on frequent inspection trips along the rail lines. They were exhausting journeys from which Father returned haggard, but he kept pushing himself, drawing on seemingly inexhaustible reserves. He talked about these trips only with Mother, quickly changing the subject if I came into the room. Still, I caught bits that Buzzy deciphered.

"Your father's been behind Japanese lines with the KMT!" he whispered, face lit with excitement.

"He was inspecting the rail lines," I protested.

"What if the Japs catch him?" asked Donald.

"What do you think?" said Buzzy.

Donald and I both stared, wide-eyed, as Buzzy slowly drew a finger across his throat.

As the Findlay-Wus' departure drew near, Yuri came down from Mukden to visit Irene. He'd grown terribly thin. Clothes hung on him like a scarecrow's. Once again there was talk of marriage, but Yuri would not allow Irene with her delicate health to hazard the primitive conditions of Manchukuo.

"You'll be better off away from the madness of China," he pleaded. "The war can't last forever. There will be a time for us."

"We're never coming back," Irene said. "I'll never see you again."

"Then I'll go to England," said Yuri, putting on a brave face. He might as well have proposed going to the moon. A stateless Russian without money or connections had no way of getting out of China and into Britain. That night he slipped out of the house and caught the first train back to Mukden. Afterwards, Irene blamed Father for not having moved Yuri out of Manchukuo. Whether he could have done so but did not, or whether, as Mother maintained, Yuri was too stiff-necked to accept a charitable promotion, I cannot say.

A huge farewell party was organized for the Findlay-Wus. The string orchestra that played the Beijing Hotel was hired for dancing.

Dressmakers bustled in and out of the house with bolts of fabric and designs for the ladies' gowns. Zhang flew about, supervising, delivering instructions, re-arranging furniture. Cook shouted happily at the extra kitchen help. Everybody who was anybody was invited.

For weeks the Legation Quarter had been buzzing with news that the dapper middle-aged Frenchman, Monsieur Claude, a perennial bachelor, had finally met his match in the person of a French woman he had met in Shanghai. It was whispered, with raised eyebrows, that the lady was an *artiste*, from the Folies-Bergère.

"What's Folies-Bergère?" I asked my father.

"Eat your carrots, dear," Mother smiled. "They make your eyes sparkle."

"Father?" I persisted, shovelling buttered shredded carrots into my mouth.

My parents exchanged looks of alarmed amusement.

"You'll learn, when you grow up." Father's smile was conspiratorial but no further information was forthcoming.

As usual, Buzzy had the answer. "The ladies of the Folies-Bergère prance around with no clothes on," he informed Donald and me.

Donald, who was prone to illness, muttered something about catching a death of cold.

"It's true!" Buzzy hissed, shoving his face into Donald's. "And feathers stick out of their arse!"

"Only chickens have feathers coming out their arse," Donald said, blinking behind his thick glasses.

"I'll show you my father's postcards," said Buzzy. "Fifty cents a peek!"

Neither Donald nor I had any money so we dickered. Finally a deal was struck. For a dozen marbles in mint condition Buzzy would show Donald and me the picture of a lady of the Folies-Bergère. We were sworn to secrecy with a special handshake.

At the appointed hour we met behind the statue of Joan of Arc in the park. Donald and I handed over our favourite marbles, and Buzzy took a postcard from his breast pocket. A plump, scantily dressed young woman with feathers protruding from her derrière leered at the camera. It was the first time I'd seen a near-naked lady.

"Does Madame Claude look like that?" I asked dubiously.

"She'll catch cold," sniffed Donald.

"You two are so dumb!" Buzzy tucked the postcard out of sight and stalked off.

Days before the party, Father carefully coached me in greeting his guests in their own language. At a certain point, Zhang would bring me to the reception room and Father would present me to the designated guests, whom I would greet as instructed. Then supper would be announced, and Zhang would whisk me up the stairs, where I would have my supper and go to bed.

At seven o'clock the guests began to arrive. From the top of the stairs I watched Mother, in a white evening gown, and Father, in evening clothes with a chest full of medals, welcoming the arrivals – motley artists and writers; bankers, captains of industry, and diplomats; various exotics in turbans, saris, and silk robes; and a sprinkling of dubious Romanovs who assiduously avoided one another. I was all agog waiting for the woman with feathers, but no one fitting that description appeared.

Finally, dressed in a new charcoal grey suit of some summer-weight material with a handsome dark tie, my unruly hair damped down with water, I was led down the stairs. Zhang flung open the door, and my father crossed the room in a few swift strides, smiling broadly. With one hand on my shoulder, he steered me through the guests towards the great Buddha's head, where a knot of people had gathered. Monsieur Claude, whom I'd met before, shook my hand solemnly and then winked, his waxed moustaches jiggling with delight at my newly acquired French.

Then I was presented to a tall thin woman who seemed to grow out of the pool of white satin swirling about her feet. Madame

Claude's arms were encased in long white gloves that ended in a slender black cigarette holder. A white turban adorned with a single jewel was wound around her head. She was beautiful but as cold as the stone Buddha's head behind her.

I murmured the greeting I had learned by rote – "Bonsoir, Madame, et bienvenue" – darting quick glances to see if there were feathers attached to her rear. Monsieur Claude engaged my father in conversation before we could move on, and for an awful moment I was stranded as Madame Claude gazed down at me from her great height.

"Stop starin' at me arse," she said. "Piss off, you little 'aff-caste."

I saw red and planted my foot on the train of her gown. Madame Claude's eyes widened in horror; then, smiling, she said between her teeth, "Git off me bleedin' dress, monkey!"

I smiled up at her and ground my foot into the satin.

"Ah'll box yer ears, I will!" she hissed.

"I'll kick you," I whispered back.

She tweaked my ear. I wiped both feet on her dress.

It must have been close to daybreak when I woke. The few voices coming from downstairs sounded distant, unreal. Someone was playing snatches of songs on the piano. The clink of glasses told me it was probably my parents and the Findlay-Wus having a nightcap. Mother launched into a tune everybody knew and Uncle George's rich baritone floated up the stairs:

"After the ball is over,
She took out her glass eye;
She put her false teeth in water;
Hung out her hair to dry . . ."

Though his health had been precarious, he was well lubricated and in good spirits that evening.

"She put her false leg on the doorstep,
Hung her wooden arm on the wall.
There wasn't much left of her beauty

After the ball!"

They were having so much fun I could not stay in bed. I tiptoed down to find the door to the reception room ajar. I could see them clustered round the piano. Uncle George ended the song with a flourish and reprised it on the piano in a comical, stiff-fingered way, left hand thumping out a hard one-two-three, one-two-three. Father bowed to Mother, and they danced. Irene slid onto the piano bench and took over, while her parents danced. Then Mother played while Irene danced with Father.

One of the maids tidying up discovered me.

"Join us, young man!" cried Uncle George from across the room. I raced to him, and he swung me up and plopped me into an empty chair. Father's eyes were grave, but before he could say anything, I blurted, "I'm hungry!"

"We'll see what we can do," he said, and gestured to Zhang across the room. In a moment a roast beef sandwich and a glass of milk materialized. The grown-ups watched me eat, talking desultorily. Suddenly they were all tired, especially Uncle George. After I polished off the food, Mother led me back to bed. As I drifted off, I heard the others going to their rooms.

There was never another party like it in my father's house. It was the last time all of us were together under one roof. The next day the Findlay-Wus left for Tienjin to board their ship. Waving goodbye, Auntie Hester told Mother she was sorry to say goodbye, but would not feel completely safe until she set foot in Hong Kong.

A few days later Mother closed the house for the summer. We would go to Beidaihe for June, July, and August, far from the war. Yet the war, we discovered, could be felt there, too, partly in the tensely luxurious indolence of summer, partly in the distant gunfire that often shattered the nights. One learned to avoid the Japanese soldiers in town like rabid dogs. Mother always took care to walk on the opposite side of the street, head high, eyes straight ahead. She was determined that war would remain a disaster that happened to other people.

The same ebb and flow of guests passed through Father's villa. All my schoolmates whose families had summer retreats came to Beidaihe as well. Though our parents saw each other regularly, we seldom met. The other children had swimming lessons, riding lessons, went to the tennis club with their parents where they took ballroom dancing classes on certain afternoons. Chinese lessons took up my mornings. Midder found me a new tutor, who came up from Beijing and lived in the house with us. However, tutors didn't last long. Either they did not measure up to Father's expectations, or I did not measure up to the tutors'. I could not wait for the lessons to end to escape and race through the fields bare-foot in search of Xiao Hu.

My friendship with the tenant farmer had not gone unnoticed. Father had no objection, but Mother was painfully caste-conscious, and perhaps even more germ-conscious. "Keep a distance," she pleaded. "They have TB, and goodness knows what else. And promise not to eat anything!"

I promised, but nothing was better than Xiao Hu's pancakes, and Wuowuo Tou – a hollow cone of steamed corn meal – eaten with roasted grasshoppers, freshly picked hot peppers, and garlic smelling of earth.

Midder came up often that summer, nearly always accompanied by two or three Chinese men in wide-brimmed straw hats whose pasty faces showed they were more at ease in the dark than in daylight. On a few occasions the General came, too. I thought it funny that he altered his appearance each time, using clothes, glasses, moustache or beard, even a stiff wig.

The General was a strong swimmer and a good horseman. Often he and my father went on long rides. One night they didn't return, and Mother waited up, huddled under a blanket on the veranda while Zhang and Lao Zhao patrolled the grounds. In the morning the two men came home dusty and exhausted, but oddly excited. Mother was so relieved to have Father back that she even smiled at the General, whom she distrusted and disliked.

Midder sometimes slipped away from the others to talk with Xiao Hu in the fields. There was a signal between them. Midder cupped his hands over his mouth and imitated a cuckoo. Whenever Xiao Hu heard that sound, he dropped whatever he was doing. If the cuckoo's call came again, he made an answering call and told me to go into the cornfields or among the towering sorghum.

"Why?"

Xiao Hu scowled, and I went. From my hiding place I strained to make out what was being discussed, but the drumming of my heart blotted out what I tried to overhear.

As the summer wore on, we harvested corn and sorghum, and dried sweet potatoes in the sun for winter. Xiao Hu and his grey donkey, laden with food, often disappeared into the mountains, sometimes for days. When I asked where he had been, he would only say, "Market." He knew I knew he was lying.

"Where?"

Xiao Hu smacked himself on the forehead. "Questions!" he exclaimed.

He managed to change the conversation, and we returned to harvesting. A day or two later he was gone again. I knew he had gone into the mountains and assumed he was taking food to "the bandits." Every time I heard gunfire coming from up there, I quivered and felt lonely, frightened, and terribly left out. Father knew what Xiao Hu was up to. So did Midder. So did Zhang. Why couldn't I?

There was no one I could talk to except Buzzy. Lying on the beach one hot afternoon, I said, "There are bandits in the mountains."

Buzzy flipped over on his stomach, squinted at the mountains, and said, "They're not bandits. They're guerrillas."

"Like King Kong?" The movie had made a tremendous impression.

Buzzy tweaked my nose. "Not that kind of gorilla. Like the black chamber. Secret agents. . . ."

I groaned. I could believe in King Kong, but this other stuff was beyond me.

In August of 1941, the resistance derailed a Japanese troop train north of Beidaihe. Fierce fighting lasted throughout the day. With the sound of gunfire raging, now near, now far, the town shrank into itself. Train service in and out of Beidaihe was halted for several days. The reprisals were savage. The Japanese rounded up people from nearby villages at random, torturing them before shooting them in the back of the head. During those steamy, ominously quiet days, nobody left the house.

One afternoon we were having tea on the veranda when a car flying a Japanese flag drove up, and a Korean in Japanese uniform alighted and marched unceremoniously up to the veranda. My father excused himself from his guests and went to meet him.

"We have a man called Hu San in custody." The Korean spoke Chinese in a stiff staccato accent without preamble. "Does he belong to your household, Administrator?"

Although I did not know Hu's full name, my chest tightened and I could hardly breathe.

"He is my tenant farmer," my father replied. "Why are you holding him?"

The Korean's flat, round face crinkled nastily. He told Father in the same sharp voice that Xiao Hu had been captured in a nearby village. "We suspect he was in the mountains," he said. "The question is why?"

"You are mistaken," Father countered. "He went to market," and he named a small market town north of us where local farmers sold their produce. The Korean paced up and down, slapping his thigh with his swagger stick. He had switched to Japanese, and I did not understand the rest of their exchange. But I had heard enough. I was trembling so hard I could barely bite into my sandwich. Mother took my hand between hers. She did not understand a word of what was said but knew something was wrong. Father never raised his voice. When he was angry he rumbled. He was rumbling now. Something he said made the Korean pivot stiffly on his heel. Father continued without pause until he was done. By now the Korean was sweating profusely, his swagger stick beating an erratic tattoo against his leather-booted shin. Both men were livid. Father had one more remark before the conversation ended. The Korean sputtered angrily, stamped back to his car, and drove away.

"Father!" I cried as soon as the car was gone.

"Just a little misunderstanding," he said. His smile included everybody on the veranda. "We'll clear it up quickly."

As soon as train service resumed, Father said he had to leave for Beijing.

"Must you go?" cried Mother, choking back tears.

"There is a Japanese aristocrat I must see," he said, "a moderate attached to the High Command. He might be persuaded to help."

"And if he doesn't?" Mother countered. She suggested we all go back to Beijing, but my father vetoed the idea.

"We must keep our heads and act normal," Father warned. "I'm going back on business. In a day or two I'll return . . ."

Evidently Father's personal appeal worked and the nobleman exerted his influence, because the Japanese soon released the remaining hostages at Beideihe. Meanwhile, the town emptied early that summer. The war had come uncomfortably close. The few summer residents who remained gathered on the veranda of my father's villa in their crisp summer whites, sipping drinks.

Just when I despaired of seeing Xiao Hu again, there he was one afternoon, leaning on a crutch at the edge of the field. I ran to him, shouting his name. He didn't move or even acknowledge me, merely gazed pensively at the fields. His nose was broken. Teeth were missing. His eyes were swollen half shut. One leg was in splints. A thick wad of bandage bound his ribs. At the sight of the helpless tears running down my face, he shook his head and scowled. I dashed away the tears, and we stood grinning at each other. The toes of his good foot burrowed into the earth as though rooting him. He was the earth.

Xiao Hu had fallen into the hands of Korean collaborators, who were a law unto themselves. Their zeal for their Japanese overlords combined with their contempt for the Chinese made them the worst torturers. Xiao Hu was one of the last prisoners released. Only later did I grasp that, if his tormentors had been able to break him, we all would have been summarily executed.

Xiao Hu was free but not out of danger. He could be arrested again at any moment. Father decided he had to be moved to unoccupied territory and began quietly making arrangements. Later, when we were back in Beijing, he casually remarked that Xiao Hu had been safely smuggled into free China.

"Is he all right?" Mother asked. "He was so badly hurt."

He gave her hand a reassuring squeeze.

"Will I see him again?"

Father took just a second too long to answer. "Perhaps. One day."

8

第八章

ENEMY
ALIENS

B Y THE AUTUMN of 1941, when we were back in Beijing, the dogs of war were baying at our door. From my bedroom window I watched the Japanese troops drill and parade on the dusty no-man's land that separated the Legation Quarter from the Chinese city. Mother, a stony look on her face, came in and drew the curtains to deaden both the raucous cries of "*Banzai!*" that accompanied the bayonet drills and the brass band that played out of tune. When she left again, I crawled under the curtain, fascinated by the spectacle of so many men with weapons moving with the precision of a machine, all controlled by a diminutive officer who had to climb a stepladder to mount his beautiful Arabian horse almost twice his height.

Japanese ambitions to dominate east Asia, long speculated about in the corridors of power from London to Washington, were finally being taken seriously. Mr. Burton and Captain Wood, who regularly went off to Washington, often came to the house for long discussions with Father in his study, from which they all emerged looking grim. Yet the hectic pace of social life within the quarter was maintained, even accelerated, as if everyone was seeking to drown out the disquieting reality beyond the walls with the sheer volume of their gaiety.

Several new faces appeared among the distinguished visitors to Father's house, including Yue. A rotund, fussy little banker, he groomed his moustache with a tiny comb and wore spats long after they had gone out of fashion. He had connections to both Chiang Kai-shek and Wang Jingwei, head of the puppet government in Nanking. Yue's wife was an American-born Chinese with sunken cheeks and eyes like hot coals. Both spoke in such a flowery, affected manner that one felt something quite different lurked behind their words. Mother considered them coarse. I disliked them by osmosis.

Count Yamashita, like my father a connoisseur of Chinese art, became the first Japanese to cross our threshold. The two men had known each other for some time, but the count had not been invited to view my father's collection till then. Mother objected vehemently, but she was over-ruled. "Such people come in handy in times like these," Father told her.

From my aerie at the top of the stairs, I watched Father guide the count through the main floor. When they came to a pair of early Qing vases, as tall as I, that stood on either side of the door to the reception room, Yamashita paused, standing stock-still as if he were in the presence of something sacred. Father looked on impassively, hands clasped behind his back. The two men talked in Japanese, exchanging many smiles and bows, and then moved out of sight.

Curiosity made me tiptoe down for a closer look at the tall man who moved with such cool detachment. He and my father had gone into the reception room. The door, ajar, framed them in front of the huge Buddha's head. The count half turned as he spoke to my father. A glimpse of his face brought back what my father had said to the trader at the Temple of Heaven when he bought the head – a tall man, with a bullet head, thick glasses, and a moustache. This had to be the man who also wanted the head! Both men were smiling; the count seemed to be admiring the finer details of the piece, his hand tracing its supple lines as he spoke. When he turned back towards the door, my heart leaped into my throat. It was too late to dash up the stairs – I hid behind one of the vases and held my breath.

They stopped before the vase on the other side. Now I could see his face clearly. Though he did not touch the vase, I could feel his eyes caressing it and hear him sigh. When he turned to my father, his eyes were gleaming. My father's back was to me, but I could hear his low voice between thoughtful draws on his cigar. The count, smiling broadly, bowed in the stiff, formal Japanese style. My father responded in kind, and they disappeared into the study for tea.

I was indifferent to the vases, but when I came home from school a couple of days later and noticed they were missing, I flew into my parents' room without knocking. "The vases are gone!" I cried.

Father spoke. "I gave them to Count Yamashita."

"Why?" I don't think I would have minded had he given them to anyone else.

"They are only things." Father laid his hands on my shoulders. "Right now they are where they'll do the most good." Father regarded himself as mere custodian of all he possessed, a custodianship that must pass inevitably into other hands at appropriate moments. Though he did not elaborate, I guessed that the vases were payment for the intervention that had led to the freeing of the hostages taken after the troop-train incident near Beidaihe. Without that intervention, many more people would have died, Xiao Hu among them.

That fall my cousin Julian came back from America. The son of Father's oldest brother, he returned to teach at Yen Ching University (the present-day Beijing University). While in Chicago he had married a fellow Chinese student. Rebecca was vivacious, head-strong, and modern; he was conservative, quiet, and even-tempered, with flashes of wry wit. Julian studied literature and history; Rebecca, social work. To the horror of their feudalistic families, both were thoroughly westernized.

Julian became Father's confidant. Both understood that Japan's expansionism would lead to world war but they disagreed on China's future. Father believed that hatred of the Japanese would eventually unite the Chinese, giving them the sense of nationhood necessary to fight the aggressor. And he thought Chiang Kai-shek's Kuomintang was China's best hope for democracy and the establishment of a true republic, not in Father's own lifetime, but possibly in mine.

Julian had no illusions about the Kuomintang. Sick of its appeasement of Japan, its cronyism and unbridled corruption, he flirted with Communism. His was the first generation of Chinese intellectuals intent upon closing the gap between the haves and have-nots. He joined the outlawed Students' Union, as Eddy Findlay-Wu had done, believing that only violent revolution and the restructuring of society in the Soviet mode would solve China's problems. Rebecca shared his convictions.

They became frequent visitors. They took me boating on the man-made lakes in the Summer Palace or in Beihai Park behind the Forbidden City. They also took me into the older parts of Beijing which I would never have seen. In tortuous little alleys with names like Candle-maker's Hutong or Mat-weaver's Hutong, craftsmen had once lived and worked side by side. There were still mat-weavers and candle-makers, but there were even more young intellectuals, writers, actors, and artists, printing clandestine newspapers and pamphlets spreading communist propaganda. The ramshackle courtyard houses I visited with Julian and Rebecca were communal dwellings whose inhabitants shared everything. They were a jolly bunch who yelled at each other good-naturedly over copious pots of tea. Rebecca had the knack of making everything an adventure. I helped her fold flyers into neat bundles that could be stuffed into coat pockets or handbags, to be distributed later in another part of the city.

"We won't tell about this part of our outing," she told me, "because it's special. Just between you, me, and Julian."

I did not understand what Julian and his friends discussed, but I picked up the odd word.

"What does 'strike' mean?" I asked him.

He tried to explain in ways that I could grasp. As the words did not particularly interest me, I quickly forgot them. But this much I did learn: not all Communists were bandits, and not all Kuomintang were honourable men.

More often than not we left with a parcel, neatly wrapped in red paper from some shop in the Chinese city, or in a box tied with red string. If it was not bulky, I was allowed to carry it. I assumed these were presents – surely everyone liked Julian and Rebecca as much as I did. The parcels probably contained political literature that they helped distribute.

An even stronger bond between Julian and my father was their love of art and literature. Soon after his return from America, Julian began cataloguing Father's art collection and his library. In those uncertain times, Father kept his more precious items in the huge attic at the top of the house. With Julian I discovered these treasures, including a pair of bronze stirrups that had belonged to our illustrious ancestor, Guan Yu, who lived in the second century A.D., during the Three Kingdoms period of the late Han dynasty. Through Julian I learned how such artefacts linked me to the past and the future.

Rex sometimes followed us up to the attic, but he found it a struggle. Outside he no longer romped and played, but lay panting in the shade. During the summer in Beidaihe, he had become quite breathless running on the beach and approached the sea gingerly, getting only his feet wet, grumbling under his breath. The journey back in the train's baggage compartment had sapped him further. The English vet could find nothing wrong with him. "He's old," he told Mother. "It's a wonder he's lasted this long."

Though I had expected the end, I was not prepared for it. Rex was the only true friend I had in the first seven years of my life. I was not conscious of being the only non-caucasian at school, but I felt an instinctual sense of *me* and *them*, so that bonding with the

other children was always superficial. Rex's devotion was uncon-
ditional. I was lost without him. Father's response to my copious
tears gave little comfort: "Life is a series of goodbyes. There will be
many more before you're done."

Starting with American Thanksgiving, the parties in the Legation
Quarter moved from one house to the next without a break. Already
a pair of geese and a turkey were penned at the back of our house
for Christmas and New Year. Midder stocked the house with sacks
of rice, flour, dried sweet potatoes, jugs of peanut oil, and urns of
pickled turnips. He also filled the coal shed to last the winter.
Mother lined the pantry shelves with canned food and laid in a supply of cod liver oil, essential for a boy prone to chest colds.

Buzzy's father, Captain Wood, returned from Washington towards
the end of November, around the time Christmas trees began arriving at the houses in the quarter. Meetings involving him, Mr. Burton, my father, and now Mr. Yue, often lasted late into the night.
Sometimes Chinese military types, ill at ease in civilian clothes,
joined them. The General also came at least once. During these
sessions Mother waited upstairs in the living room with the light
off, pacing the floor. The even tenor of my life was largely undis-
turbed, but my parents' anxiety showed in the dark rings under
their eyes.

As war in the Pacific became a real possibility, there was talk of
closing the International School and sending the children home.
Huddled behind the schoolhouse, smoking cigarettes taken from
his father's dresser, Buzzy speculated confidently about the future.

"The Japs won't dare take on us Yanks!" he sneered. "We're not
softies like you Chinks."

It snowed that day in December, tiny, stinging flakes that made
the roads slick. People and cars moved cautiously. There was a
breathless hush in the air. The tailor delivered Mother's gown in the
nick of time for a gala ball that evening at the Beijing Hotel. Julian
and Rebecca, who went everywhere with my parents, arrived for

cocktails, served in front of a crackling fire. Father allowed me a small glass of wine. All of them were excited at the prospect of a splendid meal followed by dancing. After they left, Zhang set my supper tray beside the fire as a treat. By bedtime the snow was coming in large wet flakes, and I seemed to float off with them, into sleep.

Loud banging and shouting woke me in a panic. Zhang scooped me out of bed and ran up the stairs to the attic. We heard the heavy front door ripped terrifyingly from its hinges and land with a thud that shook the entire house. Hobnailed boots raced through the ground-floor rooms and up the stairs. Zhang dropped me into a tall laundry hamper.

"Don't make a sound. I'll be back," he whispered, lowering the lid over my head.

Guttural shouts in unintelligible Japanese rose from the floors below. Men seemed to be everywhere. Furniture was smashed, tables upended, glass shattered. Then came silence, more terrifying than the noise.

Zhang returned stealthily with my clothes. "Dress," he whispered in a no-nonsense tone. I pulled my clothes on over my pyjamas and did up my shoes with trembling fingers. We could hear the bedrooms directly below being ransacked. Zhang held me to still my trembling. A strident Japanese voice rang through a loudspeaker mounted on a truck in the street outside, but the echo made a jumble of the words.

Another loudspeaker crackled. This time the words were in Chinese. "Come out at once for an important announcement! Loiterers will be shot!" The last word reverberated like an explosion.

The commotion in the house ceased. Zhang led me down a back stair to the kitchen. The other servants were gone. We slipped through the back door into the street, where other people – mostly servants, old folk, and children – were streaming into the falling snow. Japanese soldiers in olive-green uniforms and leggings herded us, at the point of their bayonets, to the small square in front of the church. The only sounds were the lowing wind, and a bonfire crackling and sizzling in the snow. A disembodied voice dinned across the square.

"The Imperial Japanese air force has destroyed Pearl Harbour. We are at war with America! *Banzai! Banzai! Banzai!*"

Japanese soldiers invaded every house except the one that flew a swastika, carrying out books, papers, and magazines, which they tossed on the fire. As flames shot high in the air, I glimpsed Buzzy's frightened face, and then saw Miss Kramer, our teacher, huddled under a blanket. My other classmates must have been there, too, but I did not see them. In the flickering light the soldiers who encircled us seemed strangely disembodied – a waxy face, the top of an olive-green peaked cap, a shiny brown leather belt cinched around the waist, the gleaming tip of a bayonet reflecting the flames. We waited in the biting cold for an interminable time with rifles pointed at us. When the blaze finally abated and we were all numb with cold, we were ordered back to our houses.

Our front door lay in the entrance foyer. Shards of chandelier covered the floor under a thin layer of snow blowing in through the gaping doorway. Father's library was a shambles. The Japanese had burned every book, magazine, and newspaper in English they could find. Gramophone records with English labels had disappeared too. Ironically, pirated recordings of Glenn Miller's "Moonlight Serenade," Artie Shaw's "Stardust," and Arthur Fiedler's rousing rendition of "Stars and Stripes Forever," all bearing Japanese labels, had escaped destruction.

The Japanese sealed the Legation Quarter, and it was daybreak before my parents, dazed and indignant in their evening wear, were allowed back in the house. Count Yamashita came in the morning to survey the damage. Only the reception room was untouched. Perhaps the huge Buddha's head had deterred the invaders. From the doorway, the count gazed at the room and sighed. He said that he had tried to intervene, but the commanding officer had been overzealous. "It is one of the unfortunate facts of war," he told Mother in stiff but correct English. With that, he clicked his heels and left.

Wind-swept snow danced in the empty streets. Japanese sentries stood at intervals, their savage shrieks sending the few hardy souls who ventured out scurrying back indoors. Father set off as usual for his office in the main railway station. Mother put on a brave face, but after he was gone she wandered through the house like a lost soul. The telephone lines had been cut. All the radios in the quarter had been destroyed. There was no newspaper. We'd become completely isolated.

Everyone in the Legation Quarter had to be registered. Residents fell into three categories: friendlies, neutrals, or enemy aliens. Each category was issued a colour-coded identity card and a corresponding armband: green for friendlies; white for neutrals; red for Americans, British, Canadians, Australians, French, and Dutch, the enemy aliens.

Mother, then, was technically an enemy alien. According to British law, however, she had forfeited her citizenship by marrying a Chinese. Count Yamashita solved our problem. Since my father had diplomatic immunity, the same courtesy was extended to his family and household. The vases turned out to have been an excellent investment.

After registration, life took on a routine. We could go out, provided we wore our white armbands, but gatherings were forbidden. Those who wore red armbands were confined to the quarter. Father slipped a bottle of Johnnie Walker to the Japanese officer in charge of guarding the main gate to the quarter. Thereafter his car passed in and out unmolested. In this way he smuggled a short-wave radio into our house and Captain Wood out of the quarter for meetings in the Chinese city.

It was a dismal Christmas morning that year. Though my parents did their best to be cheerful, their hearts weren't in it. Towards noon there was a tentative knock at the door. Miss Kramer had braved the Japanese guards to visit each of her pupils. She had circles under her eyes, and her fingers worked nervously in her lap.

"They destroyed our schoolhouse. It's all gone," she said. "What do you think will happen next?" she asked Mother.

Mother tried to be reassuring. "Things will settle down. There's still the Geneva Convention. I'm sure we'll all be treated with courtesy and understanding."

Not everyone shared Mother's faith, having already seen what the Japanese did to the conquered. Somehow Miss Kramer's helplessness and distress finally brought home that we had been living in a dream.

"What will you do?" Miss Kramer asked.

Mother set her chin at a proud angle. "I will be where my husband and son are." She reached across and squeezed Miss Kramer's hand.

"I'll be all right." Miss Kramer blinked away tears. "He brought me to China, so He'll look after me." It was the only time she spoke of her god. She looked about the room, which she had visited many times, as though committing it to memory. Then, with a sigh, she got up to leave. I accompanied her to the door and helped her into her thick wool cloak.

"What will you be when you grow up?" she asked me, taking my hand.

"Buzzy wants to be a soldier and fight the Japanese. I guess that's what I'll do."

"Be something useful."

"More useful than a soldier?"

She smiled wistfully. "You'll know when the time comes."

She squared her shoulders and sailed past the Japanese guard outside without so much as a sidelong glance.

Julian and Rebecca came to share our Christmas dinner; they must have bribed their way into the quarter. Cook roasted a goose and proudly unveiled the plum pudding that had been hanging mysteriously in the pantry for at least six months, to which brandy had been added at regular intervals. Afterwards, we tried singing carols around the piano. Joy to the world. The words caught in our throats, and left us gaping at each other in a daze.

My present was one of those gramophones you wind with a crank, but our pirated American music could not be played in the circumstances. The only selections we found that seemed safe were Caruso singing "Una furtiva lagrima," sounding like he was caught in a downpour, and Lawrence Tibbett roaring out "The Toreador Song" from *Carmen*. Neither lightened our mood.

"Let's hope next year will be better," Father said, as I went dispiritedly to bed.

The days were long, grey, and cold. As I had no school to go to, Mother tried to keep me busy reading and making cardboard toys. But I was restless. Now and then I would see one of my school-mates in the street. Occasionally, Donald came to play, or I went to his house, but Buzzy stayed away.

"He's angry at everybody," Donald whispered. "The Yanks took a real beating."

On a blustery morning towards the end of January 1942, when a cold sun shone through a veil of yellow desert sand carried in on the howling wind, we were summoned from our houses. Several canopied military trucks, emblazoned with the Japanese flag, stood outside the quarter with motors idling. Japanese soldiers, reinforced by Chinese police in black uniforms with white leggings, surrounded us. Those of us wearing red armbands were quickly separated from the rest. It was swift and efficient. The only sound was hobnailed boots on cobblestones. With mounting horror, I watched the soldiers shove my school friends onto the trucks. At the last moment Buzzy caught my eye and mouthed something angrily, something I did not catch. I tried to communicate with my eyes but then the tailgates were slammed and the trucks set off. It happened so quickly, with so little warning, that people went with only what they stood in.

That day, the vacated houses were systematically looted. The Japanese and their Chinese collaborators flooded in and took up residence. Our Magic Circle was shattered.

9

第九章

QINGDAO

WITH THE INTERNATIONAL SCHOOL destroyed, my parents had to make other arrangements for me. Dressed in a navy blue jacket with the stiff turned-down collar favoured by Dr. Sun Yat-Sen, matching pants, and a peaked cap, I was sent to a prestigious Chinese elementary school in the western section of the city. It was Julian's alma mater, and I set off eagerly, expecting a larger version of the International School, except that the language of instruction would be Chinese.

The first day, my father delivered me to school. The headmaster was expecting us. A bespectacled fellow with a bald head and a fawning manner, he was surprised I could read the text he produced. Because I did not know much arithmetic, I was put in the first grade.

The headmaster propelled me into a classroom where thirty-six boys were seated at double desks. The teacher's desk and chair stood on a small platform in front of the blackboard. Next to the window was an unlit pot-bellied stove whose metal flue ran through a hole cut in the pane. On the back wall were pictures of Wang Jingwei and of Tojo, prime minister of Japan. Over their heads were the crossed flags of the puppet Nanking government, five horizontal bars – red, yellow, blue, white, and black – and Japan's red sun in a white sky. A banner that read "The Great and Glorious United Asia" was strung across the top.

A bird-like woman was reading from a primer, while the class repeated after her. She bobbed at the headmaster and cast a jaundiced eye over me. I removed my cap and bowed. The teacher smirked and the class giggled. I was pointed to an empty seat in the front row.

The headmaster cleared his throat, folded his hands across his chest, and intoned, like an actor onstage, "This is your new classmate." He had already forgotten my name and had to consult a slip of paper tucked in his sleeve. "Kwan's father is an important man, so . . . what do you say?"

"Welcome to our class!" piped the children. The teacher glowered at me behind his back.

The lesson resumed. The mindless repetition continued, the teacher beating time with a willow switch as though conducting a chorus. A huge bronze bell hanging under a mouldy wooden canopy inside the school gate was struck at the end of each period. The great bell bonged, and the class swarmed for the door. The teacher joined the mêlée, vigorously laying about her with her cane.

I wandered into a corridor where the other boys horsed about. The only light came from two grimy windows, one at either end. The rest of the corridor was in permanent twilight. The air stank of the latrine somewhere down the hall. The floor was slick with spit and snot. The dingy walls, dark with soot and cobwebs near the ceiling, were covered with graffiti at eye level.

"There's the new one!" someone shouted.

Leering faces surrounded me.

"A foreigner!"

"Naw! Just a stinking half-caste!"

"His father's an important man!"

Someone hawked and spat in contempt.

They joked about my hair, my nose, jeering and jabbing at me. The teachers monitoring the corridor averted their eyes.

The bell finally rang, ending recess. The bird-like teacher re-appeared and began a most curious lesson. In a strident voice she told the class, "Foreigners are evil. Especially the British, who poisoned our bodies with opium, and the Americans, who ruined our minds with their god and other silly ideas!"

The class chorused, "Evil! Evil! Evil!" as she beat time with her willow switch.

I found myself shouting with them in spite of myself, until the teacher's stick cracked down on my desk. There was instant silence. Her eyes narrowed. "What are you yelling about?"

I was bewildered. The tip of her stick flicked my hair.

"What colour is it?" she sneered.

"The colour of shit," someone said from the back of the room.

Everybody laughed. The teacher bared her teeth in a grin, and the tip of the stick travelled down my forehead to rest on the bridge of my nose.

"*Yang bi zhi*," she spat, and "Foreign nose" became my nickname. My formal education had begun.

Each day I went off to school more disheartened. The lessons were mind-numbing. We spent the day repeating after the teacher, except during the daily political harangues, which usually ended with the entire class shrieking, "Long live Emperor Hirohito! Long live Wang Jingwei! Long live the Glorious Asian Circle!" – the mythical empire the Japanese hoped to create.

Even arithmetic was learned by rote. Arithmetic did not come easily to me. Miss Kramer had just started teaching me the multiplication table, and now I found myself learning it all over again. In Chinese it was twice as confusing. There were addition, subtraction, and division tables to memorize as well. The daily session on the abacus was torture. The secret of speedy calculations was memorizing tables, a skill I have never mastered. The teacher reeled off numbers: "Two thousand eight hundred and one, minus two hundred and fifty, plus one thousand and eight, multiply by five hundred and four, divide by eight hundred."

Thirty-five abacuses rattled, while I gaped at mine in helpless confusion.

"What are you waiting for, Kwan?" she shrieked. I looked up, my mind a blank. The palm of her hand cracked across my face, causing a nosebleed. Thereafter she used my failure to master the abacus as proof that *yang bi zhi* are stupid.

"Is this the race you can look up to? Do you want to be like them?" she yelled, pointing at me.

"No! No! No!" chanted the class.

Early on I made the mistake of asking a question. The teacher flew into a rage and lashed me with her willow switch. Outside class, my attempts at being friendly met with rude curiosity or rebuff and derision. I dreaded recess; I was an animal in a zoo, except that zoo animals are protected from human predators. I fell prey to every bully and came to hate the school.

Once, Lao Zhao, who drove me home, noticed a bruise on my cheek. To the rear-view mirror he said, "Kid, you've forgotten what I taught you."

I shook my head. "Too many of them."

Lao Zhao decided to do something about it. Next day, when school let out, the usual swarm followed me out the gate, pushing and shoving, landing sly kicks and punches. Lao Zhao singled out the biggest of the lot, a sixth-grader, seized him by the ears, and lifted him off the ground. The bully's squealing and kicking stopped the others dead in their tracks. Lao Zhao whispered something to his squirming victim.

"Guys, lay off the *yang bi zhi*," the sixth-grader cried.

Lao Zhao gave the culprit's ears a twist.

"I don't know his name," bawled the boy.

Lao Zhao gave the ears another twist and told him my name.

"Lay off him. Lay off Kwan."

Lao Zhao shook him, and the bully wailed, "If anybody touches him again, this guy will come after me!"

A dark, wet stain spread down the bully's pant leg. The others couldn't help snickering.

In a movement too fast to follow, Lao Zhao let go of the boy and slapped him hard on both sides of the face. The bully crumpled. His followers turned tail and ran.

After that I was left alone. But I made no friends, and I learned very little. The headmaster wrote unctuous letters to my father praising my progress and soliciting donations, which Father never refused. When Julian asked how I liked school, all my woes tumbled out. Mother was in the dark about the conditions at school; Father shielded her from the less pleasant facts of life in China as best he could, but he himself was not ignorant. Lao Zhao would not have taken matters in his own hands without my father's say-so, and the generous donations my father made to the school were no doubt intended to ease my lot. Instead they produced report cards that lulled him into believing I was getting an education.

My stay at the school did not last long. I contracted trachoma, a highly contagious eye disease. Within days both eyes were swollen shut. The treatment involved turning the lids out and scraping their insides after the initial swelling had subsided. It was excruciating, and the recovery was slow. Mother put her foot down. "He is not going back to that school!" she told Father.

He grumbled a bit, but I never went back.

In the first months of 1942, Japanese successes had serious reverberations in Chungking. Many observers were convinced Japan would soon spread herself too thin. The mines and factories of Manchukuo in China's northeast were already strained to breaking point. The long distance that war materials had to be transported was another formidable obstacle.

An old American proposal to land marines on the Shandong peninsula and strike at the Japanese homeland from the rear, abandoned before war broke out, was seriously reconsidered. With Chiang promising his support to cut the lifeline sustaining Japan's war effort from within, thus opening a back door to the island empire, the plan seemed not only feasible but desirable. Qingdao andWei Haiwei, with their fine natural harbours, were the favoured landing sites. The powerful ally that Chiang had been waiting for finally materialized, reinforcing people's belief that the Kuomintang would be China's salvation once the Japanese were driven out. An unspoken by-product of the plan was the establishment of an open trade policy after the war, a policy that America had been angling for ever since 1911 and that Chiang's middle-class merchant supporters heartily endorsed.

The General visited several times after Pearl Harbour, trying to persuade my father to take a direct role in the resistance. Up to that time, Father, as a concerned citizen, had operated a complex web of listening posts and wireless links, passing military intelligence to Chungking and its British and American allies. Now the General wanted him to become an official member of his Ministry of Military Intelligence.

"The man is a snake," Mother remarked with a shudder. "Why must you have dealings with that sort?"

Father replied simply: "It's the times."

Father was reluctant to align himself formally with the General, for good reason. The General had been an underworld figure in his native Zejiang province, Chiang Kai-shek's birthplace. Paranoid about real and imagined enemies, Chiang gathered a coterie of Zejiang thugs around him whom he trusted implicitly. As the powerful head of Military Intelligence, the General operated according to the gangsters' protocol, which made him extremely dangerous. If you were not for him, you must have been against him. He was never photographed; few knew him by sight and nobody spoke his name. For a time Father managed to avoid becoming a full-fledged operative by citing the importance of keeping the two major railways functioning. After Pearl Harbour, however, it became increasingly difficult, even dangerous, for my father to demur. He was in too deep.

The General moved with uncanny speed and efficiency across the length and breadth of China. Around the time of the battle of Midway, in May 1942, he began concentrating his efforts on the coastal areas of Shandong. The banker Yue, another Zejiangnese, became his liaison and deputy in the north. Aside from being a part of Chiang's clique, Yue also had connections with Wang Jingwei. Thus, in the spring of 1942, Yue was able to insinuate himself into the position of mayor of Qingdao, which was under the control of Wang's puppet Nanking regime. Yue quickly installed KMT operatives in key positions in his administration. He earmarked the post of Commissioner of Finance for my father as a front for the gathering of military information, especially on the movement of the Japanese navy, which maintained an important base in Qingdao.

Father held out. Gradually, however, the influx of Japanese residents into the Legation Quarter made it uncomfortable and possibly unsafe for Mother and me in Beijing. When Count Yamashita was recalled, Father was finally persuaded it was time to move. In the summer of 1942, he left for Qingdao to take up his new position, and to find a house, and a school for me. Having Julian painstakingly catalogue his possessions had not been a whim. He had foreseen the day when we would have to quit Beijing. His postcards somewhat ameliorated my disappointment at not spending the summer at Beidaihe, as did my knowledge that Xiao Hu would not be there: "We will live by the sea all year round!"

We left Beijing without fanfare. Father went first, with Midder, who stayed on as his secretary, and Lao Zhao, to get the house ready. Cook followed. The other servants were let go one or two at a time, each with a packet of money to tide them over and a

letter of recommendation to my father's wide circle of friends
and acquaintances.

A house about to be deserted acquires a peculiar quality. It
shrinks. Sounds become muffled. Shadows pool in corners, poised
to spread as soon as the key turns in the lock. Memories inundate
the inhabitants; conversations begin out of nowhere with "Do you
remember. . . ." For an eight-year-old there was a need to break
toys, run up and down the stairs, sing and yell, make noise till I
was red-faced and breathless. Only then could I dull the nameless
ache in my heart.

Mother, Zhang, and I were the last to board the train for the
two-day journey to the coast. On a blistering August day Julian
hired one of the cars the Japanese were building – noisy things with
a huge tank at the back that burned charcoal instead of gasoline.
Zhang had quietly taken the baggage to the station earlier so that
anyone seeing us would think we were going shopping. Except for
a few small items, all our furniture, books, and artefacts – the
accumulated memories of a lifetime – were left behind in Beijing.

Rebecca arrived on the platform as the whistle blew. Julian
doffed his fedora as the train rumbled out from the station. We
stood at the window watching them shrink into the distance.
Nobody waved goodbye. The city receded, its grey ramparts slowly
blending into the sun-baked earth. The landscape gradually changed,
becoming greener, less flat, as the train rattled on. I darted in and
out of the compartment, gaping out the windows, crowing with
excitement at everything we passed. Mother sat nervously knitting, speaking to me in urgent whispers.

"Please be still," she repeated over and over. "No one must hear
you speaking English!"

She shoved a colouring book and crayons at me. For a while I
applied myself, but there was so much to marvel at that I could not
stay still for long. I spent hours at the window. At last, on the second day, I spotted an endless gleam on the horizon.

"Look! The sea!"

"You've seen the sea before," Mother implored. "Sit down and be quiet."

China had ceded Qingdao to Germany in 1898. The city was largely built by German émigrés who set up factories and introduced brewing and sugar refining, which became important industries. The Japanese seized it after World War I. For a short period the Chinese wrested it back, only to lose it to Japan a second time. In 1942 Qingdao still resembled a white-walled, red-tiled Bavarian town, the twin spires of its Catholic cathedral sharing the skyline with slender smokestacks. But it was the miles of white sand beaches and the wide sweeping arc of the harbour, filled with ships, that captured my fancy.

Father installed us in a house on the crest of a hill on the outer edge of the city. The hill was sparsely settled except on the far side closest to a popular swimming area known as German Beach. At the foot of the hill was a huge Buddhist monastery whose bell at dawn and drum at dusk could be heard for miles around. A narrow unpaved road snaked through pine woods full of shifting shadows and wind song. Except for foxes and rabbits scuttling through the underbrush, there was scarcely a soul about.

The two houses at the top had stood empty for years. Father had taken the more remote one. From the road all that could be seen was a grove of green-black pines behind a granite wall. The house was built into the side of the hill like a seabird about to take flight. It was the smallest house we had lived in, but bright and cheerful and sufficiently secluded, Father believed, for Mother and me to be reasonably safe. From the sun deck at the back of the house we had a sweeping view of the bay and the city. Most of all we had a bird's-eye view of the Japanese naval base.

The house faced a sunny garden with a row of spindly rose bushes. At the far end of the garden, hidden among the pines, was a stone coal shed cut deep into the rock of the hillside and ventilated with air shafts cleverly camouflaged among the trees. A kitchen garden took up most of the backyard. A haughty rooster and his harem shared a coop to one side. Another smaller garden was accessed by a narrow passage behind the house. A huge old pine dominated this forgotten strip sandwiched between the high wall separating us from the empty house next door and our own hillside. Nestled among its branches, which spread across the wall, was a tree house made of rough planks. A stout rope ladder dangled from it. I had recently discovered Edgar Rice Burroughs, and the tree house fired my imagination. I became Tarzan and claimed the tree house as my own.

Few of my father's new associates came to the house, and those who did were all Chinese. Wives never came, which was a good excuse to keep Mother out of sight. Occasionally she and I went downtown. Qingdao still boasted a sizeable European community, mostly Germans with a sprinkling of Italians and Russians. Mother did not stand out as long as she kept her mouth shut.

Once we stopped to look in the window of an antique shop. Inside was an old upright piano with candleholders built into its face board, where painted nymphs, amorous shepherds, and naked cupids gambolled. Mother's fingers tapped the window pane involuntarily. She missed her piano, though she would not admit it. A plump, white-haired European lady in a black dress with white lace collar and cuffs beckoned us in. Mother hesitated, but the woman's beaming smile won the day. The woman opened the piano.

"Please try," she said in accented English.

Mother's hand flew to her throat. The older woman smiled. There was something warm and reassuring about her that dispelled fear, and Mother played a bit of Bach. When she finished, the old woman shut the instrument.

"I'm Italian," she said. "My son in America, maybe army. I want go there but"– she shrugged – "the war."

That evening, when we recounted our adventure, we discovered that Father not only knew the shop, he knew the old lady,

Maria Contini. A few days later the upright piano was hauled up the hill to the house. We had music again.

When we first arrived in Qingdao, Mayor Yue came frequently to the house. His American-born wife's lips curled disdainfully at our comfortable but simply furnished lodgings until she stepped onto the sun deck.

"Look at this view, darling!" she exclaimed. "You're the mayor now, and where do we live? Without a view!"

Turning to Mother she continued in flat, nasally English, "You have such a clever husband, my dear." She glanced at Father, who busied himself with lighting a fresh cigar. Mrs. Yue lay a long-nailed finger on his arm and cooed, "Now that you're here at last, maybe the mayor will have a little more time for society. We really must entertain! But first we must have a suitable house!" Her gesture encompassed the view again, as she darted a meaningful glance at her spouse.

"Darling," the mayor began timidly, dabbing at the sweat beading his brow, "I was thinking maybe . . . German Beach might be nice."

Mrs. Yue's eyes widened. "Yes!" she hissed. "Then we will entertain the way we used to. Yes, I want it!"

Before long they had moved into a mansion on German Beach, and the mayor began to enjoy his newfound importance. He became a fixture on the social circuit. Photos of him and his wife hobnobbing with the Japanese appeared regularly in the newspaper.

"He has to," Father explained to Mother. "We all do. It's part of the job."

The truth was, though, that Yue was distancing himself from the resistance movement that had put him in the mayor's chair. Father had become the unit's real leader.

10

第十章

THE REIGN
OF TERROR

UILT by German teaching brothers at the turn of the century, St. Michael's School for Boys stood on several acres
belonging to the Catholic archdiocese in the middle of Qing-
doa. The cathedral and the bishop's house stood at the centre, a convent school run by French nuns stood opposite, while St. Michael's
erupted like an unsightly carbuncle on the cathedral's flank.

By the time I attended, only one of the European brothers
remained. The others had been replaced, over time, by Chinese.
The Chinese replicas looked like the originals, but they were neither men of God nor dedicated teachers. Amid the uncertainties
of China, I suppose it was a reasonably secure life for them, though
not without its disadvantages, since celibacy was contrary to feudal Chinese ideals of family, filial piety, and ancestor worship.

The brothers came to class armed with rattan canes that were
liberally applied to hands and backsides. The ancient Chinese adage
"*ku xue*" – or "painful learning" – was the order of the day. All the
brothers were brutes. Those who did not wield their canes devised
other means of humiliation. A favourite form of punishment was
being made to kneel in the middle of the playing field with signs

pinned to one's back and chest that read "I did not do my homework" or "I failed my test."

Only Brother Wang, our acting headmaster, did not carry a cane. A round little man, not an inch over five feet, with a fringe of bristling white hair around his bald head, and round startled eyes, he resembled a genial, timid gnome. He always seemed to be scurrying off somewhere, giving the impression that the less he had to do with the school and the students, the better he liked it. Nobody took any notice of him.

School was a curious blend of religion and politics. A picture of a very blond Jesus, pointing to a bleeding heart wrapped round with thorns, a tiny flame spouting from the top, adorned the front wall of each classroom. From the back wall Wang Jingwei smiled blandly and Tojo glowered. We were sandwiched between an alien god and the faces of aggression and national humiliation.

My fellow students were all Chinese Catholics, supposedly from a better class than those I had encountered at the school in Beijing. Xenophobia was just as strong, however, and often abetted by teachers. The teaching was lackadaisical and eccentric. Religion and war propaganda were spouted in the same breath. God's love and mercy seemed impotent in the face of the casual killings that sake-crazed Japanese soldiers indulged in daily in the streets.

Brother Wilfred, an ancient Corsican who taught arithmetic, was an odious man with red, gummy eyes and a scraggly beard matted with food and the spittle he drooled. He had a bean-shaped lump the size of a tennis ball on the back of his head, for which the boys nicknamed him "Chan Dou" or "Broad Bean." He was fluent in Chinese, and he might once have been a good teacher, but a lifetime in China had hardened and soured him. In his seventies, he had a mind that wandered unpredictably and he could often be heard muttering, "I'll die in this cursed place!" There followed a string of obscenities.

On my first day Brother Wilfred hauled me before the class. Adjusting his pince-nez and tilting his head at an angle, he examined me like a bug under a microscope.

"Do you know where I'm from?" he thundered.

I shook my head.

Brother Wilfred yelled at the class, "Where am I from?"

"Corsica!" chorused the boys.

Brother Wilfred stroked his beard, as though being Corsican was a singular achievement.

"Who else came from Corsica?"

"Napoleon Bonaparte," I answered.

Brother Wilfred's lips formed an O. It was a sign I would learn to be wary of, for at such moments he teetered between rage and a sudden fit of giggles.

"I'm related to Napoleon," he said, spraying me with spittle. "Don't you forget that!"

"No, sir."

Drawing himself to his full height, he attempted to shove his beefy hand between the buttons of his cassock in Napoleon's familiar pose. Buttons popped off and the class giggled. Brother Wilfred raised his cane and brought it down on my shoulder. I yelped in terror, which inflamed him further. The blows came hard and fast. I dodged as best I could, finally crawling under a desk. As suddenly as the rage erupted, it subsided. Brother Wilfred slumped into his chair, breathing raggedly. A minute later he was smiling and pleasant, and the lesson commenced.

Brother Wilfred's method of teaching arithmetic consisted of reading problems from the text and muttering a few unintelligible words of explanation, often lapsing into French or German. After going through half a dozen problems this way, he would crack his cane on his desktop and ask gently, "Any questions?"

Nobody spoke. Nobody breathed.

"Any questions?" he said again. There was a slight edge to the voice now. One never knew what to expect from Brother Wilfred.

"Homework," he said, and announced the pages.

We called Brother Wilfred's class "The Reign of Terror," for he believed that what he did not instill in us he could beat into us.

Failures were caned in front of the class, one stroke for every mark below the passing average of 60. I was utterly lost and never achieved more than zero. That was worth a hundred lashes, which could be administered all at once – which would probably have given Brother Wilfred a heart attack – or on the never-never plan, ten strokes a day. The offender could choose. I dumbly chose the instalment plan. At the end of ten days, both hands were so swollen that I could barely hold a pencil. As a result my calligraphy suffered, and for that I was made to go about with signs pinned to my chest and back that read "I am stupid."

After the Chinese school in Beijing, I was leery about reaching out to the other boys. I did make one friend, though, quite by chance. I had been made to kneel on the playground all afternoon, as punishment for something or other. The last period was usually catechism followed by benediction. A group of boys came out of one of the classroom buildings ahead of the last bell, chattering excitedly – they were probably choristers and altar boys.

"Look, the new boy!" one of them chirped.

The whole group veered towards me.

"Leave him alone," said one of them. The speaker was about a year older than I, with a small heart-shaped face that was almost pretty, and the wise, sad eyes of a Botticelli angel. I did not know his name, but I recognized him. The first time I'd heard his pristine soprano voice at benediction, my hair stood on end. It was as though the painted angel hovering over us from the cathedral dome had come to life.

I bowed my head, feeling the blood rush to my face. I wished he would go away. Instead, he tilted his head the better to read the sign pinned to my chest. Then he turned and strode briskly towards the gate in the high wall that separated the school from the churchyard behind the cathedral. The others followed.

A few days later, during recess, as I leaned against the building warming myself in the sunlight, trying to be inconspicuous, someone leaned against the wall beside me. I looked cautiously out of the corner of my eye. It was the same boy.

"French?" he said, barely moving his lips, meaning did I speak it.

"English," I whispered back. There was a pause. He shut his eyes and faced the sun.

"I guess we're birds of a feather," he said as though he was talking to the sun. Members of minority groups have uncanny ways of recognizing each other. I felt a peculiar rush of warmth as though all the blood had suddenly been squeezed out of my heart. He turned his back to the sun, cushioning his forehead on folded arms pressed against the wall.

"Shao," he said, addressing his shoes.

"Kwan," I replied, without moving.

Shao sauntered off, hands in his pockets.

I made no effort to get to know Shao. He was always surrounded by other boys, sometimes talking earnestly, sometimes jabbering like a crazed magpie, now and then running about in a fit of sheer exuberance. I looked on, wanting to be part of the group but afraid of making a fool of myself by approaching them.

My separateness made me an easy target. Once after benediction I was swarmed. I don't quite know how it started but Shao, coming out of the cathedral, intervened in the nick of time.

"Stop it," he said, driving his fist into the back of the boy nearest him.

"What did you do that for, Shao?" the boy whined.

"He's my friend," Shao replied evenly. "Understand?"

He put his arm around my shoulders, and stood there until the others drifted off. He took me under his wing from that moment.

"To live in this place, we have to be special," Shao explained. He had a Chinese father and Belgian mother. A survivor, he sounded older than his years.

"Are you good with your fists or quick on your feet?"

I was neither.

"Then you better have a gimmick like me," he said, "something you do better than anybody else. Something that makes you shine."

The archbishop himself said Shao's voice was the glory of the choir. As soloist he was essential to daily Mass and benediction. That was enough for the brothers and fellow students to treat him with kid gloves, despite his mixed background. Because he sang so beautifully, the only gimmick I could imagine was singing. The catch was that I could not carry a tune.

Christmas was approaching, and the choir practised every afternoon for midnight Mass, which the archbishop would celebrate. After benediction one day, I stayed in the church to hear Shao rehearse. A sacristan discovered me and dragged me into the vestry by the scruff of my neck.

"You're not supposed to be here," he growled suspiciously, as though I had tried to steal money from the collection box. "Father Schmidt will deal with you."

I expected an ogre. Instead, the choir master and parish priest turned out to be an affable man in his early forties with greying hair and beard and an easy grin. Father Schmidt must have guessed I was Eurasian; he spoke fluent Chinese but peppered his conversation with German and French. When that drew a blank, he tried a few words of English. I started to reply and caught myself. Father Schmidt chuckled. Pointing to the little red light that shone day and night on the high altar, he continued in English, "You have nothing to fear in God's house." Switching to Chinese again, he asked what I was doing in the church. I said I had stayed to hear my friend sing.

"Ah, then you like music?"

"Yes, Father."

"Do you play an instrument?" In those days, owning a piano and being able to play were the mark of middle-class respectability. I said, "My mother plays piano very well, but I don't."

"Why not?"

"My hands are too small," I said, hiding them behind my back.

"Show me! Show me!" teased Father Schmidt. I showed him one caned hand in embarrassment. He grimaced, though surely he had seen other hands that resembled raw pork chops.

"Would you like to be in the choir, with your friend Shao?"

"I can't sing." I ducked my head. Shao did everything better than I.

"Are you Catholic?"

I nodded.

Father Schmidt mulled that over. "Would you like to be an altar boy?"

"But I don't know Latin."

"I'll teach you," said Father Schmidt. He went over to a calendar on the wall and studied it, frowning.

"If you like, we can start next week," he said. "Monday, Wednesday, and Friday, after benediction." His steady, smiling blue eyes permitted no contradiction. It was settled.

Father Schmidt gave me a bilingual prayer book, Latin and German. He did not attempt to teach me Latin as a language, merely the prayers and responses of the Mass. The lessons were like a drama class; I was an actor learning lines by rote. Father Schmidt, the stage director, blocked my every move – when to stand, when to kneel, when to ring the little bell, how to genuflect without falling over sideways.

Catholic ritual drew me irresistibly into a mesmerizing vortex of colour, music, and drama that contrasted starkly with the drabness of school. The business of turning thin white wafers into the body of Jesus and swallowing it smacked of ritual cannibalism, horrible but fascinating. For a lonely, imaginative boy it was a powerful opiate, a high from which the letdown was so terrible that I ached to repeat the experience. I had been fascinated by Napoleon, Lincoln, Beethoven, and Alexander the Great. Now I was preoccupied with the lives of saints. In a childish way I fancied myself a martyr. Only by emulating their stoicism was the daily pain endurable.

My parents, who did not subscribe to any organized religion, came to see me carrying the archbishop's mitre at Midnight Mass on Christmas Eve. I had the most envied position among the altar boys. Afterward, I gleefully said to Shao, "I think I have my gimmick!"

The archbishop and my father became fast friends, drawn together at first by a legal matter. The Japanese coveted the land on which the cathedral and the two schools stood. An excuse to seize the property had presented itself a year earlier when a captured member of the resistance named our headmaster, Brother Feng, as one of his associates. The Japanese sealed and searched the school. Despite the archbishop's protests, they also searched his house, the convent, even the cathedral. Brother Feng was thought to have escaped to a guerrilla band in the mountains outside the town. The Japanese could have seized the property then and there, but were stymied because the land was legally owned by their German allies. Thereafter taxes became so exorbitant that the archdiocese found itself in danger of losing the property. The archbishop sought Father's help and, as commissioner of finance, he intervened. Citing international law, as well as Japanese and Chinese law, he initiated a series of hearings into the matter that dragged on indefinitely, and the land was saved.

The archbishop became a regular visitor for Sunday lunch. He was a big, soft-spoken, saintly man whose religion was his life, yet he never invoked his god, even obliquely. He did not speak English but was fluent in German, as most educated Chinese in Qingdao were. Therefore, the conversation at table was mostly in Chinese, with me interpreting for Mother. The archbishop loved roses and knew a thing or two about gardening. This he shared with Mother. Gradually the two were able to communicate, quite animatedly at times, as they puttered in the garden.

On quiet Sunday afternoons, as my father and the archbishop played chess, their conversation often turned to the war. The archbishop was well informed. He believed, as did Father, that the world was about to change forever and that the eventual shape of China was unpredictable. The masses would follow whoever put a roof over their heads and food on their tables. Thus it had been in historic times, and thus it would always be. Though it was impossible to predict who would emerge as the eventual leader, both men distrusted Mao and saw his land reforms as a cynical means of gaining the support of the rural poor by robbing the rich urban population.

"The resulting class wars could lead to a third, even less palatable outcome," warned the archbishop. "A return to warlordism."

"After the war China will need massive amounts of foreign aid to get on its feet again," opined Father. "Chiang is more likely to get that support than Mao."

The archbishop agreed. "Whatever the outcome," he sighed, "we must be prepared by building national pride now. Starting with the young."

Early in 1943 slogans that read "Chinese are the sick men of Asia" began appearing in the street. The authorities scraped them off walls and lamp-posts, but new ones appeared. Before long they were also plastered on the external walls of the school buildings and even seeped into our classrooms. Nobody knew how they got there.

Using the poster as leverage, and countering with the saying "Healthy minds in healthy bodies," my father went to the commissioner of education, asking him to organize an inter-school sports meet.

"An inter-school sports event has not taken place for a long time," the commissioner argued. "The Japanese banned large gatherings."

"Will you agree if I speak to the Japanese?" Father persisted. The commissioner agreed so long as he stood clear of the proposal.

Though the Japanese authorities did not applaud the idea, they did not veto it. Once approved, the games became the commissioner of education's brain-child, which nothing must compromise. Thus, my father's scheme to combine traditional Chinese gymnastics and martial arts with the usual track and field events met with stiff opposition. "The Japanese might consider their inclusion seditious and stop the games!" the education commissioner blustered.

Father offered to take personal responsibility by participating in the martial arts segment of the program, which mollified the commissioner. Unfortunately, Father knew nothing about martial arts and had to learn, quickly. Soon after we arrived in Qingdao, he'd made the acquaintance of the abbot of the monastery near our house where monks practised martial arts as part of their spiritual and physical development. Father persuaded the abbot to allow one of the monks to teach him the use of the broad sword and to give a demonstration during the games. Lao Zhao, who'd had some martial arts training, asked to join as well.

Master Sun, the young monk who came to teach Father and Lao Zhao, was different from any religious person I had encountered. His piety was not worn like a cloak, but glowed from deep within, permeating every word and gesture. A foundling raised by the monks, he was an innocent. With no knowledge of the world, he probably would have been content to spend his life behind monastery walls. Preparing my father for the games propelled him out of his cocoon. Though Father made sure nothing disturbed his serenity, or violated the strict rules of his faith, the excursions into the outside world must have had an impact on the young monk. For one thing, it brought him into a home.

Master Sun took dinner with us after teaching Father and Lao Zhao. In keeping with monastic rules, Cook prepared a separate strict vegetarian meal for him, which was served at the far end of the long dining table that comfortably seated twelve. Mother was almost certainly the first woman Master Sun had encountered at close quarters. He ate hurriedly with eyes averted. My father's attempts at conversation drew brief, halting replies, always preceded with a murmured "*Ah-mi-tuo-fuo*," a devout invocation of Buddha's blessing. Though Master Sun usually finished before we did, he sat, eyes downcast, fingering his beads until he could politely extricate himself from our company. Occasionally, a word or a sound caused him to look up. If Mother happened to look his way, he would turn beet red and duck his head. I counted three round scars burned into his scalp, each scar representing one step forward in his spiritual evolution. (The maximum was a dozen, which meant Master Sun had a long way to go.) He steadfastly refused to be driven back to the monastery. He walked, Lao Zhao accompanying him a few paces behind out of respect.

"What did you talk about?" I asked Lao Zhao.

"We prayed," he replied.

The games were held on the last day of school. The stadium, closed for years, had been given a thorough facelift and gleamed under a blazing sun. Those of us who did not participate crowded the stands to cheer our school team.

The part of the program I was waiting for came in late afternoon. Monks stripped to the waist performed amazing acrobatic feats. Then Master Sun took the field and drew amazed gasps with his demonstration of strength. Finally, Father stepped into the ring with Lao Zhao and Master Sun for a three-way combat with broad swords. Blades flashed in the sun, thrusting, parrying, slicing the air. Bodies gyrated, leaped, and dodged. The crowd roared. The commissioner of education, seated next to Mother and me, applauded wildly. Even the usually staid archbishop clapped and cheered. Mayor Yue's wife, on the other side of Mother, stared disinterestedly at the proceedings through black sunglasses until Master Sun appeared. She could not peel her eyes away from him.

"Darling" – she interjected the English word in an otherwise Chinese conversation – "that man must teach you too."

The mayor's several chins shook with disbelief. "Darling," he countered, matching her tone, "I'm not the athletic type."

The collar of his wife's Chinese robe was so high and stiff that she had to turn from the waist to face him. "I wish it, darling." The emphasis on the endearment made it sound like a threat, her fingernails digging into her husband's hand like the talons of a bird of prey.

"Impossible! The man's a monk!" the mayor hissed.

But she had turned away, absorbed again by Master Sun.

Father gave an impassioned closing speech. Without veering from the theme of healthy minds in healthy bodies, he urged the crowd to do their best to shake off the indignity of being called "the sick man of Asia." It was a subtle call for national pride, couched in simple, even humorous terms that everyone could identify with. The commissioner of education was ecstatic, and the archbishop beamed. The mayor scowled fearfully as interpreters jabbered in their Japanese masters' ears. Ever vigilant, the Japanese could not find fault with Father's carefully chosen words, even when they were reprinted in their entirety in the next day's newspaper. The inter-school games became an annual event, and physical education became an integral part of our school curriculum.

Again I contracted trachoma, more severely this time. The illness made for a long, painful, lonely summer circumscribed by the stone wall around our hill-top. When the bandages finally were removed, and the searing pain of sunlight bored into my brain, I sought out the shaded calm of the tree house.

To my surprise, the house next door, which had been boarded up for years, was being cleaned and painted inside and out. Gardeners were mowing the overgrown lawns and turning flower beds; bricklayers and carpenters were constructing a gazebo close to the wall that separated our houses.

"An admiral, the new commander of the naval base, has taken the house," Father said matter-of-factly at dinner. He knew this long before the workmen appeared, of course, but shielded Mother from the disturbing news as long as possible. The question on her mind – on all our minds – centred on the radio transmitter hidden in our coal shed, and the nocturnal rendezvous held at our house with other members of the resistance.

Father was not perturbed. "The admiral's proximity is actually an advantage," he reasoned. "Who would dream clandestine activities were happening under his nose! Of course, precautions have to be taken. The important thing is to act natural."

My parents did not like my going to the tree house in the first place. Now, with the admiral ensconced, there was the added fear of trigger-happy guards. In fact, the Japanese sailors posted to the house had already discovered me in my roost. One fellow pointed his rifle at me, grinning. I froze, and heard the wings of death flapping by. But the sailor only made a lewd gesture and sauntered off. Soon other guards came to gawk up at me. I pretended to mind my own business, certain they could hear the wild hammering of my heart.

Despite my terror I went back to the tree house the next day, and every day thereafter, impelled by an irresistible force. Eventually I lost my fear, and the Japanese soldiers lost interest in me. One afternoon a lady in a white kimono appeared in the new gazebo. Twirling a parasol gently with her porcelain-pale hand, she stood contemplating the view. When she turned, our eyes met. She smiled and inclined her head; I did the same. Presently she left. The garden suddenly seemed incomplete, even desolate, without her.

The admiral arrived a few days later. A tall, spare gentleman with courtly manners, he wore his uniform and medals with an air of weary resignation. I'm sure my presence in the tree house must have registered somewhere behind his expressionless eyes. Though he never gave any sign of being aware of me, the guards were withdrawn from the garden. Soon their numbers were reduced to one at the front gate and another at the rear.

The admiral lived by the clock. Promptly at four-thirty, his charcoal-burning car wheezed up the hill. His wife waited in the gazebo, fanning a brazier, over which sat a smoke-blackened teapot. Bowls were laid out on a low table placed between deep cushions. On another table to one side stood a wind-up gramophone. Beside it was arranged an orderly stack of record albums. Soon the admiral appeared, having changed into an earth-coloured yukata fastened round the waist with a wide black sash. Husband and wife bowed formally, exchanging pleasantries in low voices. He sat cross-legged on one of the cushions, facing the sea and the setting sun while she served tea. After the first cup, the admiral inclined his head towards the gramophone. His wife wound the machine and put on a record. The most wonderful music floated up to the tree house. I too sat facing the westering sun, imitating the man and woman next door, as music wove wild patterns of light and shade against the lids of my closed eyes.

The music did not stop until the sun dipped beneath the horizon. The admiral and his wife sat silently together until the light had faded. After they'd made their way indoors, the orderly noiselessly removed everything from the gazebo. By then it was almost dark; from the tree house, only his white gloves were visible, darting about like nocturnal birds.

Sitting cross-legged in my tree house day after day, I became a vicarious part of this ritual. A wonderful sense of well-being settled over me as the music took its place in my life, the key to a world apart. In a most unlikely way, I had discovered my own magic circle.

第十一章

HOUSE GUEST

MY FRIENDSHIP with Shao went by fits and starts. We saw each other only at school. He was the centre of a rather boisterous group. Too shy to propel myself into its midst, I clung to its fringes, where I was mostly ignored. Occasionally Shao sought me out during recess or walked with me after benediction as far as his home on the edge of the town's business centre. Now and then I caught a glimpse of his mother peering fearfully through the lace-curtained front window of their tall, skinny house. She was sitting out the war like Mother, except she never left the house and was more cut off. Shao never invited me in, nor did it ever occur to me to invite him home.

My gimmick, not as showy as Shao's, did not net me the recognition or the precarious friendships he derived from his. At best it kept me out of harm's way some of the time. Because I learned the Latin responses quickly, I was much in demand as a server, especially when the archbishop officiated. That did not go over well with the other altar boys. His excellency's friendship with my father made some of the brothers less ready to punish me, though nothing deterred Brother Wilfred.

The drama of Catholicism enthralled me. Mass and benediction became beacons in the darkness. In the candle-lit cathedral, with the organ booming and the choristers sounding like an angelic host, my spirit soared. Away from it, the struggle between a supposedly loving god and the brutality of some of his servants weighed heavily upon me. I came early to a bleak appreciation of the unfathomable contradictions of this world.

Clattering down the steps of the cathedral after benediction one day, I almost bumped into a white-haired old lady dressed in black. I apologized, and her face lit up in recognition. I thought it was because she had seen me carrying the archbishop's mitre.

"The piano," she said softly in English, "in my shop . . ."

Of course – the elderly woman from whose antique shop my father had bought our piano. Since she lived on the far side of the hill where we lived, we walked home together, conversing in a mixture of English and Chinese, liberally laced with gestures. Maria Contini had come to China from Italy with her husband when she was young and had lived in Qingdao ever since. "It reminds me of Napoli," she said, gazing out across the harbour, "where I was born."

She had walked to the cathedral twice a day for many years, first with her husband, then with a son as well. She never missed a day. Her son had gone to America to enter college and had stayed on. When her husband died, she remained in Qingdao to run the business alone.

"I pray every day the war will end," she said.

Some weeks later Mrs. Contini came to the house with a bottle of goat's milk and a slab of cheese she had made. She'd noticed I hadn't been serving the eight o'clock Mass or benediction. When Father Schmidt told her I was ill, she came with the gift. Maria Contini and Mother became fast friends. Thanks to the old lady, Mother's life became less constricted. Maria Contini showed her where she could shop safely, including a bookstore run by an old Russian and his son, who saved stacks of English books by disguising them behind covers in other languages. Mrs. Contini taught Mother to grow yeast in a jar and to bake tasty bread and biscuits with flour ground from millet and bitter sorghum, since wheat flour was scarce. Cook grumbled but no longer threatened to quit if "missy in kitchen."

We lived in a kind of vacuum, aware that fierce battles were being fought somewhere far out at sea, but the details were sketchy. The Pacific theatre covered a vast area stretching from the Aleutians in the foggy North Pacific south to tropical Fiji and New Caledonia, from Java to Hawaii and Midway in the Central Pacific. At the outbreak of war, to obtain oil and other raw materials it needed, Japan planned to seize not only the Philippines, but Burma, Malaya, Thailand, Borneo, the Netherlands East Indies, and various island bases in the south and central Pacific. Japanese successes in the first months of the conflict far exceeded their wildest expectations. In May 1942, a Japanese invasion force sailed for Port Moresby on the Papuan Peninsula of New Guinea. Forewarned by intercepted and decoded Japanese messages, the Americans had a carrier task force lying in wait in the Coral Sea. The battle that ensued was fought entirely with carrier aircraft. Both sides were hampered by bad weather and human error; in the end, the Port Moresby invasion force was turned back.

The following month, the Japanese launched an even larger strike at the American base at Midway, an island about 1,000 miles west of Hawaii. Their objective was to disperse and destroy the American fleet. Again, the Americans learned of the Japanese plans through intelligence reports and had their aircraft carriers waiting in ambush. The Japanese suffered a major defeat; losing four large carriers in a single action ended Japan's hopes of further offensives in the Central Pacific.

In Qingdao, the local newspapers exaggerated Japanese victories and omitted their reverses. From Tokyo, Tojo's daily propaganda broadcast exhorting his troops to fight and die for the glory of the empire was piped into our classrooms. It didn't matter that we did not understand a word. The important thing was to drum into our minds the Japanese empire would last forever.

Father sometimes shared disjointed bits of war news gleaned from his wireless communications. Port Moresby and Midway were the first tiny dots he pointed out to me in an atlas, with the help of a magnifying glass. In the summer of 1942, the struggle for control of the strategic airfield on Guadalcanal developed into a brutal, six-month slugging match. U.S. possession of the airfield on Guadalcanal gave the Americans a long-term advantage that Japan would never overcome. Father saw that American victory as a pivotal point in the war.

Back in 1941 the Americans had agreed with the British that if the United States entered the war, the main Allied effort would be concentrated on defeating Germany and Italy. Offensives against Japan would have to follow victory in Europe. No overall plan or agreement was made between the American and British High Commands regarding Japan until the Casablanca conference in January 1943. While the British balked at committing almost a third of the Allied resources to defeating Japan, they did agree that the Americans could go ahead with further offensives against the Japanese. The long-anticipated American offensives in the Pacific got under way in June 1943. The new advance across the central Pacific involved thousands of tiny islands, from the Gilberts, near the equator, north and west through the Marshalls, the Carolinas, and the Marianas. This had long been recognized as the shortest route to Japan; now it was seen as the most advantageous way to deploy American naval and amphibian strength.

The island-hopping war began shakily, with the battle for Tarawa in the Gilbert Islands. The United States suffered enormous casualties, but the campaign proved the efficacy of bypassing and isolating strong garrisons and assaulting weaker ones.

The names of other islands we did not know existed were soon stamped on our consciousness: Majuro and Kwajalein in the Marshalls; Saipan, Tinian, and Guam in the Marianas. The list seemed endless. Each little dot on the map was the scene of unbelievable bloodshed.

Japan's loss of the Marianas in June 1944 had serious repercussions. Japan's inner ring of defences had been penetrated. As a result, Tojo's government fell. The islands of Saipan, Tinian, and Guam also put the new American long-range B-29 bomber within reach of the Japanese homeland. Although the press was muzzled, news that Tokyo had been bombed leaked out in China. Father said it was the beginning of the end of the war.

Air-raid drills were held frequently. One morning the siren wailed during Brother Wilfred's arithmetic class. We rushed down to the cellar, our air-raid shelter, leaving Brother Wilfred ranting and shaking his fist at the sky. The original brothers probably built the cellars under the school buildings for brewing beer. A faint smell of fermenting hops still clung to floor and walls. The bare, musty space had been divided into cubicles, some fitted with a thick wooden door that locked. A few square, iron-barred windows along the front of the building, level with the ground, admitted weak light through the dirt-encrusted panes.

Shao always sought me out on these occasions. I think it was because he was claustrophobic and didn't want his cohorts to know about his horror of confined spaces. I was glad of his company because I was terrified of the dark. Our separate phobias became our bond. We huddled together against a wall where there was a faint patch of light, though we'd been told to stay clear of windows. Shao sat with his arms wrapped tightly around his legs, knees propping his chin.

"I wish I was somewhere else," he moaned.

"Where else?" I tried to divert him.

Shao started to say something and then stopped mid-word. I followed his gaze. In the dim light a shadowy face, no more than a thin layer of skin stretched over the skull, seemed to leach out of the wall opposite us. The eyes blazed from deep sockets. The lips, pulled back from teeth and gums, formed silent words: "Be quiet!"

The man – for it wasn't a ghost – slithered away, sending a cold, clammy feeling down my spine. We buried our faces against our knees, shivering until the all-clear sounded. Then we raced out into the blinding noon sun, teeth chattering. We ran around the playing field, pumping blood through our bodies, running till our legs ached and our breath came in short, painful gasps, until everything became a yellow blur and our knees crunched against the hard-packed earth. We lay there panting, dazed, gritty sand in our teeth.

"It was Brother Feng," Shao gasped.

My scalp crawled. The Japanese had turned the school upside down searching for him, and all this time. . . .

"It can't be." I busied myself inspecting my scraped knees. "Everyone knows Brother Feng is a hero, fighting with the guerrillas in the mountains." I shook my head to rid myself of the awful apparition.

"It was Brother Feng," Shao insisted, dusting himself off. "I recognized him from before, and he recognized me. We mustn't tell." Shao grabbed me and shook me violently. "We didn't see him . . . you hear?"

We sealed our silence with our secret handshake, clasping one another's wrists.

Shao put the incident behind him but I had nightmares, petrifying visions of a cadaverous face seeping out of a wall, bidding me to keep silent. Neither of us went into the cellar after that. In the confusion of air-raid drills, we dawdled while the others rushed out of the room. Then we sneaked into the classroom closest to the cellar door and hid there, waiting for the all-clear. It was easy enough to mingle with the crowd when the boys came streaming back into the building.

The only other person who didn't go to the cellar was Brother Wilfred. The air-raid siren turned him into a raging beast. Armed with his cane, he prowled the corridors as the sirens wailed, shrieking incoherently and striking out at invisible attackers. Once we heard him coming down the hall towards the room where we were waiting. We scurried under desks in the back row. He came in, sniffing the air like a bloodhound. We watched his big boots pace up and down, his cane beating time on desktops. The all-clear sounded. As if a switch had been thrown, Brother Wilfred, instantly composed, moved with stately serenity into the front hall as the boys burst through the cellar door.

Apart from such random moments of excitement, my narrow world blurred into grey monotony. Education was a cacophony of propaganda mixed with random truths. The story of George Washington and the cherry tree, for example, was held up as an example of personal honesty. Yet this same man was reviled as the father of a nation of vicious imperialists. Between the daily tyranny of the Japanese in the street, and the casual cruelty of the brothers, what little faith I had eroded. The colour and the music of the Mass became an empty show. The little red light on the altar was no longer the all-seeing eye of God, but the symbol of my flickering faith. My mind wandered during Mass one morning and I dropped the censer. Afterward Father Schmidt demanded I make a confession.

"I have nothing to confess." I was adamant.

Father Schmidt was close to losing his temper. His long harangue did no good. "You will not be permitted to serve until you learn humility," he said, at his wit's end.

"What happened, Da-vee-day?" Maria Contini asked later, pronouncing my name the Italian way. She had witnessed my mishap. I was having a hard time milking her goat because my hands were perpetually swollen from caning. I smiled brightly and said, "Nothing."

"You can tell me."

Maria Contini was so kind, so good, it was hard not to. But there was too much to tell; it was too complicated, too mixed up in my own mind to make sense. Somehow it would all lead inevitably back to my nightmares and Brother Feng hiding in the school cellar. I knew that if he were discovered because of something I let slip, life wouldn't be worth living. So I just smiled at Mrs. Contini and the secret festered inside me.

One morning in the summer of 1944, the air-raid siren sounded. By then Shao and I had perfected our tactic and roamed the deserted building at will. Just another false alarm, we thought. There had been raids before, but nothing more lethal had been dropped than leaflets and packets of biscuits and candy. The pom-pom-pom of ack-ack guns hidden in the mountains behind the town sounded almost perfunctory. Shao was already out the door to investigate. I raced after him onto the playing field.

Planes were directly overhead. We stood on the deserted play-ground, gleefully watching little black dots falling out of the sky until a high-pitched whine ended with a concussive bang that knocked us backwards off our feet. We lay there, stunned, fright-ened, and disbelieving. There were explosions all round, then a sort of hush, then the crackle of flames mixed with the haunting screams of the wounded and dying. The street by the school quickly filled with people, wailing and crying, shouting through the din the names of friends and relatives. Buckets of water were passed along a human chain, hand to hand, from hydrants to burning buildings, but the effort was futile. Fires seemed to feed on themselves, burn-ing out of control. Some of the bombs intended for the naval instal-lations had fallen on the town, just missing the cathedral and St. Michael's School for Boys.

When the all-clear sounded, the boys raced out of the cellar. Terrified by the smoke-blackened sky and the reek of destruction, they stormed the school's iron front gate, which was padlocked at the first bell each morning and not unlocked till the last bell at the end of day. We were penned in. Even so, it took a while for cane-wielding brothers to restore order and herd us back inside.

We found Brother Wilfred in our classroom, slumped in his chair, feet outstretched, head lolling to one side. His eyes and mouth were wide open, fear frozen on his face. Urine had stained his cassock and pooled around his boots.

One of the bigger boys sauntered over and snapped his fingers in Brother Wilfred's face. The rest of us squeezed into the room, cautiously at first, then in a rush. Somebody chanted, "Chan Dou, go to hell!" Others picked it up: "Chan Dou, go to hell!" Though the rancid man's ugly death made my stomach heave, I found myself yelling with the rest of the class. I looked up at the picture of Jesus and his flaming heart and realized I should feel something in the presence of death. I felt nothing – no awe, no grief, no pity, not even relief at having cheated him out of the last fifty of the hundred strokes of the cane I had earned by scoring zero on yet another test.

Brother Wilfred was laid out in the assembly hall. Even under a blanket of flowers he was grotesque. His head remained twisted to one side. Neither eyes nor mouth could be made to shut. Chinese dread the eyes of the dead that will not close, for it is a sign that the spirit is not at peace. What forces had driven the man to beach himself on the rocky shore of Shandong? What demons drained him of enthusiasm, soured his faith, exhausted his heart, leaving a decaying hulk to rage? Against what or whom? China's endless needs suck the marrow out of the unwary; her shores have always been littered with the burned-out shells of do-gooders. I felt no pity for Brother Wilfred; I felt only the pain in my swollen hands.

I became an agnostic the day Brother Wilfred died. For me, hunger, disease, the senseless killings of war, and the grotesque death of one of his own gave the lie to the existence of a compassionate god. Ironically, Father Schmidt relented and asked me to serve the high requiem Mass for Brother Wilfred.

"I won't. I hope he burns in hell," I said boldly. I could see from Father Schmidt's expression he knew about Brother Wilfred's brutal ways. "Why didn't you stop him?" I demanded.

Father Schmidt talked about the virtue of forgiveness. But nothing would move me, not even the showy but useless task of carrying the mitre of the archbishop who, Father Schmidt reminded me, was my father's friend. A tiny piece of ice had formed at the core of my being, and Father Schmidt's platitudes were not about to melt it.

During the raid that frightened Brother Wilfred to death, an American aircraft ditched offshore. Four crewmen were picked up by Chinese fishermen and hidden by the resistance. For two days the Japanese made massive sweeps through the mountains trying to flush out the American airmen, but to no avail. The resistance managed to stay one step ahead of them. One by one, the Americans were spirited to free China. The last man should have been taken behind the lines after an attack on a Japanese munitions train outside Jinan, but the Japanese had been tipped off and the attack went sour. Many members of the resistance group were killed and the rest dispersed. The American, who was ill, had been left behind.

It was rumoured that the mayor had been the turncoat, though nobody could prove it. Mayor Yue's life had grown increasingly decadent. He had taken a concubine, a pretty, fourteen-year-old girl from a poor family. Master Sun, the naïve young monk, had succumbed to temptation and left the monastery to be Mrs. Yue's plaything. Meanwhile, both the mayor and his wife had become addicted to opium. As the Japanese regularly shot users and traffickers alike, it was by no means out of the question that Yue would betray his compatriots to stay alive.

One day after school I overheard Midder and my father in the study, arguing about the mayor. Midder was all for "pulling the weed up by the roots." My father, the group's de facto leader, argued vehemently against drastic action without positive proof.

"We are all human. If one of us is overcome by fear, that should not be held against him. Besides," Father reasoned, "Yue has the General's confidence. Any rash action could boomerang in our faces."

"I hope we don't live to regret it," said Midder. The conversation ended abruptly when they saw me in the doorway.

A few days later, home for breakfast after one of his nocturnal forays, Father casually mentioned, between his last cup of coffee and his first cigar, that we had a "house guest." We'd had a number of house guests since we arrived in Qingdao, resistance fighters who had been wounded or separated from their group. We fed and sheltered them until they could be guided to safety. Mother had behaved with her usual sangfroid, but harbouring an American airman was more than she could handle. She chided my father vehemently for giving more importance to the war than to the safety of his family.

Previous "house guests" had stayed in the coal shed, but Zhang thought it inappropriate for an American. By volunteering his quarters and moving in with Lao Zhao, he more or less shamed Mother into agreeing to have the man in the house. Fearful for our safety, she made no excuse for wanting him gone. It became Mother's personal mission to get our house guest well enough to leave. Since he was weakened by dysentery, she administered a Chinese remedy Father obtained from the abbot of the monastery – raw garlic, to combat the amoebae in his system. Maria Contini provided goat's cheese and milk, as well as home-made pasta when there was flour. "Too thin," she clucked at the American with a rueful shake of the head. "Maria make strong again."

The house guest – we were not permitted to exchange names – was a personable young man with blond hair that fell over his startling, cornflower-blue eyes. His complexion and easy-going Yankee swagger made me think of Buzzy, but all grown up. I saw him only during meals when he joined us at table. Cook provided a tiny dish of grated raw garlic which Mother placed before him.

"Eat it," she ordered.

He wrinkled his nose at the pungent fumes, but did as he was told.

The American's saving grace was his sense of humour. He had the knack of seeing the funny side of the sticky situation he had plunged us into and making Mother laugh in spite of herself. Being Catholic and from New York endeared him to Maria Contini at once.

"Tell to me, the Liberty Lady," Maria beamed. She never tired of hearing about New York. "And the Empire Building . . . so tall! Is wonderful, no?" She embraced me enthusiastically. "Da-vee-day, we go New York one day soon! See my son!" She blew effusive kisses to the absent Vittorio.

The American's recovery was painfully slow. Sometimes after school I sneaked down to the servants' quarters and caught him standing on a chair, sucking in air through the open window high on the wall or just gazing at the tiny patch of sky it framed.

Gradually he grew less frail, and when he was well enough Lao Zhao showed him martial arts exercises to build up his strength. "I'll be strong enough to get out of your hair soon, ma'am," he announced one evening. He always spoke with his hand over his mouth, conscious of his overpowering garlic breath.

When autumn darkened into winter, an opportunity finally arose. Midder was going to Chungking. The American would go with him. "You will impersonate a Russian trader," Midder explained. "You'll be provided with papers and suitable clothes. You'll carry a small valise. Your host will tell you when."

A few nights later, wearing a Russian bearskin cap, the fur collar of his heavy coat turned up, the American was smuggled out of the house. He and Lao Zhao went over the back wall of the garden and made their way down the rugged tree-clad hillside to the road that curved along the harbour. From there they zigzagged through a labyrinth of crooked side streets to the train station at the centre of town. Midder was waiting there.

As Father explained it, the journey, though long, was not particularly difficult. The trick was to get off the train at just the right spot outside Japanese-held territory. A guide would take the American across the lines while the Chinese were busy killing one another.

"I'll come back one day to thank you properly," the American told Mother. "And as for you, buster" – he pretended to box with me – "don't grow up too fast, okay?"

"Do you think he'll be all right?" I asked Maria Contini after he'd left.

"I pray for him," she whispered. "I pray for everyone."

Wang Jingwei's mysterious death in Japan on November 10, 1944, sent shock waves through his Japanese-sponsored government in Nanking. Although the death was attributed to illness, rumours of assassination persisted, especially when a successor stepped quickly into the breach. Collaborators everywhere wondered who would be next to die mysteriously. Mayor Yue, distrusted by the resistance and despised by the Japanese – who fed his opium habit for their own ends – was caught between the devil and the deep blue sea. His wife only added to his troubles by flaunting her affair with the defrocked monk.

The guerrilla activity around Qingdao intensified. Power plants, telephone exchanges, radio stations, and newspapers were targeted. Ever concerned about his own skin, Mayor Yue now tried to distance himself from the Japanese, whom he had courted so assiduously. His position grew more precarious by the week during the long, dark winter.

The newspapers now had blank spaces where columns had been excised. Through my father's transmitter we learned that Nazi Germany was disintegrating. Our concerns, however, were more immediate. The new year of 1945 brought bitter cold, and the frigid temperatures added to the misery of food and fuel shortages. Long lines formed outside food stores where ration coupons were exchanged for slivers of meat or a few measures of flour, to which unscrupulous merchants added sand or cement for bulk. Coal was scarce, rice as precious as gold. At home the wrought-iron stove in the living room was lit only in the afternoon, so there would be one warm room when Father got home from the office.

Maria Contini's goat died. It was more than a provider of milk and cheese; it was a link to the past. The laughter went out of Maria that frigid winter. She still talked about going to see Vittorio in New York but the words sounded hollow. She had turned from a bright, energetic woman whose hair happened to be white into a frail, wistful old lady.

At school we wore our coats in class. The concrete walls and floors were like slabs of ice. The cold crept up through my feet, and after a while the ache spread insidious numbness through my body. The teacher's voice faded in and out, and I felt a terrible need to sleep. We were driven outside with canes to run round the playing field; we could see our feet but couldn't feel them. We were too numb even to feel the cane that drove us on, or the stones that cut into hands and knees when we fell.

One day I fell asleep in class and couldn't be wakened. Father was notified and Lao Zhao came to take me home. I became mortally ill and for days hovered between life and death. Dreams and waking became confused; consciousness was fleeting. Mother was there whenever I opened my eyes, smiling her half-sad smile.

While I fought deliriously to regain my health, the war in the Pacific raged on. From our terrace I watched the blackened remnants of the Japanese fleet limp in and out of the harbour, and white-clad kamikaze pilots, mere boys in their teens, jogging to their death planes shouting, "*Banzai! Banzai!*" Waterfront patrols took pot shots at passersby who appeared the least bit suspicious.

As I was recovering, a letter that had been passed from hand to hand finally reached Mother. It was spring, when I was feeling better, before she read it to me, stopping frequently to steady her voice. Uncle George, Auntie Hester, and Irene, who'd been so eager to get to Hong Kong, had been caught in the Japanese attack on that city a few days after Pearl Harbour. All had been killed.

"You shouldn't know about death," Mother said, dabbing at her eyes, "before you begin to live . . ."

Without a word I went outside and, though weak, hoisted myself into my tree house. Mother did not object too strenuously. I think she understood how deeply the deaths of the Findlay-Wus affected me, knew I had lost my moorings to the past. I'm sure she was bitterly disappointed I did not turn to her in my pain. I don't think she realized the tree house was the portal to another sphere, where there was no war, no grief, only the tranquillity of ceremony and sunset and music. She never spoke of the Findlay-Wus thereafter.

I heaved myself up, shaking with exertion, afraid no one would be next door. As always, the admiral and his wife, in flowing robes, sat with their backs to me, facing the late afternoon sun. Nothing had changed except the music. Instead of rich orchestral sounds, a handful of instruments played, music that was unfamiliar but reassuring, balm for the heart and soul.

As the spring of 1945 deepened, the war in Europe teetered to an end. Hitler committed suicide on April 30, and on May 8 Germany surrendered. Half a world away, in Qingdao, the thunder drew ever closer, and we braced for the promised landing by American Marines. By then Chiang Kai-shek had made his token gesture of fighting the Japanese. As foreign aid flowed into his deep pockets, the guerrilla activities ceased.

August 6, 1945, was an unusually hot, still day. The sun blazed through a high white haze of extraordinary brilliance. The cicadas whirred and fell silent. Flowers drooped. Even the birds seemed to gasp in the trees, fretful, songless. The air was so dense breathing was an effort.

Father did not go to his office that morning. He had been up most of the night wrestling with the radio transmitter. I could smell his cigar through the cracks of the study door and hear him pacing back and forth. Mother was in her room. The servants remained in their quarters. Only the chickens in their coop went about their usual business.

From the terrace, the sea gleamed, flat and hard as burnished steel. In the naval base, a few ships rode at anchor. Nothing moved. I needed something to shatter the awful stillness; to run about; to yell. But my limbs felt leaden, and some mysterious force smothered my voice.

There was no relief from the oppressive heat even in the tree house. I must have dozed off when the droning of an airplane made me come to with a start. The plane glowed like a jewel against the washed-out sky. The sound, though far off, drew Mother to her window. She called to me to come inside. I pretended not to hear.

"Come inside!" She sounded edgy.

I started down the rope ladder as a trail of tiny dots fell in the plane's wake. "It's all right, Mother. They're only pamphlets."

I was mesmerized. I had a collection of pamphlets hidden in a shoebox under my bed. As the first of the leaflets fluttered down, I let out a whoop and raced about snatching them out of the air. Father came out and picked one up. Mother joined us, and Father translated for her: "Today the atomic bomb was dropped on Hiroshima. The war will soon be over . . ."

"What does it mean?" she asked anxiously.

"It's the new weapon," Father said, putting a reassuring arm around her.

"What will happen now?"

"Japan will give up," he said.

"Then what?"

Father sighed. "China is her own worst enemy."

In town there was a complete news blackout. People sensed something momentous had happened and kept to their homes until they knew what it was. Meanwhile, Mayor Yue appeared at our door, wan and sweaty and anxious to speak with Father.

"None of us were collaborators," he said in English, for Mother's benefit. "We were agents of the national government in Chungking. Oh, some of us may have taken advantage of the situation, yes."

"Some people certainly did," said Mother.

"But that was only camouflage."

"That's what you call it?"

"It was for the cause!"

"Was it."

I waited in my tree house that afternoon, but the admiral and his wife failed to appear. There was no movement, no sound from their house. The shadows lengthened across the garden. Still they did not come to the gazebo. Finally Zhang called me in to dinner. I knew the admiral and his wife had gone from my life as mysteriously as they had come.

Later, as I was preparing for bed, the doorbell rang. When Zhang answered, no one was there. Two stacks of record albums had been left outside our gate – the complete symphonies of Beethoven, Haydn, Schubert, Schumann, Tchaikovsky, Brahms. Nearly all the concerti in the popular repertoire. The operas of Wagner, Puccini, and Verdi, as well as a dizzying assortment of chamber music by Beethoven, Brahms, Dvorak, Schumann, Schubert, Haydn, Mendelssohn, and Mozart. Along with the albums was a note in Japanese: "For our young friend in the tree."

12

第十二章

MAROONED

I T T O O K a second atomic bomb, dropped on Nagasaki on August 9, to bring Japan to her knees. Six days later the emperor, Hirohito, broadcast his surrender. Qingdao went mad. Church and temple bells rang joyously. The municipal government's call for calm fell on deaf ears as the pent-up hatred of so many years was let loose. People ran about, shouting and whistling and cheering. Japanese homes and shops were smashed and looted. None of us left our hilltop until the fury spent itself. By then, the Japanese had disappeared from the streets as though they had never set foot on them.

Chiang Kai-shek's Kuomintang regime quickly replaced the puppet government in Nanking. Then began a headlong dash between Chiang's KMT and Mao's Chinese Communist Party (CCP) to take control of what had been Japanese-occupied territory. While the municipal government in Qingdao strove to maintain the status quo, the two sides clashed in the surrounding mountains. For several days and nights gunfire rattled our windows. The lulls, strangely, were even more frightening. Though it was unclear which side would enter the town, it was widely assumed the KMT would prevail.

One of Chiang's first public statements as head of the new national government was to declare that all those who had links with the defunct puppet government, or who lived and worked in occupied territory, were collaborators and traitors until proven otherwise. Father and Midder worked round the clock, sorting documents relating to their resistance work, worried about the impending takeover. Father, an idealist, clung to his belief that his actions would speak for themselves. He had accepted the post of commissioner of finance as a cover for covert activities; he had harmed no one except the enemy; most importantly, he did not enrich himself. Midder, however, had grave misgivings about Mayor Yue's trustworthiness.

"He will do anything to save his own skin," Midder cautioned.

"I'm guided by my conscience," Father replied. "Therefore, if they pound on my door in the dead of night, I have nothing to fear."

"I hope you're right."

The reality of politics, especially Chinese politics, is connections. Father wasn't without them, but Yue, like the General, came from the same province as Chiang Kai-shek, who trusted only his fellow Zejiangnese. That explained how a petty underworld figure such as Dai Li – that turned out to be the General's name – had become head of Chiang's all-powerful Military Intelligence.

"If they come after us," said Midder, "and I'm sure they will, they'll come for you first. I'll take these documents and keep them safe."

"Where will you put them?"

"It's better that you don't know."

Though the war was over, there were still long nights of curfews and blackouts when the electricity failed. Mother saved candles for emergencies, so we often sat in the dark. To while away the time, Father talked about what we would do after we left Qingdao and returned to Beijing.

"You will go to a good school," he told me. "Perhaps abroad."

"Where, Father?"

"What would you say to England?" His voice sounded reassuring. "Then Cambridge, or some equally venerable university."

Sometimes he talked about mundane things – café au lait and croissants at a sidewalk café in Paris – that he made sound so enticing I could taste them. "Then we'll stroll over to the Louvre." I saw the Mona Lisa, the Venus di Milo, and many other great works through my father's eyes.

Mother never joined in our fantasies. Instead she knitted in the dark, murmuring her soft litany: "Knit . . . purl . . . knit . . . purl." Or she played the piano, Bach and Mozart, mainly, with a little Beethoven and Schubert. I think Father dreamed aloud for the same reason Mother played – to help us through those long, dreary evenings. In his heart he believed everything would go back to the way it used to be, and there would be no need to leave.

All that changed the day the Kuomintang entered Qingdao in the fall of 1945. A new national flag – white sun in a square of blue sky over a field of red – flew over the town. Gigantic portraits of Chiang Kai-shek appeared everywhere, and slogans on bright paper plastered every wall and lamp-post.

"Welcome, conquering heroes!"

"Down with the Imperialists!"

"Long live eight years of resistance!"

"Long live our glorious victory!"

"Long live Generalissimo Chiang Kai-shek!"

Generalissimo was one of three titles Chiang Kai-shek used. He was also chairman of the KMT and president of the republic. The latter title he had conveniently inherited when the incumbent died just before the Cairo conference in 1943, enabling him to attend as an equal to Roosevelt and Churchill.

The euphoria in Qingdao was shortlived, replaced by sullen wariness the day a rag-tag collection of filthy, half-starved men straggled into town. Their uniforms were in tatters. Many were shoeless. Others had wads of straw tied to their feet. Some were without weapons; others dragged ancient hunting rifles, even bird guns, by the barrel, looking more like an army in retreat than conquering heroes. The officers riding in American Jeeps were smartly turned out and well fed. American aid clearly did not filter down the ranks.

Father was eager to hand over his portfolio and return to the railway. He soon discovered that returning to civilian life would not be so simple. Dai Li refused to dissolve his connection with Military Intelligence when hostilities ended, as he had promised. Neither was Father offered a new post or permitted to retire in Beijing. Father assuaged Mother's fears by assuring her these were temporary measures the new government had to take to ensure a smooth transition. In fact, we were marooned in Qingdao.

The national army descended on the town like locusts, grabbing anything, including homes and businesses, that caught their fancy on the flimsiest excuse. The people eager to curry favour with their new rulers and to ensure some degree of personal safety denounced one another as traitors, collaborators, or war profiteers. Though my father no longer had an official position, people still came to him for help. When he could, he spoke out for those who could not defend themselves against unjust accusations or official avarice. Though he saved some businesses and properties from being taken by force, he did not endear himself to those in power.

It was only a matter of time before the Board of Recovery, set up to probe the assets of enemy aliens, took a fancy to Maria Contini's antique shop. An army officer, representing himself as a board member, visited the shop and demanded several delicate antique Easter eggs as gifts. Maria Contini refused. The man went away muttering threats. When she mentioned it to my father, he counselled hiding the pieces. "In these lawless times it is better to minimize one's losses."

Maria Contini, however, would not bow to tyranny without a fight. When the officer came back, the items he wanted were still on display. "I must have them," he said arrogantly.

"Then buy them," she told him.

The man pointed his pistol at her. Maria crossed herself and waited for him to pull the trigger. He backed down.

A few days later the Board of Recovery seized the shop. They painted the words "*Di chan*" ("Enemy Property") across the show window and sealed the door with strips of paper bearing official stamps, signatures, and the date. Just like that, Maria Contini lost her livelihood. Father did what he could to get the property released but to no avail. He even appealed to Yue, who still had some say in local affairs though he was no longer mayor. Yue knew full well that Maria Contini was not a collaborator of the Japanese.

"It's a pity," he shrugged. "But she *is* Italian."

Father's intervention brought the Board of Recovery down on our heads. Soldiers invaded our house, turning out drawers and cupboards, fingering everything we had. Father had been lured to the Municipal Hall for "consultation" just before the soldiers arrived and could not be reached. Mother was close to hysteria.

Electric lights, the telephone, and especially the toilet intrigued the dozen men who occupied our house. They watched it flush again and again, chortling with glee like children. They washed hands and feet and even their faces in it. They were used to cooking their midday meal wherever they were, and at noon they prepared to do so. First the rice had to be washed. They emptied half their day's ration into the toilet and pressed the lever. Before their amazed eyes, the rice disappeared.

"We've been robbed!" they cried, storming out of the bathroom waving guns.

The toilet that delighted them had become an instrument of sabotage. They wanted to seal the bathroom.

"Come now, let's not be hasty," soothed Zhang. "The cook will fix you something to eat, and while you wait let's have a drop of something in my humble quarters."

In his room he plied the men with harsh sorghum wine. When Father came home, he put through a call to the Commissioner of Recovery, complaining that the men were drunk and disorderly on duty. A lorry came and took them away, but Father knew our troubles were just beginning.

A few days later the General flew into Qingdao, met with Yue, and flew out again. Shortly afterwards, an editorial appeared in the local press lauding the former mayor's exploits with the resistance, in anticipation of the American landing in Shandong. Father, Midder, and others who had actually taken risks were not mentioned. Later editorials called for the arrest of collaborators and the confiscation of their property.

"The Generalissimo must be told the truth!" Midder cried. Over Father's objections, he wrangled a seat on a train and went to Nanking. Father remained calm. If he felt the country he loved and served had betrayed him, he never said so. His devotion to China never wavered, though he was disillusioned by her leaders.

When weeks passed and there was still no word from Midder, Father decided to move us back to Beijing without permission. A timely letter from Julian, though, warned against the move. Rumours of a full-scale purge were rife following a failed attempt on Dai Li's life by a disgruntled member of wartime resistance. In the time it took Julian's letter to arrive, the KMT, Father discovered, had seized our Beijing house and its contents. After the authorities sealed the place, Julian crept in through a basement window. What the Kuomintang had not carted away, they'd destroyed. Julian salvaged only a few small artefacts.

The KMT had also seized Father's substantial bank accounts. Mercifully, he had been able to transfer some funds into Mother's name in the nick of time – the accounts of foreigners couldn't be touched, at least for the moment, since the National government still dreamed of attracting foreign investments.

A new regime also took charge at school in Qingdao. Like Lazarus risen from the tomb, Brother Feng emerged from the dank cellar where he had been hiding for almost two years. When school reopened, he was given a tumultuous welcome. He was cadaverous. The planes and hollows of his face were covered with grey stubble like mildew on a skull. Only the burning eyes gave any sign of life. The man possessed the voice of an orator, and he used it to spine-tingling effect. He spoke about his imprisonment, and the devilish torments devised by Korean and Chinese collaborators. I broke out in a cold sweat, assailed by waves of nausea as I listened to him, haunted by the wraith-like apparition in the basement. The voice suddenly rose to a banshee shriek.

"But victory is ours!"

The hall exploded in applause.

"Who are these devils?"

"Collaborators! Traitors!" shouted the assemblage.

"We must root them out! Destroy them! Drive foreigners from our land! China belongs to the Chinese!"

Brother Feng flayed the air, and the audience leaped to its feet, clenched fists raised. "Down with Imperialists! Down with traitors and collaborators! Down with foreign devils!"

Swept up in the hysteria, I shouted the slogans until I was hoarse and dizzy from excitement. Afterwards we marched into the cathedral for High Mass, giving thanks for our deliverance in a dead language to a foreign god.

Kneeling in the candle-lit church, I trembled uncontrollably, desperately needing to believe the defeat of the Japanese made the world a better place. To that end I was even willing to subscribe to the myth that China had won the war, not ridden to victory on American coat-tails. In spite of candlelight, incense, and music, God was absent from the cathedral and the world did not feel like a better place.

Chiang Kai-shek's portrait was the new icon that adorned the classroom wall. Teaching was replaced by propaganda drummed into us for hours on end. My school day began with the singing of the dirge-like Nationalist anthem, "San Min Zhu Yi" – "Three Principles of the People." We then recited an oath of allegiance while facing the Generalissimo's portrait. This was followed by the Lord's Prayer. With all the propaganda bases covered, class began.

Brother Feng was nicknamed Submarine after his habit of sneaking in, interrupting the teacher, and taking over. His harangues about the war, his graphic descriptions of Japanese atrocities, his poisonous hatred of everything not Chinese – except the church – sometimes lasted the rest of the day. At other times we were made to do calisthenics or run around the playing field literally until we dropped. A spirited, lengthy tirade followed.

"It's because you're weak that foreigners take advantage of you!" he stormed.

These episodes drained me emotionally and physically. Shao, on the other hand, took it all in stride. He even seemed to sing more beautifully than ever.

One day great lumbering American airplanes filled the skies, so big and heavy-looking one wondered how they stayed aloft. The landing we had waited for was finally happening. Once more the harbour filled with ships. Great grey hulls tied up at the docks the Japanese, and the Germans before them, had built and left behind. This was a different invasion, not with guns blazing but with star-spangled flags snapping in the wind and bands playing. It was infectiously festive and the Chinese, starved of gaiety, turned out to welcome the Sea-Bees.

The municipal government, decked out in medals from here to Thursday, greeted the American commander on the steps of city hall. Yue, the archbishop, and even Brother Feng were there. Father was not. The bells of the cathedral pealed, and the whole official party moved into the church, where a Te Deum was sung.

I went only because I had to. As usual, the music transported me beyond those walls, and it took me a moment to realize something was amiss. As Shao reached for those spine-tingling top notes, he faltered in mid-flight and fell silent. I looked up at the choir loft and saw him doubled over, both hands covering his mouth.

"What happened?" I asked as soon as he came out of the sacristy. He was white as a sheet. He tried to speak but there was no sound. The dried blood around his mouth frightened me. I put my arm around his shoulders, and we stood shivering in the warm autumn sun.

After school a few days later, I went to the tall, skinny house where Shao lived. When I knocked, his mother opened the door a crack. I could see only a wisp of colourless hair, one greenish eye, and part of a mouth.

"What is it you want?" she hissed.

"I'm Shao's friend," I faltered.

She glared at me. "The other half-caste," she said matter-of-factly. "He is very ill," she added, and slammed the door. Shao's voice was changing and forcing out those high notes had ruptured his vocal cords.

"My father's pleased," Shao croaked on his return to school a few weeks later. "Since I can't be a singer, I guess I'll have to follow the old man's footsteps and be a banker."

Secretly I was pleased at Shao's devastating fall from grace. Since he was no longer useful to the cathedral choir, Father Schmidt washed his hands of him. Up till then I'd envied the gimmick that had elevated him above the casual tyranny of the hoi polloi, envied the friendships I pretended to disdain. They had all turned against him except me; we were truly birds of a feather now. Aside from being despised Eurasians, we had a more serious strike against us: our fathers had held important positions during the war. Teachers used us as whipping boys. Schoolmates ostracized us when they were not bullying us. Shao and I spent recesses and lunch hours away from the others. One day Brother Feng came upon us eating lunch in the empty bleachers facing the soccer field.

"Hmmm," he grunted, circling as we clutched our sandwiches, scrutinizing first one then the other. "Are you *yang gwei zhi*?"– foreign devils – he asked in a gentle voice.

"We're Chinese," I replied.

He hauled me up by a handful of hair, so that I danced on tiptoes.

"What colour is this?"

"Brown, sir." I winced.

"Is it the proper hair colour for a Chinese?"

"I don't know, sir!"

He let go and I crumpled.

"I never forget faces," he said, a long finger tracing an arc through the air from Shao to me and back again. "Even faces glimpsed in a dark place."

Folding his hands behind his back, he left.

"He meant that day in the cellar," Shao whispered. "Everyone believes he's a hero. We must never tell."

I got a pair of scissors and cut my hair as close to the scalp as I could. Mother was aghast and pressed me for a reason. "I hate the colour," I said. A barber finished the job. The reflection in the mirror was bald, blank-faced, as anonymous as the other boys. Perhaps now I could disappear into the crowd.

Later, I heard my parents' hushed voices behind the closed door of their room. Mother was crying, and Father was doing his best to comfort her. "Life is hard," he told her. "The sooner he learns, the better, because it won't get easier. He's –" I knew all the expressions meaning "half-caste" that Father was trying to avoid.

"Whose fault is that?" Mother cried. "It's so unfair!"

I retreated to my tree house. Silence and shadows filled the house next door. Every door and window was crossed with white paper seals. The grass around the gazebo was knee-high. Chrysanthemums, heavy with bloom, fought a losing battle against encroaching weeds. I was not aware of my father's presence until he reached up and grasped my knee.

"Come down," he said.

I scrambled down, glowering, jaw clenched. He reached to touch my bald head and I flinched. He withdrew his hand as though it had been stung.

"You want me to be strong, don't you?" I screamed. "Well, I'm being strong!"

Was it so wrong to want to be like the rest? He did not understand the pain of being set apart, couldn't, and I wanted him to leave me alone. He spoke in a low voice about being proud of one's heritage. Switching to English, he quoted from Shakespeare: "This above all: to thine own self be true." He added, "You'll always be who you are," and somehow made me feel that was a good thing. Suddenly I wanted the touch of his hand. He reached out and cupped my head like a fuzzy watermelon and pulled me towards him. This time I did not back away.

Shao's father was a tall, reedy, bloodless looking man. With heavy glasses precariously balanced on a slender nose and a thin humourless mouth, he seemed the epitome of a conservative banker. Meeting him on the street one day, Father remarked, "You can set your clock by that man." And indeed, Mr. Shao was utterly predictable. He inhabited a narrow world bounded by the cathedral to the north, the harbour to the south, the Banque de l'Indochine, where he worked, to the west, and his home on the eastern fringes of the city's business centre. He navigated this cramped space through the war without mishap, not only preserving the bank's interests but showing a small profit. However, the reward he expected was slow to materialize. One morning Mr. Shao left his house for the bank at precisely eight-thirty, as he did every day, but never got there. He vanished.

Shao's mother went to pieces. Like so many western women of her generation who married Chinese men, she was completely dependent on her husband. The twilight world she inhabited during the Japanese occupation must have worn her down further. She became quite ill. The servants absconded, taking whatever valuables they could. When she recovered, Shao's mother became obsessed with getting out of China before galloping inflation ate up what little savings she had. Sure that her husband was dead, she wanted out at once. The repatriation process was heart-rendingly slow. Through sheer persistence she found a clerical job with the United Nations Relief and Rehabilitation Agency (UNRRA), thinking it would shorten the wait. When it did not, she took up with an American officer to help move things along. She became so self-absorbed that her son faded into oblivion. Shao, still coming to terms with the loss of his voice, had lost his father and was now becoming estranged from his mother. He turned wild.

The American Sea-Bees brought in heavy machines that flattened a building in minutes. Others, with giant claws, lifted the debris like so many matchsticks and loaded it on trucks to be hauled away. The whole town came to gawk. The Japanese barracks – surrounded by watchtowers, electrified fences, and a moat – were replaced by half-cylindrical structures of metal. No one had ever seen a Quonset hut before. The new U.S. Marine camp was open and airy. Spaces between the huts were packed down with rollers so that the wind wouldn't raise the dust, and plots for grass and flower beds were marked off for planting in the spring.

Locals swarmed around the site. Enterprising souls stuffed cards into the pockets of off-duty servicemen, offering everything from curios and food to drugs and sex. Word got around that the Americans had chewing gum and chocolate bars. At school the myth was perpetuated that these goodies contained mind-altering drugs, but the warning was disregarded. Most of us had eaten candy dropped by the planes before the war's end and were still sane. Nevertheless, the camp was declared out of bounds and being there was made a caning offence. The Submarine and his cohorts patrolled the site after school in civilian clothes; woe betide the poor miscreant who got caught. We were easy targets in our blue blazers, grey pants, white shirts, and blue and gold striped ties. There were more of us than there were brothers, however, and we led them on a merry chase.

Qingdao changed. American servicemen filled the streets. Garish neon signs flashed everywhere. What had been Maria Contini's antique shop sported a sign that spelled B-A-R. Heavily painted young women in slinky Chinese robes slit to the hips lounged in the doorway, while a jukebox blared within. Inflation ran wild, since no one trusted the Kuomintang-issued paper currency, called Fa Bi. Officially pegged at twenty yuen to one U.S. dollar, it had slid to 320 yuen by early 1946 and was still plummeting. Shops quoted prices in U.S. dollars or in gold. Red Cross and U.N. relief packages wound up on the black market, together with American cigarettes, candies, nylons, canned food, even K-rations. Most of the racketeers were government officials. While Chiang strutted before his people as the man who'd catapulted China into the ranks of world powers, and his wife made impassioned pleas to the American Congress for more aid, members of their inner circle became immensely rich. The people, however, sank deeper into poverty and despair.

Public resentment mounted against the Kuomintang as a vicious civil war raged. Qingdao was safe as long as the American forces were there. Though the townsfolk welcomed them for the money they brought in, posters shouting "Yankees go home!" and "Down with Yankee Imperialism!" mysteriously blossomed everywhere. Even the archbishop added his voice to the anti-American babble. "They are the new imperialists," he railed from his pulpit. "Guard against their corruptive ideas and lifestyle that fascinate our youth and run contrary to all our ancient beliefs and traditions!"

My father spent those troubled days writing, sitting perfectly still, except for the wrist guiding his brush tip in a long flowing motion down the page. Once I asked what he was writing.

"Things," he replied, without looking up. "Things that must not be forgotten."

While Father wrote, Mother and Maria Contini made new curtains for the bedrooms, turning old ones into a slipcover and cushions for the daybed and armchair in the guest room.

"What are you doing, Mother?" I asked, noticing the strained looks on their faces when I entered the room.

"Sewing!" she snapped. "Surely you have better things to do than watching us sew."

Winter gales churned the grey sea into frothing whitecaps by the time Midder finally came back to Qingdao. He had been caught in an endless tangle of bureaucratic red tape in Nanking. Chiang Kai-shek was surrounded by sycophants, jealous of their positions, suspicious of one another. Nobody and nothing got through to him. Midder had beggared himself, offering bribes to one official after another, and returned with his faith in Chiang's government in tatters. He described the Ministry of Military Intelligence as an enclave of gangsters bent upon looting the country before it fell to the Communists. For reasons known only to themselves, those close to Dai Li were urging him to discredit all those who had been part of the resistance operating in Japanese-held territory, with the exception of a select few. Many people Father and Midder knew had already disappeared. Others had been dragged from their houses in the dead of night and shot.

"They will destroy us," Midder warned. "Why don't you leave while you can?"

Father shook his head. "I've done nothing to be ashamed of."

I wondered whether Shao's father had been dragged off somewhere. "Did Mr. Shao do something to be ashamed of?" I asked Father.

He mulled the question before answering. "I don't know," he said wearily.

Work with the resistance had brought both Father and Midder into close contact with the Kuomintang as well as the Communists. Midder weighed one against the other and found the Kuomintang wanting. Like many disillusioned young men before him, Midder decided to take his chances with the Communists. My father was deeply concerned because Midder's upper-middle-class background made him anathema to the CCP. Ironically, it was disaffected young men and women of his class who had helped hasten the Kuomintang's defeat.

Father must have also ruminated over the pros and cons of the KMT and CCP, but he remained committed to the former. A known evil is preferable to an unknown. Thus two brave men, who had been through thick and thin together, calculated the murky future of the country they both loved and came to a parting of the ways.

At school, the U.S. Information Service showed a propaganda film about the Japanese incursion in China, starting with the incident at the Marco Polo Bridge and proceeding to the dropping of the atomic bomb on Hiroshima. I have never seen a more graphically violent, gory film; every atrocity imaginable, every shriek, wail, cry, and groan was captured. At the end scenes of carnage at Hiroshima faded into a concert hall with Marian Anderson singing Schubert's "Ave Maria."

"Down with Imperialism!" Brother Feng's voice boomed over our heads before the last strains of the song faded and the lights came up.

"Down with Imperialism! Down with Imperialism!" The chanting became a frenzied babble. Fear, rage, and confusion turned us into mindless creatures, easily manipulable. I emerged from the screening shaking like a leaf. We saw that film again and again. After the first viewing, I shut my eyes and stopped my ears at the most gruesome bits, but the ending always left my stomach in knots.

Shao never saw the film because he was truant for days on end and sullenly refused to explain his absence when he got caught. He took his punishment as though it was the outcome he'd had in mind all along.

"Where do you go?" I asked.

Shao circled me, hands folded behind his back, his gaze almost hostile.

"Want to come along?"

I was curious but lacked the nerve. "I can't . . ."

"Then it's none of your business," he rasped, and stalked away.

Shao's open-hearted grin and easy-going grace were gone, replaced by an edginess. He'd turned inward, secretive, the blackness in his eyes infinitely lonely and sad. He'd picked up some English with a peculiar American accent. Whenever I saw him, his pockets bulged with Hershey bars and Lucky Strikes, sometimes cash too. Outside school he smoked openly, flashing a military-issue lighter. His prized possession was a Marine's cap that he carried under his shirt, next to his heart. The badge and the lieutenant's bar he kept separately, wrapped in a handkerchief.

"How did you get them?" I asked, nibbling a chocolate bar he gave me.

Shao shrugged, munching chocolate and smoking at the same time. "I'm getting out," he said, squinting at me through the smoke.

"Has your mother got papers?" Everybody was getting papers except my parents.

"I said I'm going." He stretched his arms out and raced round me making airplane noises.

"You can't. You're only thirteen!" I shot back. "You're not old enough . . ."

Shao pushed his nose up against mine. "Fourteen," he said. "And old enough for lots of things."

Registration of stateless persons was a first step in repatriating foreigners. Some, like Maria Contini, had adapted to China and were leery about their ability to fit in elsewhere. Others, like Shao's mother and mine, watching their privileged lives disappear, hankered for greener pastures. Many had no documentary proof of where they'd come from or who they were. Some, like Mother, had lost their citizenship through marrying Chinese. All they could do was fill out endless forms and wait.

Meanwhile the International Red Cross broadcast short messages from all over the world from people hoping to find friends or relatives in China. Mother and Maria Contini huddled over our radio every afternoon, hoping for word from Tim, from Mother's relatives, or from Maria's son, Vittorio. It was like looking for a pin in a haystack. Every broadcast was a disappointment. Maria comforted herself, saying softly, "One day Vittorio will speak." She sighed. "I think I die in China, like Giuseppe. Is not so bad. I'm old. Ha! New York."

It was so unlike Maria that Mother was seriously alarmed. To brighten her spirits, Father bought Maria another goat. How he came by the animal was never clear. Nor would he permit her to pay for it, so long as we shared the milk and cheese. The arrangement pleased everyone. With an animal to care for, Maria was more her old self, though she never again talked about going to New York.

Not long afterwards, my brother Albert appeared on our doorstep unannounced. He had eloped the previous year. Father's main objection to the match was the bride's family. A gaggle of wastrel siblings had squandered the family's considerable wealth in less than a decade. It was not the sort of family he wanted his son to be entangled with. Albert did not see it that way, and since the marriage there had been little contact between Albert and Father until Albert appeared on our doorstep.

Father had cut off Albert's allowance when he married, adamant that he shoulder the responsibility of supporting a wife on his own. Albert, however, had always harboured the notion that Father owed him a living because of his deafness. Albert had received the best education possible, was an excellent draftsman, and had a good job largely through Father's intervention. Expecting to inherit considerable wealth, Albert cultivated expensive tastes, which left him horribly in debt. In addition, his arrogance and a caustic tongue alienated his colleagues. Albert was discovering he could no longer rely upon our father's influence to keep his job.

Money had brought Albert to Qingdao. His wife was pregnant. Shanghai was once again the business centre of China and he wanted to try his luck there. For that he needed a stake. Lately, newspaper editorials had been urging the government to seize the assets of all Chinese with connections to the Japanese. Albert wanted his inheritance before Chiang Kai-shek and his minions appropriated it.

At that time we were living simply. Father, in his fifties, without an income, facing an uncertain future, was deeply provoked by Albert's demands. They locked horns, their arguments becoming so fierce that Zhang had to break in to the study and forcibly remove Albert. Separated, they calmed down, kept their distance for a time, but then quarrelled again. Albert went on a rampage, wrecking furniture and threatening Father with a carving knife. He was a veritable tornado that took all three servants to subdue.

I crouched in my tree house, arms folded over my head to shut out the noise. Presently, when it stopped, Albert came looking for me. There was barely enough space in the tree house. We had to sit with our legs dangling over the side. Albert had once been an elegant dresser, but he had lost so much weight that his clothes bagged and hung loosely. I recoiled, though my heart ached for him, as he hugged himself, rocking back and forth, muttering, "Deaf . . . deaf . . . deaf . . ."

Stormy sessions between Albert and my father over money usually ended predictably: Mother made the peace, and Albert got what he wanted. This time, though, was different. Whether Albert's demand was prompted by need, deep unhappiness, or greed, it violated the most sacred tenet of the father-son relationship in Chinese culture and stung my father to his soul. Demanding an inheritance from a living parent was tantamount to wishing him dead.

Father took ill with chest pains that very night. His malady was treated as severe indigestion brought on by something he ate or by stress. He was ordered to bed. Albert caught the next train back to Tienjin empty-handed, without apologizing or even saying goodbye. Father was soon on his feet again, but he had changed. Overnight he had aged. "He will be the death of me," he said to Mother.

Almost daily, the newspapers published lists of Allied prisoners being repatriated from Japanese prison camps. Mother always scanned these lists. One day she spotted the names of Captain D. Wood and son, and Mr. J. Burton.

"Can it be them?" she asked Father. "I must go and see!"

Mother and I went to the station early on the day the POWs were to arrive, hoping to get as close to the platform as possible. Others had got there even earlier. Foreseeing the problem, the Red Cross had cordoned off the platform, keeping the crowd outside the station, leaving a path wide enough for two or three people to walk abreast from the train to waiting lorries. We pushed our way through the throng until we reached the wooden barrier at the foot of the steps outside the station's main entrance. The train was late. Red Cross and UNRRA workers ran about distractedly. Chinese military policemen in American-supplied khakis yelled at the crowd to stand back.

Finally, a trickle of dazed, exhausted scarecrows emerged from the station. Young and old looked alike. Hunger, illness, and unimaginable hardship had robbed them of individuality. As they shuffled into the light, a Red Cross worker gently pointed them towards the vehicles lining the curb.

Names shouted from the crowd hung eerily in the air. Mother gripped my shoulder with a quivering hand, alternately dabbing her eyes and scrutinizing the line of grey faces as they passed. Then I spotted him.

"Buzzy!" I cried, pointing excitedly at a gangling, tow-headed youth squinting in the daylight. "There, on the steps!" I pointed, waving and shouting. "Buzzy! Buzzy! Over here!"

Mother gasped when she finally singled him out. Buzzy was all legs, hollow-eyed, grey like the rest. I shouted his name and waved more vigorously. He shuffled forward and two men followed, the taller supporting another whose head lolled sickeningly from side to side.

Mother waved, calling through her tears, "Woody! Woody!"

"Buzzy!" I shouted, straining against the rope that held us back. He shuffled past without so much as a glance.

Mother reached out and clutched Captain Wood's sleeve. He stopped, and a light of recognition flickered. A toothless smile slowly suffused his face.

"We made it," he rasped.

The man he was supporting lifted his head fitfully.

"It's all right, Jack . . . just old friends."

Mr. Burton's head drooped again.

"Mavis? . . . Donald? . . ." Mother asked in a choked whisper. Captain Wood blinked, and Mother covered her mouth to keep from crying out. Then a Red Cross worker interposed herself.

"Move along, mustn't hold up the line," she chirped. With a fixed smile, she pointed the two men towards a lorry.

As the lorry drove away the word Buzzy had mouthed at me that cold day in 1942 when the Japanese took him away flashed through my mind. The word I could not decipher then was crystal clear now: "coward." To Buzzy, anyone who'd escaped going to a concentration camp was a coward.

We seldom had visitors any more. All Father's fair-weather friends had vanished. Even the archbishop, hailed as a hero for saving church property from the Japanese and with a cardinal's red hat in the offing, stopped coming. Mother laid down her sewing apprehensively one day when the doorbell sounded.

Zhang was quite breathless when he announced, "American . . . come back!"

A tall, big-boned fellow filled the doorway, his sandy hair glinting in the sunlight. "Remember me, ma'am?" He stuck out a big hand, grinning from ear to ear.

"You're . . . you're – " Mother stammered. Realizing she didn't know his name, she exclaimed, "Our house guest!"

The man chortled.

"It's Captain Perry!" I exclaimed.

Mother wheeled in surprise, but we were already shaking hands. I had asked our house guest his name and he had told it to me, though it was against the rules – our secret.

Captain Perry had gone to Chungking after he left us and followed the Kuomintang government to Nanking after the war. He had come to renew a wartime acquaintance and to deliver a letter from G2 Section of the U.S. Fleet Marine Force Western Pacific Headquarters in San Francisco. The letter commended Father and his group for their work monitoring Japanese military activity in the Shandong peninsula and aiding downed U.S. airmen. There were also letters of commendation for Midder and other members of the resistance.

Captain Perry brought a carton of gifts – brandy and cigars for Father, perfume and nylons for Mother and Maria Contini, as well as a ham, and enough tins of Spam, condensed milk, and candy bars to feed a small army. I ran to fetch Maria, Zhang set the table in festive fashion, and Cook bustled out to the market for vegetables. There was still a bit of fine wine in the cellar and this seemed as good an occasion as any to open it.

Captain Perry was now stationed in Qingdao awaiting discharge, and he and my parents became fast friends. He kept Father informed about world events, since the censors left many blank columns in our local newspapers. George Marshall, the former chief of staff of the U.S. army, had arrived in China towards the end of 1945. The Marshall Aid Plan, combining massive economic aid with liberal helpings of propaganda about the virtues of union and federation, was giving the recovery of battered but still resourceful European economies a great boost. With Marshall at the helm, President Truman assumed the plan would succeed again. What is good for the goose is not always good for the gander. Truman failed to recognize that the Europeans had come to see the error of their ways at war's end and were ready to rebuild and move forward. The Chinese were not.

Marshall's mission – to stave off the civil war through a compromise between the two sides, and help the Nationalists establish their authority over as large a portion of China as possible – was bound to fail. My father was hardly unique among the Chinese intelligentsia who saw the American scheme of a coalition between the Kuomintang and the Communists as a forlorn hope. Chiang and Mao were both rooted in millennia of feudalism and separated by bitter class hatred. Chiang gravitated towards the urban, mercantile middle class who cynically embraced corruption as a way of life. Mao, on the other hand, understood the down-trodden rural population who saw city dwellers as exploiters. And he recognized the potential of properly motivated masses that represented eighty-five per cent of the population. While Mao was winning adherents through his radical land reforms, everything Chiang did further alienated the people from the Kuomintang.

As the American-brokered negotiations went on fitfully, civil war gathered momentum. Inflation that had begun in Chungking during the war spread like a plague throughout Nationalist China afterwards. In his capacity as party chairman, Chiang Kai-shek promised economic reforms and a national election in the near future. As a first step, the Kuomintang sought to curb runaway inflation by issuing a new national currency. The Chinese, however, had no more confidence in the new currency than in the one it replaced, since it was widely suspected its gold backing had gone into the pockets of Chiang's immediate circle. Besides, a largely illiterate population could not be expected to elect a government for itself. Father saw it all as a sop to placate the Americans, many of whom were beginning to feel they were backing the wrong horse. As long as the semblance of democracy could be maintained, however, the Kuomintang cynically knew that American aid would keep flowing in.

Meanwhile, in the relative seclusion of our hilltop, Father wrote steadily, filling page after page with his beautiful calligraphy. Early in 1946, he completed the manuscript that would be his sole defence against charges of collaborating with the enemy that loomed over his head. Calmly and carefully he translated it for Mother, Captain Perry, and me. It was a scrupulous, dispassionate account of his involvement with the resistance against the Japanese from the early 1930s to the end of the war. These were the things that self-seeking politicians were trying to sweep under the carpet to be forgotten, at the cost of an innocent man's life. Much later, my father would add four characters to the cover of his personal copy which translate as "A Heart Full of Anguish." When he finished his recital, he announced, "I am ready."

"Isn't there another way?" Mother asked, as he carefully put the manuscript away. Her eyes went quickly from Father to Captain Perry; something was afoot.

"For your sake, I wish there was," Father replied. "But I wouldn't count on it."

A couple of weeks later, in March 1946, a bomb placed on the aircraft in which Dai Li was flying from Nanking to Qingdao ended the General's life. By then he and his henchmen had chalked up over four thousand arrests of so-called collaborators, and more were in the offing. Father felt it was time to take action. He would turn himself in before they came for him.

"By surrendering myself, I show the world I am innocent. The state cannot prove me guilty without committing perjury. On the other hand, if I wait for them to arrest me, then in the eyes of the law and the world, I am guilty."

"Oh, John. Are you absolutely sure?" Mother asked.

"History," Father assured her, "is full of such precedents."

13

第十三章

A FAR,
FAR BETTER
THING

I N THE DAYS BEFORE he turned himself in, Father spent as
much time with me as he could manage. Spring came late that
year. Bundled against the unseasonable cold, we took long
walks along the seashore. Father had always taken me into his confidence, as if I were much older, but nothing in my experience prepared me for what he was about to do. I had many questions, and
by way of answering he used our revered ancestor, Guan Yu, to
illustrate his predicament and the meaning of love of country, justice, personal honour, and courage.

In the late Han dynasty, the empire was torn by war among
three factions vying for supreme power. Guan Yu, a breeder and
trainer of war horses, became blood brothers with Liu Bei, a distant relative of the tottering imperial house. Believing Liu Bei to be
the dynasty's best hope of regaining its faded glory, Guan Yu followed him into endless campaigns. For almost thirty years they
fought battles together. Eventually, Liu made himself king of a
petty kingdom and retired to a life of luxury, leaving Guan Yu

to guard an ill-equipped but strategic outpost. There, in A.D. 219, Liu's enemies overran the outpost and captured Guan Yu. Rather than betray Liu Bei, Guan Yu chose to die. The empire of Han subsequently disintegrated into three kingdoms. Though my father avoided mentioning Guan Yu's end, I had read the history of the Three Kingdoms and knew the price he paid for loyalty.

Just after the war, street executions of alleged traitors and war profiteers seemed even more frequent than they had been under the Japanese. They had also become a grotesque form of mass entertainment. The prisoner was hog-tied and paraded through the street on the flat deck of a truck, with a white dunce cap on his head, his offence scrawled in large characters pinned to his chest and back. At a prearranged street corner, where colourful posters announced the date and time of execution, the truck stopped. Trumpets blared, gongs banged, and noisy crowds, hooting and laughing, gathered to watch. One of the soldiers on the truck stepped forward, raised his pistol above his head, and loaded it. The prisoner was dispatched with a single shot to the back of the head. The crowd cheered as the corpse was hoisted onto the nearest lamp-post. Passersby spat and threw stones at it. Sometimes it stayed there for days until family members paid for the bullet that had killed it. Only then could they take the body away.

Father and I stood on top of a rocky bluff overlooking the wild wintry sea. The wind whipped up a scrim of pale yellow sand, obscuring the beach below, where he and I and Mother often swam. As Father talked about what he was about to do, a question formed in my mind – "Where does patriotism, honour, and duty leave off and love of family begin?" – and then evaporated. All I could think of was the round scar with vivid frayed edges under his left collarbone, the scar he refused to talk about, the scar that always made me shudder. I fumbled for words, but all I could utter was something out of *A Tale of Two Cities*, which I'd just finished reading.

"Father, are you about to do 'a far, far better thing than you have ever done'?"

He took off his hat and faced into the wind. Feet planted wide, newly grey hair flying, he seemed as solid and unmoveable as the cliff we stood on.

"There are far, far better things to do after this," he said.

I threw my arms around him. Though his words were reassuring, in my mind the high-minded Guan Yu, and Sydney Carton resolutely mounting the steps to the guillotine at the finish of Dickens's novel, melded with the street executions. Everywhere, it seemed, death came as the end.

I got home from school one afternoon to find the table laid with our best silver for six. I heard ice rattling in a cocktail shaker as Zhang made martinis, and caught a whiff of one of Father's Corona cigars, which came in fine plywood boxes. Everything was as before, except for the overnight bag outside my parents' room. This is the day, I told myself. I pushed aside the sliding doors to the living room and found them all there: my parents, the lawyer Mr. Shi, Captain Perry, and Maria Contini. They were talking and laughing, not what I expected. I felt rooted to the spot. For a moment, the thumping in my chest blotted out the sounds of merriment. The gathering seemed unreal. Maybe things have changed, I told myself. Maybe Father's not leaving. Maybe it's a celebration of freedom. Father crossed the room, smiling and relaxed. We shook hands formally, as we had done at so many receptions in our house in Beijing.

Dinner was early. We never ate before eight but it was barely six. Cook had stuffed a goose with chestnuts and roasted it to a turn. It was served with mounds of vegetables, small rolls hot from the oven, and the best wine left in Father's cellar. At the end of the meal, Cook came in holding high a beautiful chestnut cake, which he presented to my father. Everyone applauded. My father clasped hands with the old servant, whose eyes glowed moist in the candlelight. He murmured a few words and withdrew, and the chatter at the table abruptly died.

Mother's cheery voice broke the silence. "Aren't you going to cut the cake, dear?"

Father did the honours. As though released from a spell, everyone spoke at once. Zhang served coffee, brandy, and cigars to the men. The two women withdrew to the living room. I excused myself and pulled on a coat.

"Where are you going?" whispered Zhang.

I hid my face. "The tree house."

"Your father mustn't see you cry," he whispered, squeezing my shoulder. "Just ten minutes . . . and you be back."

I ran blindly out of the house. My innards had melted into clear liquid that streamed from my eyes. I wept in silence until a wave of nausea doubled me over the side of the tree house. All the food came up in a wild spurt. Empty, tearless, and numb, I was finally calm.

Zhang came for me. He straightened my tie, dabbed my face with a napkin, and pointed me towards the living room. With a desperate pang I noticed Father was not there. Maria Contini patted the sofa beside her.

"He change the clothes," she said. "Always he look so!" and she kissed her fingertips.

Father reappeared in a dark tweed blazer, grey slacks, and a plain tie as though off to visit a friend. Mother smiled bravely. They had made their farewells in private, and she had a firm grip on herself. Zhang brought my father's heavy navy blue wool coat that he always wore when we went for our walks, and a matching hat. Father hugged me so tightly my ribs ached. Dimly I was aware of him whispering something.

"Remember what I told you." He looked me straight in the eyes. I wish I knew what it was he'd told me; I nodded anyway. Suddenly there was so much to say, but I couldn't summon a voice. He gestured towards the living room, from where the sound of the piano flooded into the hallway. I went. At the door I looked back. Father hadn't moved, though the others had already gone outside. I waved. He waved back, jutting his chin for me to go in.

Later that night, the sound of weeping wakened me. I got out of bed and rapped on the door of my parents' room. It was dark. All I could see was the lighted tip of Mother's cigarette.

"They've locked up your father," she said, surprise and indignation in her voice. She hiccupped. As if to comfort herself she added, "Even Captain Perry said they can't keep him."

Though Father had prepared us for the possibility of his incarceration, Mother belonged to a generation of westerners who did not take the Chinese seriously — even their wars seemed to her faintly ridiculous. I don't think that she really understood Father was engaged in a life and death struggle; she viewed his turning himself in as a quixotic gesture.

Next day, the story, splashed across the front page of the *Qingdao Public Press*, was circled in red and posted on the school bulletin board. The big, bold characters of the headline struck me like a fist to the nose. Through watery eyes their meaning seeped into my brain. "Former Commissioner of Finance . . . investigation by the Ministry of Justice . . . subversive activities. . . ."

The blood rushed to my cheeks; the shoves, the sly kicks from my jeering schoolmates washed off me like water from a duck's back. I pushed my way out of the crush around the bulletin board and headed for the school gate. The bell was about to be sounded, and the old gatekeeper was ready to padlock the gate for the day. My footsteps quickened. He looked at me quizzically, a silent question: "Do you want out?" I stopped. Where could I go? I could not go home without giving some kind of explanation for missing school. Where else was there? Since my parents never gave me an allowance, and I never asked for money, I did not have a cent to my name. Without money, I couldn't even while away the day in a cinema. Wandering the streets in the cold would be even worse than school. I turned and headed back to my classroom.

At assembly, Brother Feng spoke about the insidious betrayal of the country, whipping his listeners into a frenzy of fear and hate. Afterwards a mob swarmed me, chanting, "Traitor! Traitor! Big-nose traitor!" A fight broke out. One against many, I quickly got the worst of it. Nobody tried to stop it until one of the boys hurled a rock that narrowly missed my head. A new brother, watching from a distance, charged into the mêlée, and the boys scattered.

"Are you hurt?" he asked. I shook my head, though I was already black and blue.

"What will you tell them at home?"

I started to walk away.

"What will you tell them?"

"The truth!" I shouted. "It's a sin to lie!"

Brother Jang was young, and new to the order. Mired between God and Chiang Kai-shek, he was as confused as I about the rightness of things.

When I got home, my clothes dirty and torn, men from the Ministry of Military Intelligence were going through our house, searching for subversive material. Mother sat stiffly in the living room. Her eyes widened when she saw my clothes and battered face, but she controlled herself.

Zhang's pidgin English had been stretched to its limits interpreting. "Young master, you interpret," he gasped, mopping his brow.

"Are you up to it?" The officer in charge flashed a deprecating grin. "This is a treason investigation."

"Have you finished?" Mother asked in a flash of anger. She waited for me to translate. "You even searched the toilet tank twice."

The officer reddened. "We'll seize the house!" he said angrily.

"Tell him to lower his voice," Mother snapped, "or I'll call the British Consul."

I conveyed her remark to the officer. He paced the floor. Then, as if divinely inspired, he crossed the room in a few quick strides and marked the door separating the bedrooms from the front of the house with a white chalk X. From that moment, the front of the house was no longer ours.

Next came the painful, laborious task of taking inventory of the contents of each room before the officer in charge sealed it with strips of paper bearing his signature and the ministry's seal. It was after midnight when the men finally left.

An article about the sealing of our house appeared in the morning paper. It too was posted on the bulletin board at school. More taunts and assaults were directed my way.

Mother busied herself turning the rear half of the house into our new home. The spare bedroom became a living room. Slipcovers and cushions that Mother and Maria Contini had made out of floor-length curtains turned the guest bed into a divan. Captain Perry brought us a short-wave radio so we could keep up with the news. Ironically, news of China had to be gleaned from foreign broadcasts.

Several weeks passed without any word from Father. The lawyer, Mr. Shi, dropped in from time to time. He was a compact man with lacquered hair, parted in the middle, that jutted out stiffly like the glistening wings of a bird. His small red mouth formed words with infinite care. He spoke English fluently, but every sentence sounded rehearsed. Though he always addressed Mother as "Missus," balancing his coffee cup with his little finger cocked, there was nothing servile about him. Mother had immense faith in him because of his British education.

Everyone felt the stress of Father's absence. Zhang disappeared one day without warning, and we didn't know what had happened to him until we heard he had gone on a binge. He came back a few days later, pale and dishevelled. "Master go way, Zhang very sad," he told Mother. "Promise . . . no more drink." Mother accepted his apology and welcomed him back.

A month or so after Father left us, Mr. Shi brought a form run off on a Gestetner machine on coarse brown paper similar to the toilet paper sold in the streets. The printed characters were barely legible but the blanks, filled in with ink and brush, were clear. It was a summons instructing Father to appear before a judge the following week to answer charges of collaborating with the enemy in a time of war.

"This is lunacy!" exclaimed Mother. "He's already in custody!"

"The Ministry of Justice issued the document," Mr. Shi pointed out. "That's good." He paused to let the remark sink in. "I'm told your husband is not in jail. That is also good." Mr. Shi surmised that Father was in one of the ministry's "guest houses" scattered around the city and dismissed the court appearance with a disdainful wave of a well-manicured hand.

"This hearing is really for judge and lawyers to size one another up. An astute lawyer quickly gauges how the judge can be swayed." Mr. Shi cleared his throat elaborately and, darting a quick glance at Mother, continued. "Every judge has his price, Missus." He lowered his voice. "Your husband could be home in no time."

Mother's hand shook as she poured Mr. Shi another cup of coffee. When she spoke, however, her voice was firm. "Can you guarantee my husband will stay free?"

Mr. Shi threw up his hands. To Mother's look of consternation, he said, "This is China."

There was a long pause.

"There's no money," she said finally, her tone leaving no room for discussion. Mr. Shi started to speak, but Mother cut him off. "My husband is not a collaborator. You know that as well as I do. See to it he is exonerated." She rose and offered her hand.

As soon as Mr. Shi took his leave, Mother went to her room and shut the door. When she came to dinner, I could tell she had been crying.

"Are we really poor, Mother?" I asked, then felt instantly sorry I had.

She knew straightaway what had prompted my question. "Your father would not want me to buy his freedom. He is innocent." She fixed me with her gaze. "No matter what anybody says, your father is an honourable man. They have to recognize that," she said, serving herself vegetables. "Even in this dreadful, dreadful place."

"I'll be plain," Mrs. Yue, the former mayor's wife, said in her nasally American-accented English. "We want your cook. You won't be entertaining." A haughty gesture dismissed our cramped living room with its ugly beige daybed, two mismatched chairs, and small table. "We, on the other hand, must maintain our place in society."

Mother calmly stirred her tea while Mrs. Yue drew savagely on her long cigarette holder. She look like a thin gorgon with her scarlet lips, permanently puckered from being wrapped too long around an opium pipe, and her mass of lacquered hair piled atop her head.

"I'm offering U.S. dollars. I dare say you can use the money. Lawyers and judges are such leeches." She looked even more ghastly when she smiled. "Name your price. We can afford it."

"Cook will have a roof over his head and food on the table as long as we do," said Mother. "But he is free to go."

Mrs. Yue glared incredulously. She had already spoken to Cook, but he would not budge, so she had come to Mother. In those days people routinely sold servants without the servants' consent. Fearful of offending their employers, servants allowed themselves to be indentured for life, or until they saved enough to buy their freedom. The two women eyed each other with frank hostility.

"A certain lawyer asked Mr. Yue to write a testimonial about your husband's underground activities during the war."

"I believe Mr. Shi is approaching a great many people with knowledge of my husband's efforts on behalf of his country."

"Mr. Yue has some difficulty complying, since the two men weren't exactly close." Mrs. Yue scrutinized Mother through a cloud of bluish smoke, gauging the effect of her words. "My husband would be happy to, of course. If I ask him."

"I'm sure you have great powers of persuasion, Mrs. Yue."

"But we must have the cook."

"Cook will make up his own mind," Mother replied without hesitation.

A few days later I found wonderful aromas emanating from the kitchen when I returned from school. Cook was making something special! I raced into the house thinking Father was home, but there was only Mother and Maria Contini.

It was a wonderful festive spread – chicken, which was ludicrously expensive, a carp, vegetables, rice, and custard tarts for dessert – served by Cook himself, who glowed with satisfaction as the three of us polished it off. Only after he served us a fragrant green tea did he join Zhang and Lao Zhao for his meal.

After Maria Contini went home, Cook knocked on the living-room door. He blushed when Mother thanked him again for the meal and asked for the food bill, as she usually did at the end of the day.

Cook wagged a finger at her. "Cookie . . . invite."

Mother started to protest, but Cook cut her short. "Missy pay Cookie. Cookie no work. No good man." He lowered his gaze and carried on in a small voice, "Cookie go way now. Missy please no angry."

Mother swallowed hard, smiling to show she was not angry. I think she had been expecting it. "Are you going . . . home to Tien-jin?" Although she was sorry to see Cook leave, she was probably relieved that there would be one less servant to pay out of her dwindling resources.

Cook made a droll face. "Cookie go Missy Yue house." He stole a glance at her.

"Good money?"

Cook nodded, smacking his hands together for emphasis.

Mother paid him his wages, and also a sum in an envelope which Father had prepared in advance for each of the servants. Cook accepted his wages but refused the bonus.

"If Cook not take . . . Master angry Cook," Mother said.

Cook tucked the envelope in his pocket. Blinking back tears, he thanked Mother profusely, lapsing into Chinese and insisting I interpret every word.

"I'll come to pay my respects on festivals," he said, bowing out of the room.

The next morning, Zhang put a note written in Chinese on the table. It was from the chauffeur, Lao Zhao. I translated for Mother. He explained that even though he had promised Father to look after Mother and me, he was marked for arrest and felt his presence would only cause us more grief. "I am going where I can contribute to society," he concluded, "and pray the lord Buddha will protect the Master and his family." It was clear Lao Zhao had joined the Communists.

"Me stay" – Zhang stamped his foot –"all time!"

"We'll get by," Mother assured Zhang and me, "if we pull together!"

She thrust Lao Zhao's note into the pot-bellied stove, and the three of us watched it burst into flame and turn to ash.

14

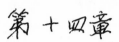

THIS IS
CHINA

NOT LONG AFTER the KMT entered Qingdao, Maria Contini had taught Mother how to sew her jewellery into the lining of curtains in the bedrooms. Other pieces they stuffed in the cushions that decorated our makeshift living room. The only piece she would not hide was a simple, oval, inky blue sapphire with a star at its centre. My father had given her the ring soon after they were married, and she always wore it.

Now, lacking an income, she began taking her jewellery out, one piece at a time, and selling it for food and fuel. With inflation rising, and one U.S. dollar – still officially pegged at twenty yuen to one U.S. dollar – fetching over two thousand yuen on the black market, we all knew the cache would not last long.

Mother announced, "I have to get a job." Maria gasped and crossed herself. Mother chuckled. "I worked before I married. I can jolly well do it again."

Maria unearthed an indestructible old Remington from her attic. Zhang carried it home strapped to his back. Then he spent hours cleaning and oiling its dusty keys. While I did my homework each evening on the little card table, Mother practised her typing and polished her stenographic skills on the kitchen table.

Captain Perry found her a job as a secretary with U.S. Marine Headquarters. Every day that Mother went off to work, Zhang pulled a long face. "This should not happen! Chiang Kai-shek, you turtle's egg!" he muttered, shaking his fist. In those days Chinese men frowned on women working for a living.

Mother did not seem to mind. Perhaps having something to do each day helped take her mind off Father. She, Zhang, and I spent most of our evenings in the kitchen where it was warm. The only people who came to visit now were Maria Contini and Captain Perry, who liked the kitchen too. The pot-bellied stove in the living room was lit only when Mr. Shi came so he would report to Father that we were doing well. And indeed, countless people were worse off.

One day five or six young men with pips on their uniformed shoulders rode up in a Jeep, broke the seals on the front part of our house, and moved in with their bedrolls. Zhang, alone, could not stop them. By the time Mother came home from work, they were firmly ensconced. From our portion of the house we could hear them tramping through the rooms, talking in low voices.

"They can't live in there," Mother protested to Mr. Shi. "There's no running water or cooking facilities."

"Ah yes, but . . ."

"Soon they'll want the rest of the house," said Mother. Being homeless was her greatest fear.

Mr. Shi shrugged.

At first the men left early and returned late at night. We never saw them, which suited us. Morale was low in the National Army, and discipline almost non-existent; soldiers were little more than thugs, and these men were no exception. Once they got used to the house they turned rowdy, hammering the locked door that separated us, shouting obscenities. They smashed glass; toppled furniture; pounded the piano till its strings snapped. They urinated on the floor and the ammonia stench filled the house. The small back garden became their latrine.

"They're making a shambles of my home," Mother cried the moment Mr. Shi came through the door, in answer to an urgent summons.

"Try to be calm," said Mr. Shi.

"Can't you smell it?" demanded Mother. "The whole house reeks!"

Mr. Shi blandly replied that he smelled nothing. In spite of his British education, he could be annoyingly Chinese – nothing would persuade him to admit bad behaviour by any Chinese to a foreigner. Besides, Mr. Shi was disgruntled. Father's trial had been put off again, for another three months, pending further investigation. Mr. Shi believed the delay and the billeting of officers in our house were due to Mother's refusal to bribe the judge.

For once Mother was not quite sure of herself. At that moment one of the men, obviously drunk, began beating on the door and meowing like a love-sick cat. Mother blanched, but forced herself to remain calm. My hands had gone clammy. Instinctively I cast about for something to use as a weapon, but there was nothing at hand. Mr. Shi just gaped at the door. Mother jutted her chin at the noise, a steely glint in her eyes. "I want it stopped!"

Mr. Shi started to protest, but she cut him short.

"Do something or I'll shoot whoever comes through that door!"

His eyes widened in alarm. "Where did you get a gun?"

Mother smiled without replying, and Mr. Shi left muttering in Chinese about headstrong foreign women who did not know their place. Mother later told me she did not have a gun. "But I do have your father's cane with the blade inside," she said with a twinkle, "and I know how to use it."

Mr. Shi, for all his protestations, must have done something, for the officers left the following week. Soldiers with sheaves of documents inspected the front part of the house, where the officers had been, and found the cupboards unsealed and silverware and small artefacts missing. Mother was deeply upset, all the more so when the officer in charge loudly insisted we had taken the articles ourselves when the occupants were absent. Mr.

Shi was hastily summoned again. He hotly denied the charge on Mother's behalf.

The two men argued back and forth, gesticulating animatedly. When it became clear he would get no satisfaction, Mr. Shi wiped his glasses and said, "I'll ask the lady of the house to speak to the Americans about this."

The officer snorted contempt.

Mr. Shi returned his glasses to his nose. "She has a very important job at their headquarters."

The officer in charge blinked uncertainly. The two men went into a private huddle. The officer issued an affidavit stating that certain army personnel billeted on the premises had pilfered my parents' personal possessions sealed by the Ministry of Military Intelligence. A new inventory was taken before the front end of the house was re-sealed.

"Missus, you are a hard woman," said Mr. Shi, mopping his brow elaborately with a silk handkerchief. "Another day like this will be the death of me!" The brandy Mother offered him restored some of his good humour.

It would have suited Mr. Shi to bribe the judge, get my father released, spirit us to Hong Kong, out of the Kuomintang's clutches, and collect a fat fee. Once he understood that it was not to be, he decided to fight the case and did so with ingenuity and thoroughness. With Mother's help he drew up a lengthy list of people who might corroborate Father's version of events.

Midder was one of the first witnesses he wanted to talk to. Shortly before Father turned himself in, Midder had gone to work for a British shipping company downtown supervising stevedores unloading foreign ships. At first he made regular visits. These became infrequent, but he kept in touch by phone. One night he told Mother he thought he was being watched by Military Intelligence and probably being investigated.

"He's afraid coming here might implicate us," Mother told Mr. Shi.

Mr. Shi smacked his forehead in dismay.

Around the time Lao Zhao left, the phone calls from Midder stopped altogether. Mother was concerned and asked Captain Perry, who knew Midder, to make discreet inquiries. In due course he told Mother, "Midder's disappeared. Vanished. At least he hasn't been arrested." Apparently, the stevedores Midder was supervising had been stamping U.N. relief parcels "A gift of the Chinese Communist Party" as they came off the ships. When the KMT learned of the practice, Midder's well-being was at risk. He had apparently got out of Qingdao one skip ahead of the secret police.

"Another good man gone over to the other side," fumed Mr. Shi. "We'll have to manage without him."

The lawyer worked like a bloodhound, tracking down former members of the resistance, trying to obtain depositions from people who had had dealings with my father from 1942 to the end of the war. It was a monumental task. Some had been killed, others had died. Those not in prison were generally too scared to testify. Nevertheless, Mr. Shi persisted, following every lead, pursuing everyone who might possibly help. Gradually he amassed a huge stack of evidence, the strongest of which was the letter of commendation from U.S. intelligence G2 Headquarters Fleet Marine Forces in San Francisco, confirming my father's connection with the Chungking forces throughout the war. Mr. Shi told Mother it was perhaps even strong enough to refute the evidence that most threatened Father – a damaging report from Yue.

Yue had been the titular head of the Shandong operation, but he did little in the resistance after Father arrived in Qingdao. In his report, however, Yue asserted that my father had joined the resistance only days before the war ended, implying he had been a willing collaborator since 1942.

"Yue is lying to maintain his false image of being a resistance hero," Mr. Shi reasoned. "While Dai Li was alive and in power, he was protected, but Dai is dead. Mark my word, there will be a reckoning."

Ironically, a young drug addict, found dead in a shabby hotel room, brought matters to a head. Death from overdose was hardly news, except that the deceased was a defrocked monk, a master of martial arts who had inspired the populace with his feats not long ago. Master Sun left a lengthy suicide note detailing his fall from grace. Though the principal players in the sordid drama of seduction, corruption, and abandonment were not named, there was enough detail to leave no doubt in the reader's mind who they were.

Temporarily unmuzzled by Dai Li's death, the local press came out with angry editorials, railing against moral degenerates who took advantage of their official positions to satisfy their appetites. Each salvo came closer to naming names. Whether Mr. Shi had anything to do with the public outcry that ensued we will never know. However, Master Sun would certainly have been one of the witnesses Mr. Shi intended to seek out. The young monk had, after all, been a member of my father's group.

In addition, Mr. Shi's tireless pursuit of the truth turned up evidence that played into the factional strife within the ministry. The reformist faction seized on the glaring contradiction between the American G2's testimonial and Yue's damning statement, making it a major sticking point.

"Police watch Mister, Missy Yue," Cook told Mother when he came for a visit. "No good time." He rubbed his bald head. "No pay Cookie." He held up four fingers. "Four month. Never mind," he sighed, "better go Tienjin. Cookie go home."

As the pressure mounted, Yue panicked. He sent word to Mr. Shi offering to retract his statement to the Ministry of Military Intelligence, correcting his "mistake" regarding Father's work with the resistance. "I was ill and upset at the time," he wrote. "Surely you must believe I would not sell out one of my own group." In return for changing his story, he added, he would expect safe conduct for himself and his wife out of China.

Mr. Shi gleefully brandished the letter, unable to conceal his satisfaction. With that note in hand, he told Mother, my father's defence was complete.

Shortly afterwards, out of the blue, Mr. Shi received word that I would be permitted to visit my father. "Twice a month, for an hour," he shouted on the phone. Holding the receiver at arm's length, Mother shouted back, "What about me?"

"The Missus is a foreigner, and not allowed!"

Mother threw up her hands in disgust.

We still had no idea where my father was being kept. Nor was Mr. Shi given any details. "Hopefully, they will let us know where and when, in time," he shouted before ringing off.

Mother was in a dither. She packed a change of clothes and a sweater she had made him. Maria Contini provided a slab of goat's cheese, and Mother baked bread. "Everything has to be practical," she kept repeating, as if to remind herself that Father was not on a picnic.

As it turned out it was all for naught. Mr. Shi had me pulled from class one morning, and we set off in his car with barely half an hour to get to where my father was.

"Keep the conversation light," Mr. Shi instructed me on the way. "Say nothing to upset your father. Be polite to the guards. Little tin gods can be very mean. Ask if there is a fixed schedule for your visits, and whether you can take your father some fresh clothes and food." He stopped the car several streets from our destination and walked me to the corner of a street lined with old-fashioned German mansions. "You will go the rest of the way by yourself," he said. "Do you know the way home?"

"Yes, sir," I said. My landmark was the U.S. Marine camp which we had just passed. From there it would be another half hour's walk.

"Good lad," he said, as he headed back to his car.

My father's prison was a turn-of-the-century German-style mansion in what had been a select residential district on the fringes of town. The hedges and flower beds in the formal garden had gone wild and the grass was knee-high. The guard in the foyer groped me while he frisked me.

"Do you have a foreign thing?" he muttered. "Never seen a foreign one before."

I ignored him.

"Do you have Lucky Strikes or Camels?"

"I'm not old enough to smoke," I stammered.

The guard looked at me searchingly. "Grow up before you come again."

Father was kept in a large corner room on the top floor with one window overlooking the street and another opening onto the garden. It was spartan but clean. There was a folding cot covered with an olive-green army blanket, a table and chair, and an incongruous old Chinese baroque wardrobe that probably went with the house.

Father seemed smaller, greyer than I remembered. Stubble covered his face, but the eyes were as penetrating as ever, the gravelly voice as firm. He bounded across the room to hug me. The guard, having followed me up the stairs, squatted by the door like a watchful toad.

Father spoke in Chinese, a signal for me to respond in kind. We talked about school. When he commented on the bruises and scratches on my face, I told him an elaborate story about soccer. Father's eyes told me he was not taken in; he knew I hated team sports. Remembering Mr. Shi's instructions, I kept the conversation light, recounting anecdotes about Mother, and Zhang, and Maria Contini that made Father laugh. It was wonderful to be able to make him laugh in that depressing place. The guard, listening closely, looked disgusted.

Father ran his hand wearily over his eyes. I realized they had taken away everything he could use to harm himself: glasses, belt, tie, shoelaces, razor, even his comb. With wry glances at the guard, Father described his daily routine in an unnecessarily loud, pleasant tone. Food was plentiful and good; he bathed every other day; he washed his own clothes and kept his room tidy; he walked in the garden once a day. "The guards are all good fellows!" he added with a wink.

"Haven't you anything real to talk about?" the guard said. He was frustrated that we did not discuss anything he could report. If we'd spoken in English he could at least have reported that we'd conversed in a suspicious foreign language.

Father apologized for the uninteresting lives led by ordinary citizens. The guard grunted. Father offered him the only chair in the room, but he waved it aside, sighing for effect, clearly getting bored. Father signalled it was time to go, even before my hour was over. "Better a shortened visit than none at all," he whispered. The privilege was entirely at his captors' whim.

On my next visit, two weeks later, I took American cigarettes. The guard, Lao Wang, groped me again, but the extra pair of pants I was wearing put him off, and thereafter he left me alone. Actually, Lao Wang was not a bad sort. Several visits later he left Father and me unattended, preferring to sleep at his desk downstairs rather than listen to our banal conversation.

A wonderful rapport grew between Father and me during those visits. We spoke with ease and mutual understanding, the constrained circumstances oddly liberating our tongues and hearts. Once I asked what he missed most. "Freedom," he said without hesitation. "Not merely to come and go, but to be useful, putting this country on its feet."

Father drew me to the window, pointing out the fountain, the stone urns in which flowers once grew, and the marble busts of grim-faced men with mutton-chop whiskers in the ruined garden below, probably likenesses of the German merchant or industrialist with more money than taste who had once lived here. When he was sure we would not be overheard, he asked, as he always did, how Mother was bearing up. How was I being treated at school? How was Zhang? I told him as much as I could.

"Time!" Lao Wang called from downstairs.

Father called back, "The boy is leaving."

He pressed a tiny wad of toilet paper into my hand as he hugged me. I retrieved my satchel, bowed to Lao Wang, and hurried home to Mother, who always waited for my reports of Father and asked me in great detail about my visit.

She unwadded the paper and tears glistened in her eyes. Father's hastily scrawled message read: "Keep your chin up, Dear. The worst will soon be over."

In the summer of 1946, after four months' detention, Father finally got a hearing. Confronted with boxes of affidavits and documents, and a long list of witnesses Mr. Shi intended to call, the Ministry of Military Intelligence admitted that it had placed my father in the position of Commissioner of Finance in the puppet government as a blind for covert activities. The case was dismissed. In the subsequent euphoria, over celebratory brandy in Mr. Shi's office, Mother, Maria Contini, and Captain Perry congratulated the lawyer on a job brilliantly done.

"And exoneration?" Mother asked.

Mr. Shi carefully adjusted the silver arms of his glasses around his rather prominent ears.

"Missus, this is China," he said. "Be thankful." Mother averted her face; for a moment, tears and laughter warred with one another. She searched for a handkerchief in her purse and dabbed her cheeks and forehead until she got hold of herself. "You're right," she murmured.

The lawyer allowed himself a small smile. "There's still red tape," he said, "but we should see your husband home in a day or two."

On the way home, still elated, Mother took me to tea at what had once been a German café. We had not been out for tea since Pearl Harbour and she was in the mood to splurge. Before leaving the café, she bought a slice of chocolate cake to take home for Zhang, who had a sweet tooth.

"The nightmare's over," she said, her heels clicking on the cobblestones. Her expression was one I'd not seen before. She was beaming.

Mother's happiness did not last long. The Ministry of Military Intelligence may have washed its hands of my father, but ominously he was not released. Instead, a few days later, the Ministry of Justice announced that the court had dealt only with the years my Father spent in Qingdao. Now it intended to delve into his years as administrator of two major railways.

Mr. Shi paced his office, seething. Everyone was angered and alarmed by the turn of events, but Mr. Shi's anger was directed largely at Mother. "I told you about the judge." He rubbed thumb and forefinger together in the familiar gesture. "Missus, I understand bribery offends your western sensibilities, but . . ."

"But this is China!" Mother interrupted, biting off each word. "How I loathe this awful place!"

The lawyer fanned the air with his soft white hand as if a cobweb had blown in his face. "Missus," he said slowly, "those sentiments won't help us. You must be careful of what you say. You too, boy."

Mr. Shi's counsel proved sage, for there was a flurry of arrests soon afterwards. In a repeat of what had occurred immediately after the KMT entered Qingdao, the terrified populace denounced one another, hoping to stay on the government's good side. A wall of silence suddenly went up around my father's case, which, even Mr. Shi had to admit, did not bode well.

The next time I visited Father, a new man was guarding the gate. He glanced at my well-thumbed permit and checked it against his register. "Isn't here any more."

"I saw him two weeks ago!"

"Not here now," said the man gruffly, shoving the book into his drawer. I dug a pack of cigarettes out of my satchel. The man grabbed it. Not knowing what else to do, I asked for Lao Wang. The man went into the garden, cupped his mouth with both hands, and shouted, "Lao Wang around?"

Someone in the house yelled, "Transferred!"

"You heard," the guard said. He shoved me out the gate and slammed it shut. "Scram!"

Blind terror propelled me from the house. I ran, bumping into people, tripping and falling on cobblestones, until I could run no more. I wanted to scream but there was no one to hear me in all the humanity swirling around me.

Mother and Maria Contini had been scouring the markets that afternoon for flour not mixed with sand, a few scoops of sugar, and some chocolate to go into a cake. Mother's cheery greeting froze on her lips when she saw me trembling in the kitchen doorway. Her hand flew to her throat.

"What is it?"

I turned my face to the wall and whimpered, "He's gone."

An unbearable silence closed in. Maria Contini took me by the shoulders and turned me to face her.

"Tell to Maria, what means 'gone'?"

I looked from her to Mother, who had sat down, hunched over as though hit in the stomach. There was a comical smudge of flour on her forehead and another on the tip of her nose.

"What means 'gone'?" Maria repeated.

In a strange constricted voice I replied, "He's not at the house any more."

Mother drew in a noisy breath.

Maria threw up her hands. "Is nothing!" she cried, trying to sound nonchalant for Mother's sake. "He go another house. Simple, yes?"

Mother nodded dully. She brushed back a stray strand of hair with a flour-covered hand, leaving another smudge. Then, trembling, she got to her feet and went upstairs to our living room. I heard her dialling the phone and asking for Mr. Shi. The lawyer didn't know where my father was, but in a day or two he found out.

Father had been moved into the grim, German-built jail on the waterfront. Black marketeers, drug traffickers and users, corrupt officials, and the worst violent criminals were kept in its crowded pens. Here the issue was not one of relative comfort or deprivation. One's survival was at stake. Our only consolation was the knowledge that Father's gifts for reason, negotiation, and empathy for the unfortunate would stand him in good stead.

With unfailing optimism, Mr. Shi saw the bright side of things. Chiang Kai-shek, he assured Mother, was anxious to repair his tarnished image. Show trials would demonstrate that he was the champion of righteousness, a fearless reformer, and the possessor of those Christian virtues his American moneybags held dear.

"The most sensational cases will go to trial first. Fodder for the propaganda mill. Our case is not newsworthy so it will be pushed back. That's good, because I need time to interview fresh witnesses."

And so Mr. Shi again set about the laborious task of locating people who might be helpful to Father's case, people who in most cases had no desire to make themselves known.

Mr. Shi came to the house one evening in September to inform us that Father's preliminary hearing would take place a few days later. "You can catch a glimpse of your husband in the street, on the way from prison to the courthouse," he told Mother. "It won't be pleasant."

Mother nodded without a word.

"You just happen to be near the prison at nine o'clock, Tuesday morning. No waving, nothing." He glared at Mother till she nodded. "Take Zhang with you. You can't tell how a crowd might behave these days."

"I'll look after her," I said quickly.

On the Tuesday morning Mother must have changed her clothes half a dozen times. Her first instinct was to dress as nicely as possible for Father's sake, but Mr. Shi had warned her not to draw attention to herself. In the end the weather solved her dilemma. It poured with rain, so she settled for a navy blue raincoat and matching hat whose broad brim hid her face, an outfit Father would recognize from a distance without difficulty.

Mother, Zhang, Maria, and I waited under a gingko tree across the street from the prison's main gate. The steady rain turned into a downpour. Zhang held an umbrella over Mother's head. She clutched my hand with both of hers. Maria, wrapped in a black hooded cloak, fingered her rosary. We were not alone outside the prison. Many others huddled together, coat collars turned up, faces averted. Nobody spoke.

The city hall clock struck nine. A policeman stopped traffic as the prison gate swung open. Police armed with truncheons hustled six men in baggy black prison uniforms into the street. It took a moment to recognize him. Though leg-irons impeded his movement, giving him an odd jerky gait, Father walked with head held high. He had lost more weight and appeared disoriented, but otherwise seemed healthy.

Mother squeezed my hand. Zhang dropped his gaze. Maria emitted a long shuddering sigh.

As the prisoners moved past, Mother instinctively started to follow, but I would not budge. She glanced at me and I shook my head, reminding her Mr. Shi had said there must be no sign of recognition. She shivered violently, rain and tears mingling on her face as the prisoners, soaked to the skin, leg-irons clattering, shuffled down the street and out of sight.

15

第十五章

BULLDOG'S
DOZEN

"THIS BOY is a disgrace!" Brother Jang cried in his peculiar Shandong-accented Mandarin. He pointed at Shao standing before the platform, holding a tall stool in one hand, dishevelled but defiant. Someone had turned his pockets inside out. His tie was askew and his shirt unbuttoned, revealing a strip of pale chest. Fraternizing with Americans was the school's latest taboo, and Brother Jang had caught Shao, in his school uniform, smoking in a parked Jeep.

Shao had been moving inexorably towards a confrontation for some time. He hardly came to school at all any more. The cathedral choir that used and discarded him; the unbridled racism at school; the disintegrating family – these were the forces that drove him to seek the warmth of an American Marine's friendship.

"What was he up to?" Brother Jang shouted to the assembly. He dropped cigarettes, then a lighter, then money to the floor. Finally, he held up a Marine's cap between thumb and forefinger as though it was something distasteful. "What is the significance of this thing found hidden under his shirt, next to his heart?"

Brother Feng took his place on stage. In a gentle, weary voice, he said that a half-caste compromising the school's honour did not surprise him. "Aren't half-castes the result of moral turpitude?" he asked. "Therefore, what must we do?"

"Shun them!" the assemblage chorused on cue.

"Guard against their corrupting influence . . ."

"Shun them! Shun them! Shun them!"

Brother Jang pushed Shao onto the stage carrying the stool. Brother Feng ordered him to bend over it. Shao, feet planted firmly apart, said in a clear voice, "You'll have to cane me standing, sir."

No one dared talk back to the Submarine in front of the whole school. Brother Feng pressed his fingertips together in a gesture almost like praying. He flexed the cane Brother Jang handed him.

"One! . . . Two! . . . Three!" the audience counted as the cane whistled through the air. It landed with dull thwacks across Shao's buttocks and legs. He clenched his fists. His head jerked back with each stroke. He emitted an occasional grunt, but that was all.

". . . Eighteen! . . . Nineteen! . . . Twenty!"

Brother Feng threw down the cane and the audience applauded.

"Let this be a lesson," he growled, breathing hard, his finger stabbing the air above our heads. Then, in a quieter voice, he added, "It's time for benediction . . ."

I waited till the hall emptied, then ran up on the stage to where Shao lay in agony. I stuffed his things into his pockets and helped him into his blazer. With my arm around him, we slowly made our way off the school grounds towards the edge of Qingdao's business centre, where he lived.

Shao unlocked the door shakily. The house felt empty. His mother was still at work. He led the way to the bathroom and dropped his pants. His buttocks and the backs of his legs were a mass of oozing welts.

"Help me," he gasped.

Blood made my gorge rise; everything swam before my eyes. I drew a basin of cold water, wet a wash cloth, and gingerly cleaned the cuts. Shao gripped the side of the basin till his knuckles were white. "Mercurochrome's in the cabinet," he managed through gritted teeth.

"It will sting."

"Do it," Shao replied, shaking so violently he could barely stand.

I wetted a wad of cotton with the red liquid and dabbed the cuts. When it was done, Shao leaned against the wall, naked from the waist down, eyes shut, breath whistling harshly through trembling lips. The blood and the pain frightened me.

I whispered the first thing that popped into my mind. "Why did you do it?"

Shao's fist slammed into my mouth. I staggered, tripped, and landed on my back. He leaped on me. We grappled in silence, blindly landing blows. Shao was a beast possessed. I tried to ward him off but his knee in my groin sent a red-hot shaft of pain through me. Everything went from red to grey. His knee kept battering me until he had me spreadeagled under him. His weight made it hard for me to breathe. I went limp and heard him yelling from a great distance, words I instinctively shut from my mind. Dimly I felt him pummelling, scratching, biting, tearing my clothes. Pain enveloped me like a hot syrup. I was drowning until a part of me tore itself loose, leaving the shell of my body to absorb the blows.

Shao grew still. He was still on top of me, but was no longer grinding down hard with his body. I felt something moist on my forehead, and realized it was his mouth. A buzzing in my ears blocked out what he was saying. Through half-closed eyes, I saw his chin and then his slightly parted lips hovering over mine. In that split second, I hooked my knee into his groin and heaved him off.

I staggered into the street filled with people, traffic, and noise. The sun made whirling discs of light in my watery, unfocused eyes. My ankles were jelly. I don't know how I got home.

Zhang drew in a noisy breath when he saw me, bruised and scratched, my tie twisted backward, my shirt in shreds, my fly undone, Mercurochrome spattered on my pants. He pushed me into the bathroom.

"I . . ."

"I don't want to know," he said severely. "Clean up before your mother comes home."

I stood under the icy shower for as long as I could stand it. The biting cold jarred me back to reality. I examined myself in the full-length mirror. I was the same yet not the same. There was an ache in my chest that was not there before. Shao had planted it there. I felt caved in, yet full to bursting. I needed to cry but I could not. I fingered the bite marks and scratches on my neck and chest. Some oozed. I pressed them with my fingertips, making them smart. The stinging made my eyes water, but still I could not cry.

I pulled on clothes, crawled into bed, and lay curled in the fetal position, hugging the pain, wondering whether I would ever be free of it. I kept going back to the moment before I kneed Shao. What if I had stayed still? I sensed that I had crossed a threshold in that flash of anger or panic, and that in some way it had changed my life.

Mother came home from work. As usual, Perry drove her in his Jeep. We had long since dropped the "Captain." I heard them talking, laughing softly, Mother sounding happy and relaxed. They were probably having a drink before Zhang served dinner. Presently, Mother looked in and asked if I wanted anything to eat. I shook my head. She saw the bruises on my face and fetched me an aspirin.

"I wish you wouldn't get into so many fights," she said, watching me swallow the pill. "You'll feel better in the morning." In that instant I wanted Shu Ma with all my heart. Shu Ma always asked the right questions, always listened and understood what was the matter with me and what I needed.

"Mother, why did you send Shu Ma away?"

For a moment she stood quite still, silhouetted against the light. Then, shrugging slightly, she shut the door behind her.

Shao dropped out of school altogether. Once or twice I played truant, trying to find him. I soon discovered the streets were even more monotonous and frightening than school. My only friend was gone and I was doomed to solitude. Dismal weeks passed. Then one day, as I trudged home from school, he came out of nowhere and fell in step beside me. I was glad to see him but also sad. He looked ill, unkempt, and he reeked of a stinging after-shave lotion, though he hadn't started shaving. We wandered down to the jetty that stuck out into the harbour. We used to speculate about the ghostly looking pavilion at its end.

"Bet you don't dare go there!" he'd say.

"I double-dare you!"

Neither of us had ever had the nerve. This day, however, we walked towards it as if by mutual consent. Up close it was just a musty old building. A powerful smell of decay seeped through the chinks in the delicately carved shutters fastened with rusty chains. Seagulls cried plaintively from its eaves, and the sighing of the sea added to the melancholy air. The noises of the city came across the water in bursts. Shao shook two Lucky Strikes out of a pack, lit them, and handed me one in the Chinese fashion.

"My old man came home," he said without enthusiasm, cigarette dangling from the corner of his mouth.

Shao's father had been detained without charge, brutally questioned, and released. He had lost his job at the bank, but he had not been idle since his return. The Brazilian government was parcelling large tracts of wilderness land to immigrants with the proviso that they make it productive. Shao's father had applied to move his family there.

"My mother harps on Europe, but my father says Brazil is a land of opportunity. With money you can go anywhere later."

The prospect of Shao's leaving Qingdao filled me with dismay.

"Can you picture my father as a pioneer? Why, a gust of wind would blow him over!"

We laughed mirthlessly, then smoked quietly as the sun tumbled towards the horizon.

"Where will you go?" Shao asked.

"Nowhere," I muttered, thinking of my own father in prison.

"Your dad will be all right." Shao had a way of reading my mind. "You'll get out too."

I shrugged, as if I didn't care.

"My father goes down to the docks every day to check the waiting list. He thinks it might be any day now." Shao dragged deeply on his cigarette. "We each have a small bag ready so we can go at a moment's notice."

A tearing pain shot through me. That horrible hollowed-out feeling came over me again. My lungs seemed flattened against my ribs so I could hardly breathe. For a moment I was as fragile as an eggshell. I gazed out at the harbour where a few ships rode the swells, anchor chains creaking. That was no help. I gazed back, eyes brimming in spite of myself. Shao's smile collapsed his face. He got up without dusting off the seat of his pants, and I followed him back to the street.

"Will you write to me?" I shouted over the roar of rush-hour traffic.

He looked at me, eyes shining, lips parted. I wanted to hug him but all my blood had rushed upward and downward, leaving the centre caved in. I could not move. We stood there awkwardly and the moment passed. He took something from his pocket and pressed it in my hand. Before I could gather my wits, he'd darted into the crowd. I stood there clutching a Marine's badge.

From time to time I glimpsed Shao whizzing past in the passenger seat of a Jeep. Once I ran after it shouting his name. I don't know whether he saw me, but the Jeep didn't stop. I never got close enough to speak to him again. When I could not stand the loneliness any longer, I went to his house. It was boarded up, with a big For Sale sign tacked to the door. I rapped. There was no answer. I hammered till my fists hurt, praying for the door to be opened. There was no fooling myself now, no telling myself there'd been a mistake, their plans had changed. Shao was gone.

At school I was more bored and lonely than ever. Bits of knowledge were doled out between heaping servings of propaganda for the contradictory values of Chiang Kai-shek and Jesus. A half-caste whose father was in prison was doubly an outcast. I now took a perverse pleasure in the films of Japanese atrocities, secretly cheering the wrong side. I became fractious, easily provoked into a fight, but, being scrawny, I always got beaten.

I found comfort in helping Maria Contini cultivate her garden, weeding and watering her vegetable patch. She must have sensed my loneliness, for now and then I would catch her gazing at me, brows puckered.

"Da-vee-day, why you no play with other boys?" she finally asked.

I shrugged and shot her a quick grin. "I don't know any other boys," I said.

Maria clucked her tongue. "I like very much you come here, but I am old lady. You must have friends, Da-vee-day," she said, gently taking the spade from my hand and looking me in the eye. "Where is nice boy sing like angel?"

"Gone to Brazil."

"I know, you sad," she sighed. "But you find new friends. Yes?" It was impossible to hide anything from those penetrating, pale blue eyes. Perhaps that's why I sought them out.

By the fall of 1946, with Chiang Kai-shek's credibility seriously eroded, his American-equipped army defected en masse. All the billboards and posters screaming about democracy signified nothing. Press gangs went into villages, forcibly taking away young men as replacements for the defectors. And the Boy Scout movement burst upon the Chinese consciousness. The idea was to create an organization of young fanatics as the last buffer against the implacable Mao Zedong. As such, the Tong Zhi Jun, meaning Youth Army, had more in common with Hitler Youth and, twenty years later, Mao's Red Guard than with Lord Baden-Powell's ideal.

Every school was ordered to form a troop and St. Michael's was one of the first to comply. Using as his motto "Many are called but few are chosen," Brother Feng recruited only boys with politically correct backgrounds. The weak, the slow, and other undesirables were excluded. In the short term, Scouting was a godsend for draft dodgers. Young men in their twenties with rich parents bought their way in. Ridiculous-looking in their Boy Scout uniforms, they sheepishly shared the activities of young boys. Membership and a serial number similar to the military's gave them the semblance of being enlisted men, and corrupt officials did nothing to prevent this evasion of service in the National Army.

Friendless, desperately lonely, and craving acceptance, I decided I must join the Boy Scouts. Brother Feng glared at me in disbelief.

"Why do you want to be a scout?" he roared.

I had a speech ready. "Because . . . sir . . . this is a democracy. In a democracy everybody has the same rights. I'm as good as anyone else . . . I'm not sick . . . or . . . or a cripple." Once I got started the rest barrelled along. "I am not stupid. I am not a coward. If it comes to it, I can fight as well as anybody else!" I was spouting bits of propaganda that I had either heard or been fed. And like all propaganda it did not have to make sense, as long as it made the right kind of noise.

Brother Feng's fingers drummed the desk impatiently till I was done. He smiled thinly. "If you come up with the money, you can join." He named a figure that made my head spin. Contempt gleamed in his eyes as he waved me out of the room.

Mother was dead set against the idea. For one thing her salary did not allow expensive extras. As winter approached, it became clear the Marshall Plan was faltering. The on-again, off-again talks between the Kuomintang and the Communists had degenerated into all-out war. As hope of an American-brokered coalition government faded, there was widespread fear that the Americans would pull out. Inflation ran wild, and the prospect of unemployment hung over her head, but Mother was adamant that what jewellery she had left be kept for emergencies. Mostly, she would not allow me to become Chiang Kai-shek's cannon fodder.

My hopes of joining were dashed, but only until I mentioned the Boy Scouts to Mr. Shi, whom Mother now consulted on practically everything. Mr. Shi was running into a stone wall gathering witnesses for Father's defence, and in my desire he saw an opportunity.

"Putting the boy in the Scouts will show where your loyalties lie," he advised Mother. "I can't guarantee it will help your husband, but we have to try everything."

Mother abhorred such tactics, but looked to Perry. He gazed at the lit end of his cigarette.

"Do you really want to join?" he asked me.

I shrugged.

"Do you?" he persisted.

In a small voice I told him it would cost several months of Mother's salary in U.S. dollars. Perry took out his money clip and started peeling off bills. Mother grabbed his wrist. For a moment their eyes locked. "You mustn't," she said sharply. "It's not your fight."

"You don't have to fight alone," Perry said. "I want to do something for you, Ellen."

The way he said it made Mother look away. The ticking of the mantle clock seemed unusually loud. Mother glanced at the sapphire on her finger, the piece of jewellery she most treasured. The prospect of having to part with it, especially for something she disapproved of, must have been disheartening.

"Let me," Perry said, almost whispering.

Mother sat there, twisting her ring. Perry reached over and took her hand. Finally she nodded.

Mr. Shi, who had become our – or, more correctly, Mother's – champion, immediately took charge. "We'll see about the fee!" he said, incensed by Brother Feng's greed. "Now, boy, tell me everything you know about this Brother Feng."

I told Mr. Shi about what Shao and I had seen in the cellar during the air-raid drill. He listened, nodding and frowning. I told him of Brother Feng's threat after his heroic return from "internment," his remark that he never forgot a face, even one glimpsed in the dark.

"You're sure of this? There can be no mistake."

"I swear it."

Mr. Shi accompanied me to school the next day. I waited outside the office while he and Brother Feng haggled. Once or twice I heard Brother Feng howl with indignation. After a few minutes Mr. Shi came out grinning like a Cheshire cat. He jutted his chin at the door, and I entered to find Brother Feng rummaging in a cupboard. He tossed shirt, pants, scarf, cap, and socks at me. In another cupboard he found a neatly coiled rope, a pocket knife, and a wooden staff. "There!" He slammed the cupboard doors contemptuously. "You're a Scout!"

Shao had despised the Boy Scout movement. "You'll never see me in one of those monkey suits," he'd said adamantly. "All that marching and saluting!" He'd done a stiff-legged, stumble-footed parody of a drill that had me in stitches. Shao could be screamingly funny. I thought I despised the movement too, but that was then. Shao was gone now, and here I was in an ill-fitting uniform, marching out of step, turning left when everyone else turned right, tripping over my staff, getting tangled in my rope. After the first day, the other boys ignored me.

Brother Jang stamped his feet in exasperation.

"What am I to do with you, Kwan!"

He put me at the back of the troop, behind the tallest boys, where no one would see my fumblings. Instead of enduring the numbing propaganda of the classroom, I drilled until I trembled with fatigue. When we weren't drilling we served as honour guards for visiting politicians, standing stiffly at attention along the street for hours, waiting to salute smartly when the big-wigs' carefully curtained limousine whisked by. We also performed civic tasks.

We patrolled the streets and directed traffic, freeing the police to round up Communists, collaborators, and black marketeers, whom they shot summarily.

Dr. Sun Yat-Sen's idea of tutelage – a period of instruction preparing the people in the ways of democracy – was accelerated, and a national election was announced. Political parties no one had heard of fielded candidates. Posters of bespectacled presidential hopefuls, all seemingly cut from the same cloth, festooned the streets. Only Communists were barred from running.

Chiang Kai-shek withdrew from public life at this critical time, but Madame Chiang's brother, Soong, came to Qingdao for a rally, ostensibly to test the waters of public opinion, hoping to lure Chiang back. Always on the lookout for anyone who might help my father's case, Mr. Shi said to Mother, "The boy must write to Mr. Soong."

I recognized his photograph in the newspaper at once. "I put a toad in his wife's bed, that time in Beidaihe!" I crowed. "I shall remind him."

Mr. Shi wagged a finger at me. "You will do no such thing. You will be serious."

Mother was reluctant. "Since he knows English, and I have entertained him and his wife, I will write," Mother said. "You may suggest what I should say."

"Missus, at present, a Boy Scout writing might be more effective," Mr. Shi remonstrated. In those desperate days Chiang Kai-shek had embraced Christianity and adopted the saying "Suffer little children to come unto me."

And so, with Mr. Shi dictating, I wrote to "Uncle Soong" in my best calligraphy, begging his help to clear my father's name. The full text of that letter appeared on the front page of the next morning's paper. Mr. Shi was elated – "A child's plea on behalf of a wrongly imprisoned father is dynamite!" – but Mother was furious at the publicity. She scolded Mr. Shi for sending a copy of the letter to the newspaper, an act that Mr. Shi hotly defended.

"I should never have consented to my son writing that man," Mother said. She still thought Father's predicament was the result of a quixotic gesture gone horribly awry. "I told you many times, I do not want my son involved in these" – she faltered – "these . . . things."

"It might seem like a silly thing," Mr. Shi said with a tinge of sarcasm, "but we are struggling to save your husband. Missus, writing the letter would have been a waste of time if it didn't get the attention it deserved."

They glared at each other. Mother was the first to look away.

A few weeks later a graceful though non-committal reply from one of Soong's secretaries proved Mr. Shi's instinct right. "It's a thread of hope," he said, inclining his head to one side. Mother smiled warily. She had not given up hope, but had learned to approach it with caution.

When I got home from school one day, a young airman in a leather flying jacket with China's Nationalist flag painted on the back was sitting in the kitchen talking to Zhang.

"Remember me, Squirt?"

"Yes, I do!" I replied. I had not seen my brother since I was four years old.

Tim's face creased into a mass of laugh lines when he smiled. His voice had taken on a gravelly timbre like our father's. He reached to touch my shaved head. I shied away.

"We've both grown up," he said. "Shall we shake hands?"

We shook hands awkwardly, sizing up each other, and Tim burst into infectious laughter. He was lean and sun-browned from years in India. He spoke English with a slight accent, American with a touch of Indian inflection. His Chinese sounded stilted from long disuse. Now the war was over he was awaiting discharge from the air force.

Tim told us about his wife and son; about the job he was going to in Hong Kong with China's national airline, CNAC. When I asked about his war experiences, though, he became as reticent as Father. "It was a job that had to be done" was all I could wheedle out of him.

Tim did not know of Father's imprisonment until he arrived. He spent the rest of his leave with Mr. Shi, trying to get permission to see our father. In the end his record of braving The Hump, as fliers called the Himalayas, keeping Chungking supplied during the war, cleared the way. At the eleventh hour, Mr. Shi finally obtained permission for Tim to see Father alone.

Through Tim, my father spoke optimistically about his eventual release, though I believe he was beginning to doubt whether it would happen before the Communists engulfed us. Fearing he might not be able to protect us from the maelstrom that was sure to come, he urged Mother to try to regain her British citizenship, quit China, and take me with her. Mother, through the Red Cross, had located a sister living in Australia. The two sisters wanted to be reunited, and Father thought a young country might also be a good place for him to start over.

"I'll look into the citizenship thing," Mother told Tim, "but I'll not leave without your father." To me she said, in that same determined tone, "You must go. And soon."

Partly, I knew, she wanted to get me away from the Boy Scouts. I was not really getting an education, and the so-called scouting was turning me hard. Even Tim noticed how I swaggered in my khaki uniform, blue and white tie, and narrow cap copied from the U.S. Marines; how I had learned to watch men and women being shot in the street without flinching.

"Go where, Mother?" I had heard of many foreign lands, but could not imagine living anywhere except in China.

"Father wants you to go to Hong Kong," Tim said. "There are good schools, and my family will be there."

"There's all sorts of papers and things," Mother added, twisting her ring. Perhaps she was again thinking of having to part with it when she said, "Tim has to look for a school . . . and . . . and . . ."

She ran from the room, and we heard her bedroom door slam. I started after her but Tim stopped me.

He left a few days later. That same evening, Mother undid another cushion.

Maria Contini telephoned, quite out of breath. Mother listened in alarm. When she rang off, she headed out the door. "I'm going to Maria," she said over her shoulder.

"I'm coming too!"

Mother started to say no, but changed her mind. "Don't get in the way," she warned.

Maria threw her arms around us as soon as she opened the door. She was in her best black dress with white lace collars, and her favourite cameo. Mr. Shi was already seated in the living room. Maria beamed as she poured the last of the wine she had been hoarding.

"We make the toast first," Maria insisted, raising her glass. "To friends . . ."

Only then was she ready to tell her news. She had had a letter from Vittorio. He'd seen action in Europe and was now home in New York, ready to go back to school.

"To be doctor!" Maria jiggled with happiness. "And he married nice Italian girl . . . Catholic, of course!"

Through UNRRA Maria would soon be reunited with her son. Amid the jollity a great deal of business was quickly settled. Mr. Shi would sell the house together with its contents on Maria's behalf after she left. She had lived there since she was a bride; now she would be leaving a huge chunk of her life behind. Moving on was not without its regrets.

"I make the novena for your husband." Maria patted Mother's hand. She had always treated Mother like a younger sister whom she did not quite understand. "One day you leave, too." She shook her head. "China not the same . . . Better we go."

Before she left, Maria asked me to accompany her to Mass. I did not relish the idea but could not refuse. It was the same cathedral that had thrilled me, but now the atmosphere made me quiver. An unknown priest intoned Latin prayers in a peculiar Chinese accent. Brother Feng hammered the organ, while the choir did its ragged best to be heard. My mind wandered in all directions, none of them leading to God. After Mass we made a detour to Giuseppe's grave in the churchyard.

For an hour we tidied the grave, working companionably in a silence broken only when Maria spoke earnestly to someone I could not see. It took me a moment to realize she was talking to Giuseppe.

A few weeks later Maria Contini sailed. Mother and I, Perry and Mr. Shi stood on the wharf as the great ship, crammed with refugees heading for a new life, slipped away from the dock. Maria stood at the rail waving, and I waved back until her face blurred and only her white hair could be seen in the distance, glowing like a halo.

At night we often heard gunfire in the mountains. One night the din of battle was so loud that we were sure the Communists would be on our doorstep next morning. The next night was dead quiet. Qingdao's municipal government panicked. Suddenly, Communists lurked under every bed, around every corner. Cash rewards encouraged people to denounce one another.

Though Communists were the main target, intellectuals, writers, anyone considered to have a public voice was caught in the same net. The books of left-leaning writers such as Lu Xun were banned. Boy Scouts made house-to-house searches. The draft dodgers in Boy Scout uniforms came into their own during those forays. Grown men, ridiculously squeezed into uniforms made for pubescent boys, were often the butt of jokes and snide remarks. Now the tables were turned. A dozen of us followed a twenty-five-year-old bruiser nicknamed Bulldog for his big square head, drooping jowls, and wide mouth full of big square teeth.

"Search party! Open up!" in the Bulldog's foghorn voice usually opened doors at once. However, there were those who cowered behind their bolted doors, hoping that, if they kept still, we would go away. Bulldog's bite was worse than his bark. His ham-like fists and huge booted feet, aided by a dozen staff-wielding Scouts, quickly splintered the door.

"Search!" he shouted, striking whoever came within reach, often drawing blood. The Bulldog's Dozen, as he called us, had arrived!

Forcing our way into strange houses, turning rooms upside down, taking armfuls of books and pamphlets without even bothering to see what they were, and burning them in street-corner bonfires gave me a tremendous charge. I didn't need to be told what to do. I was already well schooled in the art of destruction. First the Japanese, and then the KMT, had destroyed our home. The Bulldog usually helped himself to any small valuables he could pocket. Some other boys did, too. Not me. I only wanted revenge. The best part was the look of fear on the faces of the householders – their pleading, their whimpering, their sly offers of bribes. Perhaps I was giving back what I had endured at the hands of strangers.

Scout activities kept me out till all hours. When Mother realized there was nothing she could do about it, she stopped grumbling and grew resigned. We led parallel lives. The organized chaos of Scouts swept me along, Mother drifted, and Zhang went about his chores grim-faced.

Zhang had taken a dislike to Perry, who spent most evenings with Mother. He brought slices of ham and turkey, steaks and chops, wedges of cheese and quarts of ice cream from his mess, food we could no longer buy even on the black market. He also ordered a supply of steel needles from the States for my old gramophone. The PX supplied records by Frank Sinatra, Perry Como, Dick Haymes, and Ella Fitzgerald. I heard "Till the End of Time,""It Might as Well Be Spring,"and particularly "My Happiness"so many times they grated on my nerves. Those songs enclosed Mother and Perry in a fragile bubble around which I tiptoed instinctively. The weary lines disappeared from Mother's face. She laughed and joked, and for a time she was happy.

Perry waited for an evening when the three of us were together before telling Mother he was finally going home.

"When?" Mother asked, reaching for her knitting.

"In about four weeks."

The look in Mother's eyes made me think of Father. I was fiercely glad Perry was going.

During those last weeks, Perry spent as much time as he could with Mother. She insisted on taking me everywhere they went: to restaurants and cinemas and picnics on the beach. Most of the time I felt like a useless third wheel. The deep looks, the sighs, the barely audible words that passed between them reminded me of Irene and Yuri, and made my chest tighten so painfully I could hardly breathe. I felt I was being nudged out of the nest and impatiently marked off the days on my calendar till Perry's departure. I thought of smashing all the sentimental records Mother and Perry played over and over. Maybe that would show him he had worn out his welcome.

It was jellyfish season and the beaches were deserted. On a picnic at German Beach, I found a huge jellyfish in a tide pool. I prodded it with a stick and watched its tentacles work. Perry and Mother were sitting on a beach blanket, finishing their lunch. Mother was flushed and happy. Perry had loosened his tie and collar, and the back of his neck gleamed like ivory in the sun. I got two sticks and picked up the jellyfish. I walked towards Perry unhurriedly. I was almost within reach, about to fling the jellyfish on his bare neck, when Mother broke off their murmured conversation.

"What are you doing with that?" she asked sharply. Perry turned. *Now, now, right in his face!* But somehow I couldn't do it. Perry leaped to his feet.

"It's just a dead jellyfish, Ellen," he said over his shoulder. "It can't hurt anyone."

This last remark was to let me off the hook. He dug a hole and we buried it together. Neither he nor Mother mentioned it again. Perry was still friendly but a wariness had crept into those cornflower-blue eyes.

Perry asked us not to see him off, but Mother had a mind of her own. Once again she, Zhang, and I stood in the crowd on the wharf as flags and bunting snapped in the breeze and a Marine band valiantly competed with the hubbub. From the day the Americans arrived, wall posters had clamoured, "Yankee go home!" Now that it was happening, though, there was no joy in the people who'd gathered. Men who turned a fast buck in shops, cafés, and bars saw the trickle of dollars drying up. Women with Eurasian babies faced an even bleaker future. With each sailing the struggle to survive could only intensify.

We scanned the faces lining the ship's railing, faces made anonymous by uniforms. Zhang finally spotted Perry, or perhaps Zhang's blue robe and black umbrella attracted Perry's attention. He waved and shouted, though we could not hear him as the ship cast off. Mother gazed up impassively, shading her eyes with one white-gloved hand. The band blared its finale and the crowd dispersed. Still she stood there, watching the ship go.

Zhang shaded Mother from the sun with his umbrella as we made our way home. Though her hand rested lightly on my shoulder, she seemed a long way off.

"Will he write?" I asked, just to break the awful silence.

"Pardon, dear?"

"Will he write to us?"

"No," said Mother.

16

第十六章

HOUSE ARREST

FORMER MAYOR Yue and his wife were arrested as they boarded a train for Shanghai. Weak and haggard, dressed shabbily with a couple of battered suitcases, they might have got away except both were weak from opium addiction and barely able to handle their luggage. The train was about to leave, and porters anxious for business swooped down on them. Mrs. Yue, in her drug-addled state, thought someone was trying to make off with her suitcase, panicked, and started screaming. That attracted the attention of the police. The Yues were surrounded by babbling porters, and the swarm of policemen who always seemed to materialize when the prospect of bribery was in the air. Then Yue made his big blunder. He took out a money clip full of U.S. dollars, thinking to buy his way out. The officer in charge was bug-eyed. By then the train was moving. Yue was prepared to give the money clip to the man, if he would let them get on. That only confirmed the officer's suspicions. He had the suitcases pried open. In one they found gold bars and in the other opium.

Still trying to squirm out of his predicament, Yue loudly proclaimed he was the former mayor, a war hero personally known to the Generalissimo himself. He had forgotten Chiang Kai-shek was in the midst of an anti-corruption campaign. Invoking his name was like waving a red cloth in a bull's face. The Yues were arrested without further ado.

As Mr. Shi had predicted, the show trials of corrupt officials were widely publicized. Though the proceedings were closed to the public, a curious crowd gathered outside the courthouse at the centre of the town, noisily gossiping about tidbits not included in the transcripts from the previous day posted on bulletin boards. The main fun, however, was jeering defendants as they were dragged into court, and swarming witnesses as they left, bombarding them with questions. The furore surrounding the propaganda-worthy trials overshadowed the other cases, and my father's was pushed onto a back burner.

Meanwhile, as part of Bulldog's Dozen, I was directing traffic and helping keep the crowds back along the street from the prison to the courthouse. I had never liked Yue and his wife. Seeing them hauled to court, pleading for mercy, made me despise them even more.

"You should have seen them, Mother." I was still bubbling with excitement hours later. "Screaming and yelling. Mr. Yue even peed himself!"

Mother lifted her eyes from her darning, and fixed them on me without a word.

"People were laughing and jeering, calling them all kinds of names." I stopped a moment, expecting her to say something, but she just looked at me as though she'd never seen me before. "Anyway, I'm glad they're getting what they deserve!"

"I was thinking about your father," Mother said softly. She had gone back to her darning.

"What about my father?"

She just kept darning. I sensed she was angry; maybe not exactly angry, but not pleased either.

"What's the matter, Mother?" I was annoyed that she let my story fizzle.

"I was thinking about your father," she repeated without looking up, pulling her needle through the sock she was mending a little harder than she needed to. Until that moment I had not thought about my father, that he might walk the same route to the court-house one day.

I raced out of the room and went to the kitchen, where Zhang was washing up. As I dried dishes, I tried to tell him about the Yues. "Don't you have any homework?"

I shook my head, taken aback.

"You go to school. Shouldn't you be studying something? Any-thing?" He snatched the dishcloth out of my hands and waved me out of the kitchen. His eyes were black buttons, his lips pursed tight. He didn't have to tell me how he despised my Boy Scout uni-form and all it stood for.

Each day's court proceedings were reported in the next morn-ing's paper, accompanied by editorial comments. Transcripts of the more sensational trials, such as the Yues', were posted on the bul-letin boards outside the courthouse. Yue had made many enemies as mayor. The goods and services he and his wife received for which they never paid were only minor transgressions. Yue's fondness for young girls not much older than I, and his wife's seduction of the late young monk Master Sun, all came out. In court man and wife accused each other of being the corruptor.

Yue went so far as to state, "I should never have married that woman! She was born in America, and steeped in their loose ways, and I – poor fool that I am – fell prey to her wiles!" She blamed his impotence for her infidelity; her drug dependency was to assuage her feelings of guilt. The shameful spectacle lasted three days. At the end, both received death sentences, the executions to take place the following day. They were to be shot along with a dozen other corrupt officials in the sports stadium. Yue's wife escaped the executioner's bullet by hanging herself from the barred window of her cell that night.

I was among the Boy Scouts called out to maintain order at the stadium the following day. Martial music blared and anti-corruption slogans shrieked from loudspeakers. Hawkers sold food and pop guns, as well as broadswords and axes, which had been used for executions in olden days. The more enterprising peddlers sold toy guillotines complete with a kneeling victim, fashioned out of dough, whose head could be sliced off.

Yue had to be dragged off the lorry that brought the prisoners into the arena. Even then he scrambled on hands and knees, darting this way and that, frothing at the mouth, screeching, "I'm innocent! Innocent! It was my wife's fault!" The crowd jeered and spat at the arrogant little man who had ridden roughshod over so many people during the Japanese occupation and afterwards. He died badly. A coward to the end, he was shot like a mad dog.

After Yue's death, the trials of other corrupt officials received less publicity. Perhaps Chiang had gone too far trying to impress his self-righteous American allies. At any rate, things quieted down and our troop of Boy Scouts was given other tasks. In the midst of the turmoil, the Ministry of Justice quietly moved my father out of the prison and into another guest house. No trial date was set.

"I don't know what to make of it," admitted Mr. Shi.

In the meantime, there was some good news. In response to Mr. Shi's request, G2 in San Francisco sent a further cable confirming that Father had been their liaison with the Nationalist government ever since the Japanese incursion in 1931. Captain Wood, whom Mr. Shi had traced to a small town in New England, also sent a cable corroborating Father's role. Letters to the British Foreign Office and the Bank of England also turned up an old China hand, a Scot who had settled in Hong Kong after the war. Though now elderly, he wrote in detail about my father's role in protecting British and Chinese interests and keeping the railways running after the Japanese had overrun the north of China. One day a coolie delivered a package to Mr. Shi's office containing documents related to Father's involvement with the resistance in Beijing, while he was administrator of the railways. Although the sender remained anonymous, it could only have come from Midder. All of this fresh ammunition gave Mr. Shi, indeed all of us, renewed cause for optimism.

Again I was allowed to visit Father once a month. The house where he was now held was a melancholy place from which grace and charm had fled. Each succeeding owner had hastened its deterioration. The rooms were mostly bare. Discoloured patches on the walls despaired of missing pictures. Bare bulbs dangled from frayed wires in place of chandeliers. Panes were gone from windows. Still, I imagined, it was infinitely better than prison, which I had not been allowed to enter and which Tim had described with a sigh and a terse shake of his head.

On my first visit I found Father dozing in a wicker chair on the terrace at the back of the house, a thin blanket drawn up to his chin. His face was chalky, the lines deeply etched even in sleep; he was breathing so lightly he did not seem to breathe at all. Illness may well have been the reason for moving him.

He woke with a start. I dropped to my knees and buried my head against his chest. One of his arms struggled free of the blanket and circled my shoulders. We stayed that way for a long time. Father said he had been well treated, but the marks cut by handcuffs and leg-irons told their own story. At least he had a little more freedom now. During daylight hours, he could roam the house and garden and was even allowed the occasional newspaper.

Secretly aided and abetted by Zhang, I became quite good at bribing the guards. Only their preferences differed. Cigarettes, chewing gum, and chocolate bars worked on some; others fancied American movie magazines, now that Betty Grable and Esther Williams were household names among the fantasy-starved Chinese.

Father was always full of questions about Mother, Tim, and Albert, but I was the one who seemed to concern him most. Since joining the Scouts I had become sun-browned and wiry, healthier than I had ever been. The physical improvement obviously pleased Father. But he did not like the changes taking place within me. He saw that, immersed in platitudes and propaganda, I had become cynical and callous. To keep my brain alive, Father talked about history, geography, literature, and art, and their connection to daily life. He spoke at length about China's past and present, but avoided any mention of Chiang, the Kuomintang, or Mao Zedong.

In the meantime, the vaunted national election fizzled. Most of the candidates mouthed policies that echoed the Kuomintang's party line in any case. Those who dared to express divergent views were either gunned down or arrested. Chiang remained secluded in his native village, though the country was rudderless and torn by strife. The Kuomintang called a referendum to send a powerful message to assure Chiang that the Chinese people wanted him, indeed needed him, as their president.

The night before the vote, the Scouts were given a bowl of thin rice gruel and pickles. We slept on the cement floor of our classroom. At four in the morning, we were herded to Mass, then fed another bowl of watery gruel, slightly soured from having been set out the night before. By five-thirty we were ready to be deployed. Each boy had a specific task; mine was to hand out ballots.

The ballot was a letter-sized sheet of paper. Chiang Kai-shek's name and photograph appeared at the top. Beneath was a question: "Do you want Generalissimo Chiang Kai-shek to be your president?" Beneath that were two squares, "Yes" and "No." At the bottom of the ballot was space for the voter's name, or thumbprint, and address.

At daybreak, we took our places at the polling stations, near the cathedral and in the downtown core. These were made of four poles, covered on three sides with straw matting. Inside the enclosure was a chest-high ledge and a wooden box with an opening on top. Soldiers had been rounding up peasants from the countryside for days. Cold, hungry, and bewildered, they were trucked into the city to vote. They were kept in line with rifle butts.

A siren sounded at the stroke of eight, the start of voting. Soldiers began hauling people out of their homes to cast their ballots. Businesses remained shut. The voting proceeded slowly, as many were illiterate. Country folk gaped at Chiang's grainy image and muttered, "So that's what the new Emperor looks like!"

Brother Jang flapped down the long line that snaked back from the polling station, the skirt of his cassock flying.

"You!" he shouted at me. "Help with the voting!"

He tore the ballots from my hand, stuck a pencil in it, and shoved me towards the booth. I knew what to do. The next person who sidled up I asked brusquely, "Can you read and write?"

The peasant responded with a gummy smile. "No," he whispered. "Can I go home now?"

"After you vote," I snapped.

Getting the ballot marked was tricky. Aside from being illiterate, country folk often gave themselves animal names for superstitious reasons, or went by a number that fixed their place in the family. It was not surprising that many had forgotten their proper names simply from disuse. Getting a thumb mark in place of a signature and a proper address was like pulling teeth. Suspicious of a ruse to cheat them out of their scrap of land, many peasants became belligerent. Soldiers brandished their weapons to keep order.

Finally the man was ready to proceed to the next step, marking his ballot.

"Do you know how to vote?" was a mandatory question. The man shook his head.

"This is the Generalissimo," I recited from my manual, pointing at the picture. "Of course you want him to be president. So, you go in the booth and pencil a big X in this box" – I pointed at the "Yes." "After you've done that, fold the paper and drop it into the box."

"Then can I go home?"

I pushed him into the booth.

All day soldiers in lorries drove up, hauled away full ballot boxes, and replaced them with empty ones. At six in the evening a siren went off and voting stopped. Soldiers closed ranks around the polling stations and the last ballot boxes were removed.

The streets were bedlam. Drivers leaning on their horns inched their way through the teeming masses. Getting to our rallying point was like swimming upstream. For once I was glad of my staff, using it to shove my way through the throng. The country folk who had been brought in from the hinterland were left to fend for themselves, so the city now swarmed with hungry refugees. The Red Cross did what it could with meagre supplies. Fights broke out. There were food riots. The old, the infirm, and abandoned infants simply curled up and died, victims of democracy.

The counting of ballots, if it was done at all, was completed within a few days. Chiang, of course, re-emerged as president.

The referendum affected my father greatly. He saw it not as an affirmation of the people's faith in Chiang, but as Chiang's desperate, last-ditch attempt to retain power, the beginning of the end of the Kuomintang's hold on China. Mao's ultimate triumph, he believed, was now assured.

In December 1946, George Marshall reported to U. S. president Harry Truman that his mission had failed. The last hope of a negotiated peace between Chiang and Mao collapsed. Early in 1947 Marshall was recalled, signalling that American intervention in the civil war would be withheld and aid might stop altogether. The Communist noose tightened around Qingdao, though the Kuomintang still held a narrow corridor along the rail line to Beijing in the north and Shanghai and Canton to the south. Everyone with the means now fled to Shanghai, Canton, Hong Kong, or across the sea to Taiwan or even Japan. The flight was turning into an exodus. The official Chinese currency was almost worthless. On payday, workers turned sacks of money into food and fuel as quickly as possible before prices changed again. Despite instant executions for those who were caught, people bartered feverishly with U.S. dollars, gold, or jewels.

Preoccupied with its own survival, the government forgot my father. Knowing that the Ministry of Justice could incarcerate him as long as it pleased, he urged Mother to get out as soon as possible and take me with her, promising to join us when he could. Mother, however, would not go without him.

Things happened swiftly. A few well-oiled palms and Mr. Shi had travel documents for me. Meanwhile, Tim had found a boarding school in Hong Kong. "You'll get a proper education now," Father beamed, studying the brochure. He greatly admired the British school system. Indeed, pictures of grey granite buildings surrounded by vast green playing fields, neat classrooms, smiling masters in academic gowns, and happy students, many of them Eurasian, dispelled my fears of being a fish out of water again.

There was peace in his face when my father said, "Go as far as you can. Learn as much as you can. But don't forget China. . . ."

I threw my arms around him, needing something solid and rooted to hold on to. Now that my leaving had become a certainty, I could not say whether I was glad or sad. From then on, Father and I treated each visit as if it were the last, compressing years into a few hours.

As I had to travel by way of Shanghai, Father asked me to visit his mother. Even by his account, Grandmother was a formidable old woman. Xenophobic to the core, she refused to acknowledge the foreign women Father had married, or their progeny. Nor was there any assurance she would receive me. Nevertheless, Mr. Shi wrote ahead on Father's instruction.

"Be respectful," Father cautioned. "Since you were not brought up in the Confucian tradition, you need not kow-tow."

Mr. Shi withdrew me from school, which I left without regret, but Father insisted I return to bid Brother Feng a proper farewell.

"So you're scuttling off like the other rats," Brother Feng sneered across his desk, on which I laid my Boy Scout uniform, cap, staff, and the rope I had coiled in a messy lump, the best I could do. I kept the pocket knife and the badge.

"This ship won't sink! Mark my word, you'll be whining to come back but we won't have you!"

"I'll never come back!"

Brother Feng's mouth twisted into strange shapes. "Ungrateful half-breed!" he yelled, reaching for his cane.

"I'm not afraid of you, sir," I said with a recklessness I'd never known before.

"What did you say?"

"You've been afraid of me since that day in the cellar."

Brother Feng brought his cane down hard on his desk. "Get out!"

"You're no hero."

"Get out I said!"

I crossed the room unhurriedly, pausing at the door. Brother Feng was supporting himself with both hands on his desk. He'd broken his cane in half. "You're a fake," I said. "A coward. And a bully."

I had one more errand. Maria Contini used to visit her husband's grave every Sunday after Mass, in the little churchyard, which contained no more than four or five graves. She always brought flowers or sprigs of pine, cedar, or holly from her garden as the seasons changed. Before she left she had said to me, "You go sometimes to see Giuseppe . . . yes?" I'd promised I would.

Giuseppe had been long dead when I came to Qingdao, but Maria had talked about him so often, and I had seen so many photographs, that I felt I knew him. Using the tap the gardener used for watering plants, I wet the rag I'd brought and wiped the white marble gravestone till it shone. I looked around for something to replace Maria's last, long-withered flowers, but the churchyard was bare.

On the wind I could hear, distantly, someone playing the organ in the cathedral. Not the wild shrieks, groans, and yells of a demented god that Brother Feng produced, but the peaceful sounds of Bach or perhaps Handel. The sound drew me into the church. The music, the flickering candles, the light streaming through stained-glass windows, the pious faces of saints, the mingled smell of incense and flowers wove its ancient spell on me. My bony knees on the wooden pew ached distantly, pain through osmosis. Hail Mary full of grace . . . Our Father . . . Give us this day . . . Shao's voice, pure, rapturous. . . . It seemed so long ago. . . .

The tiny red lamp in front of the altar meant God was present. I wanted desperately to believe He was. I needed answers to life's great riddles. What had happened to Shao? What would happen to my father? What lay ahead for me? An inner voice told me I would not find answers here. The music, incense, candlelight, and flowers were real enough, but the rest was smoke and mirrors.

I grabbed a bunch of flowers from the Virgin Mary's shrine, returned to the churchyard, and put them on Giuseppe Contini's grave.

Approaching footsteps made me get to my feet. I turned and found myself staring into the archbishop's round, bespectacled face, only he was not the archbishop any more – he had been made a cardinal soon after the war ended. He extended his hand theatrically for me to kiss his ring. I shook his hand instead. He looked at me quizzically, surprised by the breach of protocol. Then he smiled, and for a moment he was the man I used to think of as a living saint, the sweet fellow who shared our Sunday lunch and pruned our roses with Mother.

"What are you doing?" he asked, not unkindly.

"Cleaning Giuseppe Contini's grave."

"I see. And where is Mrs. Contini?"

"Gone to her son in America."

The cardinal sighed. "Everyone is leaving."

"I am too," I volunteered.

This briefly piqued his curiosity. He asked questions – Where was I going? How was my mother? Was my father holding up all right? – but I could see he was not really interested in the answers. The armed military guard who followed him shifted his weight impatiently. The cardinal gave me his pulpit smile.

"Is there anything we can do for you?" he asked, extending his ring again.

"No thank you, sir," I said, ignoring the ring.

He snatched his hand back. He had stopped smiling.

"Your father is a good man," he said stiffly. "We would like to help, but mother church cannot involve herself in politics." He made a quick sign of the cross. "We will pray for him."

He started for his house in slow, stately strides, his red cloak billowing behind him. I stared daggers into his back. Without my father's intervention, the Japanese would have razed the church, the two schools, and his house. He would not be wearing his red hat and offering his gaudy ring for people to kiss. Yet he wouldn't even speak to Mr. Shi, let alone give a deposition on my father's behalf. To think I had once admired the man!

Mother was sanguine about my leaving home once she got used to the idea. It was time to loosen the apron strings and she did it coolly. I had the impression a great deal went on in her head. There were many worries, not the least of which was money. She still had a job, but the writing was on the wall. Often she gazed morosely at the frayed cushions, curtains, and slipcovers in our living room, pensively rubbing her sapphire ring. By early 1947 she must have been down to the last jewellery she had. Nevertheless, she scraped together enough money to buy me a brown tweed sport jacket and grey flannel pants.

"Your father always looked like a gentleman," she said. "So should you, under any circumstances."

The bag she packed for me contained only necessities, except for a cigar box holding a few treasures – Rex's red leather collar with a tiny bell attached; a few marbles I had won from Buzzy and Donald; the wrapper of a Hershey bar dropped from an airplane; a crystal that shone like gold which Xiao Hu had brought up from the bottom of the sea. There were reminders of less happy times too – a pocket knife and badge from the Boy Scouts, and the Marine's badge Shao had given me, which sent an arrow through my chest every time I looked at it.

Leave-taking with Mother was like trudging up a muddy hill. Keeping a stiff upper lip, she withdrew into silence. Words left unsaid and gestures withheld created a separateness I could not overcome. Again I longed for Shu Ma, who would have understood and to whom I could have confided my deepest fears and anxieties.

Zhang exhibited more emotion. "You're too young to leave the nest," he mused, trying for a light tone.

"No, I'm not," I retorted, "I'm almost thirteen!"

He shook his head ruefully. "I hoped to see you grown up. Married. With your own children. I guess I won't now . . ."

"Of course you will. We'll be together again. You'll see . . ."

Zhang nodded sadly, misty-eyed.

I saw Father one last time. Though it was early February and bitterly cold, we spent the hour strolling in the garden. Nothing dimmed Father's enthusiasm as he prepared me to fend for myself.

"The world is a wonderful place," he said. "When I went abroad as a young man I was afraid, too. But you'll find people are pretty much the same everywhere, though they may speak a different language and their skin is a different shade. As long as you are true to yourself, you can't be false to anyone else. And that is really all that matters. . . ."

Knowing it was our last visit, the guard, well supplied with Lucky Strikes, allowed Father to see me to the front gate.

Father put a clod of hard yellow earth in my hand. "Keep this," he said, and squeezed my fingers tightly around it. "It's a bit of China. One day, a long time from now, when you are able, come back." Later, I would add that clod of earth to my treasures. My childhood in a cigar box.

"Will you and Mother be here?"

He cupped my face in his hands. "I don't think so."

At that moment I hated China so much it was hard to breathe.

"Then why should I come back?"

"To do something worthwhile. You'll know, when the time comes."

I slipped the clod of earth in my pocket.

"Promise?"

"I promise."

We embraced, stepped apart, and bowed deeply. With a bored grunt, the guard let me out.

The fighting between Chiang's demoralized forces and the Communists was inching ever closer to Qingdao. Gunfire that used to wake us in the night could be heard above the traffic's roar even during the day. The newspapers pointedly ignored it, or exaggerated each small Kuomintang advantage into a major victory. The fighting seemed to centre on the railway line and the airport. One night hundreds of junks sailed majestically into the harbour. Mother, Zhang, and I watched from our terrace as they tacked in the wind, weaving through the crossed beams of the searchlights stationed on the two arms of the C-shaped harbour. We were sure it was a landing. Instead, the junks swept around the harbour and headed back out to sea, sails billowing. Neither side fired a shot but the message was unmistakable. The Communists could have landed that night without opposition. The Kuomintang forces were laying down their arms everywhere, and the Americans were steadily pulling out, determined not to be drawn into a useless fight.

It was a time of anxious waiting for Tim to wire a ticket. Flights were crammed, and Tim had written that I must be ready on short notice. I scarcely left the house. It was bitterly cold; even when the sun shone there was little warmth. The black-green pines clutched the wintering garden in a frosty embrace. I sat shivering in the tree house, gazing at the slate-grey sea. Except for the white walls and the red tiled roofs of the town, everything was grey. I played the records the admiral and his wife had left me hour after hour, always going back to a few pieces that struck a chord within me. The funeral march and scherzo from Beethoven's "Eroica," Schubert's melancholy yet noble unfinished eighth, Mendelssohn's genial D Minor Piano Trio. I knew I might never again see Father and

Mother and Zhang, for the insatiable world that had swallowed Shao was snapping at my heels.

Finally the call came. A ticket and reservation was held for me on a flight the following day. "Because of sporadic fighting near the airport," the operator yelled into the telephone, "planes land, refuel, and take off as quickly as possible. Schedules mean nothing, so be there early."

Mother rang off with a shudder and a sad smile. "We're ready," she said.

There were no desperate last goodbyes, just a few words of advice.

"Always have at least one set of clean underwear and socks. Take your vitamins, brush your teeth, keep your nails trimmed and your shoes polished. Especially your shoes. Father says nothing marks a gentleman more than the condition of his shoes."

When I left, Mother was exactly as she had been the day Perry sailed. There were no smiles, no tears, just a silent resignation. With one hand she shaded her eyes, with the other she held down her skirt, which was flapping in the wind.

17

第十七章

SHANGHAI

I MUST HAVE DOZED most of the way to Shanghai. Suddenly
the steady hum of the airplane ceased, and a stewardess with a
fixed smile was shoving me down the ramp, gripping my elbow.
The stewardess hustled me blearily through the teeming terminal.
Somewhere along the way she had acquired my small suitcase. I
felt myself propelled towards the swarm of humanity plastered
against a glass door. As it opened, a blast of cold air jarred me
awake. I seemed to have blundered into an alien world where people jabbered in a strange, strident language I did not understand.

Albert and his wife, Mei, were waiting outside. Albert greeted
me profusely. He was thinner than I remembered. His face had a
greenish tint that made me uneasy.

"Where's the money?" he asked in the very next breath.

"Mother did not send any money," I said carefully, even though
lip-reading was second nature to Albert. The light faded from his
eyes. He searched my suitcase the moment we reached his apartment but came up empty. From then on he ignored me.

Shanghai was dirty, noisy, overcrowded, a city in perpetual
motion. The boundaries of race and caste that once gave it form and
shaped its prosperity had disappeared at the end of the war. Now all
was chaos. Hong Ciao, where Albert lived, was a squalid warren of

damp, sweating streets lined with grim, soot-blackened tenements. The fetid air smarted the eyes and burned the lungs. It was a place of blaring radios, shrieking children, gossiping women, and shouting men. Pimps and drug pushers loitered in shadowy doorways. Dance hostesses and courtesans with chalk-white faces rode in rickshaws with their names engraved on brass plates fixed to the sides.

Albert's apartment, on the top floor of a three-storey red brick building, was one large room. A huge wardrobe separated the brass bed that he shared with his wife from a living area that contained a folding camp cot for me. In another corner was a crib where their colicky baby cried incessantly. Plywood partitions divided the far end into a tiny kitchen and a cubicle containing a slop pail. Damp diapers festooned the apartment like bunting. The windows facing the street were opaque from caked-on filth.

Li Li, a silent girl about my age with enormous sad eyes, did the chores. Mei had found her abandoned on the front stoop and taken her in. Li Li became Mei's *ya to*, or unpaid servant. Mei was a fat, shrewish, slovenly woman who did nothing but order the poor girl around. Although the practice of indenturing young girls, often for life, was banned, the prohibition was never enforced. In exchange for food, clothes, and a place to live, Li Li toiled from dawn till late at night. Afraid of being sold or turned out, she strove to please.

Albert's arrogance and acid tongue had already cost him one good job in Shanghai. Civil aviation, the up-and-coming new field, needed bright young people. Through Tim, who knew his way around the industry, Albert had been hired by China's alternative carrier, CATC. Most people would have given their eye-teeth to be part of a young, forward-looking company, but not Albert. Within a short time the job palled. He whined that his talents were wasted and the wages much less than he deserved.

Still, there was no dearth of gaiety on payday. Albert and Mei lived close to the edge. Perhaps rocketing inflation, the looming Communist threat, sudden arrests, and summary executions drove them to excess. Victor and Judy, who lived in equally squalid conditions around the corner, shared their feverish pursuit of pleasure. A burly airline pilot and war buddy of Tim's, Victor had probably befriended Albert for Tim's sake. The two men had nothing in common. Judy, who came from an old moneyed family of Suzhou and had a western education, was just as indolent and bored as Mei, but intelligent and fiercely independent. The two women, one from the north, the other from the south, were inseparable. As soon as Albert left in the morning, Judy came over. The two gossiped while Li Li juggled caring for the baby, doing chores, and running out for pastries or whatever else her mistress and Judy fancied.

Being street-smart and resourceful, Li Li stretched the food money further than Mei could imagine. With the baby strapped to her back, she took me shopping with her one day. After we'd left the apartment, Li Li handed me the cloth sack she had. "You carry the money," she said. "I'll need both hands. And for heaven's sake hang onto the money!"

She moved slowly through the market, checking the produce laid out in baskets and scrutinizing the stall-keepers. The more people clustered round a stall, the better she liked it. She never seemed to be interested in anything particular, but her hands were busy. A head of cabbage, a sprig of leeks, a few apples found their way into the bag slung around her neck under her coat. She grinned at me and wrinkled her nose.

"Isn't this fun?"

"It's stealing. What if you get caught?"

"But I won't," she replied impishly.

We stopped at a pastry shop. Mei had asked for a dozen hot pork dumplings. Li Li waited till several matrons were crowded around the counter, all jabbering in Shanghainese that sounded to my northern ear like quarrelling. Then she pushed her way to the front. The jostling made the baby cry. One of the women turned on Li Li.

"Little *ya to*, have you no manners?"

The baby roared.

"Look what you've done!" cried Li Li. "Now you've upset the baby. And what happened to my money?" She turned out her pockets. "You made me lose my money!" Confronting the matrons like an angry hen, Li Li sobbed, "She made me lose my money! It's all her fault. Now the baby won't have any lunch!"

The other women began nattering at the supposed culprit, who vociferously defended herself. Li Li was convincing. The women, strangers to one another, were soon ready to slug it out. The worried shopkeeper, desperate to make peace, scooped a few hot dumplings into a paper bag.

"Here, little girl, take them and go."

Li Li took one look at them and bawled harder.

The first woman slammed money on the counter.

"Shopkeeper, give her what she wants," she said, and, wheeling triumphantly on the others, challenged, "Let's see you put your money where your mouths are."

We came away with a dozen dumplings and some little cakes filled with sweet bean paste, not having spent a cent. "Promise not to tell," Li Li cautioned anxiously, throwing away a piece of onion wrapped in her handkerchief. The onion fumes produced her tears.

Cash was always short between pay cheques, and one morning Judy asked Mei, as if I weren't even there, "Did your brother-in-law bring money?" It sounded like a gentle reminder that Judy expected Mei to repay a loan.

Mei blew on her freshly lacquered nails, making a face.

"It's like that, is it?"

Mei waved her hands in the air irritably. "What can you expect! The old man's a jailbird. He should have given it to Albert before Chiang Kai-shek grabbed it!"

"My father's not a jailbird!" I cried. "Take it back."

Mei narrowed her eyes. "I say what I please in my house."

Their conversation continued in rapid-fire Shanghainese. I did not understand a word, but I knew it was about me, and money.

I expected to stay in Shanghai just long enough to visit my grandmother, but days passed and Albert averted his eyes whenever I spoke of her. Mei also kept putting me off. I felt utterly helpless.

One night Albert and Mei came in late. They began berating each other for losing at mah-jong in the street. By the time they reached the apartment, words escalated to blows that finally ended in violent sex. The joyless coupling – a brutal contest of wills, the expression of despair, mutual hate, and self-loathing – was a horrible nightmare for the boy on the other side of the wardrobe, trying to shut out the beastly noises with a pillow wrapped around his head.

Next day Mei was still asleep when Judy arrived with the late edition of the morning paper. Judy pointed out the headlines to Mei, who was groggy with sleep. The government had issued a new currency, and people had until the banks closed at three in the afternoon to exchange their paper money before it turned into trash. The announcement was probably timed deliberately to catch people unprepared. It was already noon. Judy raced out without waiting, and Mei dressed faster than I'd ever seen her do anything.

"Come with me!" she yelled, dragging a pillowcase bulging with bundles of money from under her bed.

The crowd in the street was so thick that nothing moved. People came from all directions, carrying suitcases, shoeboxes, brown paper bags stuffed with money. Cars honked; engines overheated; buses and trolleys inched forward, the passengers wedged half in and half out of windows and doors.

"Keep moving! Keep moving!" Mei yelled, using her bulk like a battering ram. I followed, clutching the pillowcase.

A wall of humanity separated us from the bank across the street. People were trying to scramble over the heads and shoulders of those in front of them. Someone fell. There was a scream and a roar, and the human wave surged forward. I felt something soft and slippery underfoot, but dared not look down. The crowd squeezed me so tightly that my lungs ached for air. For an awful moment I lost sight of Mei; then, inexplicably, we were both pressed against the iron shutters of the bank. It was after two o'clock. Only one person was being let in as one was let out.

On the other side of the barrier stood a man in his twenties, built like a wrestler, wearing a Boy Scout uniform. He looked mean, probably a draft dodger. Mei was determined to thrust herself through the moment the shutter opened.

"My little brother is holding my money bag right behind me," she gasped, her eyes going big and soft. The man peered around her and I gave him the Boy Scout salute. He grinned and returned the greeting.

"Which troop?"

I responded with my troop and serial number in a crisp, high voice.

"You're a long way from home, little brother."

"Visiting my grandmother, sir. This is actually for her." I struggled to show him the pillowcase.

When the next person came out, he let us in. The banking hall, though packed, was deathly quiet. Soldiers with fingers on the triggers of their rifles stood around the gallery overlooking the hall. The clock dominating the front wall ticked loudly. A fierce struggle to reach the tellers was under way. People lashed out at one another without making a sound. Mei had caught her second wind and, signalling with her eyes for me to follow, somehow cut a swath through the crowd with elbows and knees. By now it was ten to three. One person was in front of us and the teller was taking his time. Mei reached around him, grabbed the bars of the teller's cage, and pulled herself forward, squeezing the man against the counter. He tried to push her away but she had him pinned.

Five minutes more.

The crowd behind rocked forward, like waves pummelling the shore, the rhythm quickening as the seconds ticked by. The man finally turned around to go, and Mei slammed against the counter. I handed her the money.

In the street the crowd was chanting, "Four! . . . Three! . ."

Mei begged the teller to hurry. He gave her a blank stare, rattling the beads of his abacus abstractedly.

"Two. . . !"

The teller calmly reached into his cash drawer and began dol-
ing out bundles of the new notes.

"One!"

Mei scooped the money into the pillowcase. The people behind
us stopped rocking. The guards in the gallery pointed their guns
down at us.

"Zero!"

A bell clanged and the wicket shut with a bang. A roar went up
in the street. Inside, the crowd collected itself, gathering force for
one desperate rush at the cages. The safety catches on the guard's
rifles clicked off. A voice shouted over the loudspeaker, "The bank
is closed. Leave by the side doors when they open. Any disorder
and we will shoot to kill!"

The opening doors seemed to suck us out of the building. Mei
had lost a shoe. She kicked the other one off and stood on the curb
barefoot, clutching her pillowcase of money, heaving noisily. There
was a curious carnival atmosphere. Banknotes fluttered out of
windows like snowflakes, gathering ankle deep on the pavement,
while people shouted and laughed, pelting each other with hand-
fuls of useless million-yuen notes.

Mei was soaking in a tub of hot water while Li Li rubbed tiger balm
on her bruises, and I – having been banished – was sitting on the
front stoop when Albert came home. I heard Mei yelling, the
sounds of a fight; then Li Li came down with the baby, howling. Li Li
sat down beside me and crooned softly till the baby stopped crying.
When it was quiet, Li Li motioned me to follow her upstairs.

Albert was holding a wet cloth against an eye almost swollen shut.
Mei obviously gave as good as she got. The fight was not quite over.

"Don't turn your back on me!" Mei screamed, grabbing Albert
by the scruff of his neck and forcing him to face her. "Your grandmother has money. Why don't you try her? You're the first-born.
Why should she see the brat and not you? If you're afraid to stand
up for your rights, I'm not!"

Next morning Mei put on her best dress and shouted for Li Li to hire her a rickshaw. She left without saying goodbye.

"She's gone to see your Thirteenth Uncle," Li Li whispered as she bathed the baby. "She wants to get rid of you." Li Li's greatest fear was being homeless again.

"I don't want to stay here," I replied.

"But where will you go?"

"To school."

Later in the day Mei returned with a colourless, bespectacled man in a long scholar's robe of blue silk, a black waistcoat, and a black skull-cap with a red top knot. In his early thirties, Uncle Thirteen was the epitome of a feudal Chinese gentleman, completely unlike my father. My grandmother was like the old woman in the shoe – she had so many children, she called them by numbers. Thirteen was her youngest. My father was Six.

Uncle Thirteen had been expecting me ever since he received Mr. Shi's letter. That he had not immediately been informed of my arrival had already earned Mei a sharp tongue-lashing. The squalid surroundings he found himself in offended him further. Mei brushed clothes off her best chair and offered it to Uncle. He glanced at it disdainfully and remained standing.

"This must be my nephew," he said in Mandarin, waving a scented handkerchief in my direction.

I bowed. "I'm pleased to meet you, Uncle," I said in well-rehearsed Chinese. "I trust Grandmother is well? How are my aunt and cousins?"

Uncle Thirteen was taken aback. "Ah, you speak Chinese." He signalled me to spin around, while he inspected me as though I were an exotic animal. "I suppose you won't be too much of a shock," he said. "As a rule Mother doesn't allow foreigners in the house." He inspected me again. "Do you speak English?"

"I most certainly do, sir."

"We do not," snapped Uncle Thirteen. "We will converse in Chinese."

"Yes, sir."

"His clothes won't do," Uncle Thirteen observed.

Before Mei could respond, I chimed in, saying I had a sports jacket and pants, and a nice shirt and tie to go with it.

"You'll dress like a Chinese gentleman."

"I'll look silly, sir! I won't do it."

"You'll do as your uncle says!" gasped Mei in disbelief. Uncle frowned, waved the handkerchief before his nose to banish the unfamiliar odours assailing it, and headed for the door.

"We must press on. Come, boy."

Mei offered to accompany us, but Uncle waved her back. "Just the boy. I'll return him, never fear."

Uncle hailed a taxi. We drove a short distance around the corner, then Uncle told the driver to stop. He paid the fare, holding the greasy notes between thumb and forefinger with the studied disdain for money his caste loved to display. We walked to a row of rickshaws for hire at the next corner. Uncle chose a wide-bodied vehicle for two passengers and haggled with the puller in voluble Shanghainese. Finally they struck a deal. We climbed on, went a few blocks, and stopped in front of an imposing tailor shop. Uncle remained seated till the doorman rushed to hand him onto the pavement with many bows and smiles, and then to do the same for me. Uncle grandly ordered him to pay the rickshaw man, and sailed into the shop.

I was to be measured for a robe.

"Uncle, I refuse to wear it!" I protested.

The tailor raised an eyebrow, which Uncle Thirteen ignored.

"You recall the robe you made my son for the new year?" He did not wait for a response. "Use the same stuff. Send the bill to the old lady." He paused and, lowering his voice, added, "I expect my usual cut." The tailor lowered his lids.

We were out of the shop in a trice, and on another rickshaw. Doorman and tailor bowed from the pavement. The rickshaw dropped us at a taxi rank around the block from Albert's apartment, where we switched to a cab. As we drew up in front of the building, Uncle had the driver honk loudly so people would notice.

"I'll see you in three days, boy," he said.

On the third day Uncle Thirteen returned with a box under his arm. Albert had taken the day off and Mei had dressed herself in party clothes. Albert was bursting with excitement, determined to storm the forbidding bastions of my grandmother's house, his mind aswirl with possibilities. Since the old lady held the purse strings of my grandfather's considerable estate, who knew what might rub off if he played his cards right?

I balked at wearing the blue silk robe.

"You'll look wonderful in it," Mei pleaded. "Blue is your colour."

I stood my ground. Uncle looked at me as though I was an insect. "Your grandmother wouldn't like it if you failed to dress properly," he said in sepulchral tones.

"My grandmother won't know the difference," I retorted. "She's blind."

Mei was the first to react. "What a terrible thing to say," she said shrilly. "Apologize!"

"It's true. I won't look silly for nothing!"

There was a malicious glint in Uncle Thirteen's eye. "Do you know the protocol on meeting your grandmother for the first time?"

"I will bow."

"You will kow-tow!" he growled through small white teeth.

"My father forbids it."

"Your father has no say," Uncle Thirteen hotly declared. "Here, I tell you what to do."

"My father is older than you. I follow his instructions, not yours." I took off my jacket and sat down on my cot. "I'm not going."

Uncle Thirteen swayed on his heels as though he had been struck. Mei rushed to him, yelling at me to behave. Albert, who had been lip-reading, seized the moment.

"Uncle, I'm my father's first-born and his legal heir. Let me be presented to Grandmother instead of the little pip-squeak." He flung the wardrobe open. "I have the right clothes, and I'll gladly kow-tow according to tradition."

Uncle Thirteen shook his head wearily. "My mother wishes the boy, not you." He barked at me, "Put on your jacket!"

"I'm not kow-towing," I insisted.

Uncle Thirteen gritted his teeth, then propelled me down the stairs to the taxi waiting at the curb.

Grandmother's compound was located in what had been the French Concession. A high wall enclosed three two-storeyed western-style buildings, facing a courtyard with a fountain and a pond stocked with red and white carp. Grandmother occupied the main building; the families of her two youngest sons occupied the other two. Both men were supposedly in business, though neither seemed to work.

Uncle Twelve was waiting for us by the gate. He shook my hand absentmindedly and grumbled at his brother, "What took so long? You know what a stickler she is about being punctual for meals."

Uncle Twelve was a plump little man with a ready smile and a hearty handshake. Unlike his younger brother, he preferred western clothes and did not put on aristocratic airs.

"The kid looks vaguely like Brother Six." Uncle Twelve took it for granted I did not speak Chinese.

"Exactly like him in temperament," sniffed Uncle Thirteen. Uncle Twelve glanced at me speculatively and started to say something, but we were already on the threshold of a long rectangular room, and the major domo was announcing us in a high, reedy sing-song.

It was a darkly severe room. The smell of candle wax and incense hung in the air. At the far end was an ancestral shrine, from which my grandfather's photograph gazed down on his descendants with dreamer's eyes. Grandmother, regal in her Manchu court dress and a black satin cap adorned with a large egg-shaped jade, sat on a richly carved ebony chair, flanked by the wives and children of the two uncles. She was an octogenarian, stone blind but feisty. A clock chimed the hour from one of the dim recesses of the room.

"About time!" the old lady snapped. "Approach!"

Slowly I made my way with the two uncles past the curious glances of aunts, cousins, and servants hovering in the background. Grandmother's little Pekinese seeing-eye dog yawned and cocked its head at me. We stopped a few paces from her chair. Uncle Twelve caught my eye and inclined his head towards the floor, mouthing the word "kow-tow." I shook my head.

The uncles exchanged a look. Suddenly they seized me from either side and tried to force me to my knees. We grappled.

"What's the scuffling about?" Grandmother asked lightly. The old lady ruled the household with a steel fist in a velvet glove. The uncles let go of me. The assemblage held its breath.

"He . . . that is, the boy . . . *refuses* . . . to kow-tow," Uncle Thirteen stammered.

Grandmother's brows knit into storm clouds.

"Grandmother" – I recited the speech Father had composed, slowly but clearly – "I bring my father's greetings. He detests kow-towing, and forbids me to do it. Nevertheless, I offer my most respectful felicitations."

I bowed thrice. There was a murmur of surprise. Evidently Uncle Thirteen had not mentioned to her that I knew Chinese. Grandmother leaned forward, an amused grin tugging at her lips. The little dog leapt from her lap to sniff at my heels, growling and baring its teeth.

"Boy, since you won't greet me according to our customs, greet me as you would your foreign mother." The word "foreign" was used not to hurt but to emphasize a difference. I looked about uncertainly. The dog seized my pant leg and would not let go, so I dragged it along. Some of the children tittered.

"Are you afraid of me?"

Blind people with open eyes usually make me queasy, but not her. "No, Grandmother," I said, and quickly kissed her on both cheeks.

"Oh!" she leaned away, waving her hand in front of her face. "All this slobbering!" But she was beaming.

She grasped my shoulders with her small strong hands and felt me. Arms, legs, torso, head, face. "You have number Six's forehead . . . and your grandfather's eyebrows . . . probably his eyes too. Are you a dreamer?" Before I could reply, a murmur rippled through the room, which quickly subsided when Grandmother clapped her hands. "Number Six is the worst kind of romantic." She went back to feeling my face. "The nose . . . is from your mother. Stubborn chin, but . . . long ear lobes . . . Maybe life won't be too harsh on you. Too thin, however . . ." She let go of me abruptly, and got to her feet. "We dine."

A round table for adults was set at the far end of the long dining room. To one side were two more tables for the children and their nannies. There were about thirty people when we were seated. Grandmother wanted me next to her, in the seat Uncle Twelve usually occupied. He objected.

"Oblige me, Twelve," Grandmother said with laughter in her voice; nevertheless, it was a tone that brooked no argument. Uncle Twelve glared at me but surrendered the prized seat.

The major domo hovering behind Grandmother's chair announced each dish as it was laid on the Lazy Susan in the centre of the table. Uncle Twelve, ever attentive, nudged me to serve Grandmother when her particular favourites were presented. Chicken braised in a spicy sweet sauce with almonds and peppers; bean curd stir-fried with spinach and garlic; a melon stuffed with slivers of ham, bamboo shoots, and mushrooms. She ate with great delicacy, manipulating her chopsticks with grace, never dropping a morsel. She was full of questions. I described Father, and Mother, and the house we lived in as it used to be. She asked about my education. Did I read and write Chinese? She was pleasantly surprised I did. Did I know the poetry of Tang and Soong? And who were my favourite poets? Without hesitation, I said, "Li Bai and Wang Wei."

Grandmother laid down her chopsticks, cocked her head to one side, and slowly recited the first line of a poem, which I shall translate as best I can.

"The moon sets, the raven cries, frost fills the air . . ." She paused. "Do any of you children know the next line?"

There were a few nervous giggles.

"I learned that one in school," muttered Uncle Thirteen's daughter. No one else spoke.

"I know it, Grandmother," I chirped. It was one of the first poems my tutor, Master Chien, had had me memorize.

Grandmother turned to me. "Show them."

Adopting the same cadence as Grandmother, I intoned the next line:

"Fishermen's fires glowing on maple leaves stir my uneasy slumber."

A smile spread slowly across Grandmother's face as she spoke the next line: "From Han Shan Temple outside Gusoo City . . ."

". . . the midnight chime floats to my lonely skiff."

It was a poem about loneliness – a bird's cry, firelight, the sound of a distant bell magnifying the feeling of isolation. Perhaps Grandmother was thinking about my solitary journey when she chose that poem, which has remained close to my heart ever since.

The game continued. Grandmother recited one line and I supplied the next until one of us, usually me, could not continue. She and I had fun together; the others in the room did not. The two uncles made a great show of yawning from boredom. Their wives gossiped under their breath, using many hand signals, lest the old lady catch them out. The children fidgeted. The older ones shot angry looks at me for having upstaged them. The nannies did their best to keep the young children quiet. Servants cleared away the debris after the meal, and poured tea for everyone. No doubt Grandmother was aware of all this by-play, but she was enjoying herself, and it was well into the afternoon when we left the table.

Grandmother was tired but happy. Her little dog, as jealous as the humans around me, nipped at my ankles. When it was time to leave, Grandmother said, "Bid me goodbye the way you would your mother." This time she did not say "foreign." I kissed her on both cheeks, to the consternation of all present. She took my head between her hands and felt my face once more.

"You are an imp!" she exclaimed, " like your father. Go quickly." In a whisper, she added, "Lest I'm tempted to keep you."

Uncle Thirteen was silent in the taxi to Albert's, his eyes straight ahead, as though I did not exist. Our worlds had intersected briefly and would now resume their separate courses. I knew nothing about him and felt no curiosity. The taxi drew up to Albert's tenement building. I got out and I bowed to Uncle Thirteen as the taxi pulled away, but I do not think he cared to notice.

As the KMT government's credibility eroded, and China's economic situation deteriorated, the student movement became increasingly strident. Soon it was joined by a worker's movement, protesting the high cost of living and the hunger it caused. These demonstrations resulted in increased repression, which in turn prompted a mass exodus of the business class and the intellectuals out of China. Airline tickets were at a premium.

At this critical time, both CNAC and CATC suffered a series of crashes caused by the mixing of water with fuel, and gross overloading. When news broke that both carriers faced grounding, the impending shutdown prompted a riot. Mobs stormed airline ticket offices; the army, called in to restore order, fired on the rioters. The gory photos in the newspaper next morning made me tremble. For the first time since leaving Qingdao, I wondered if I would get out of China.

Albert was still chafing at Grandmother's rejection. Now the possibility of losing his job in an airline shutdown added to his chagrin. As we sat glumly at our evening meal and rain lashed the window, Victor, just back from Hong Kong, burst in without knocking. He was still wearing his pilot's uniform.

"You swine!" he snarled, waving a letter which Albert, turning quite red, tried to snatch from him. Holding Albert by the chin, Victor forced him to lip-read.

"Using the boy to extort money from your father is despicable. The boy's mother sent your letter to Tim, and he gave it to me."

Albert lunged for it again and Victor slapped him, hard. Albert fell on the bed whimpering, "Money . . . my money."

"It's none of your business!" Mei yelled at Victor.

"They'll shoot you both for kidnap and extortion if I turn this in!" Victor pocketed the letter.

Mei started to blubber.

"Get the boy's things," Victor shouted at her, "and pray he gets on the next flight." I did not wait for Mei but started throwing my few belongings into my suitcase. Abruptly I left Albert's apartment with its reek of sour lives.

Victor drove me to the airport in teeming rain. He parked the car and bulldozed his way through the milling crowd in the terminal. The clerk behind the counter blinked at Victor's pilot's uniform and quickly checked me in. We moved into the waiting room, which was packed. Again, Victor's uniform parted the crowd.

I found myself plastered against the glass embarkation gate. Victor pointed out the c-47 I would board. It was there on the tarmac, surrounded by fuelling trucks and baggage wagons, blurred by the torrential rain. Thunder and lightning shredded the night sky. The runway lights came on.

"Something's coming in," Victor said.

I strained to see, and just as I made out a dark shape streaking towards the runway, there was a terrific scream of metal and a loud explosion. A fireball whooshed past us and down the embankment beside the runway. People cried out. Alarm bells rang, and an ancient fire engine went barrelling towards the flaming wreck. I pressed my face to the glass; behind me someone bellowed, "It crashed! It crashed!" I felt as though I had stepped out of my skin.

Victor was shaking me, slapping me across the face. "Snap out of it!" He shook me till my teeth rattled. "David! David! Listen to me!"

An announcement over the loudspeaker, garbled by the noise around me, made everyone hysterical. There was total bedlam as people tried to get out of the room but found the doors locked.

Victor was yelling at me, something about the airport being shut down. I stared at his mouth, trying to understand.

"Do you want to go?"

I couldn't speak.

He shook me again. "Do you?"

"What?"

"It may be your last chance!"

"Go," I murmured.

"Good boy!"

The embarkation door opened and people began stampeding through. Victor grabbed me round the waist and we sprinted out into the rain. In a blur of tears and confusion, I was shoved up the steps and onto the plane and put into a seat. Someone fastened my seatbelt. The ramp was hurriedly withdrawn and the fuel trucks pulled away. All the baggage still lay on the ground – I could make out my little suitcase – but the plane was already moving. I caught sight of Victor on the tarmac, hugging himself against the cold.

"Victor! Victor!" I cried, blindly tearing at the seatbelt.

The woman next to me put her arm around me. I stopped struggling and snuggled against her wet fur coat. She stroked my head, speaking in Shanghainese. I didn't understand a word, but her voice was comforting and presently I slept.

I woke with a start. The cabin lights were out, and the woman in the fur coat was snoring softly.

Instinctively my hand went to the secret pocket in the lining of my jacket. I was twelve years old. My travel document, one hundred U.S. dollars, and a scrap of paper with Tim's address and phone number was all I had in the world.

I peered out the little round window. We had climbed above the storm, and the night sky was full of stars.

尾聲

EPILOGUE

I N THE SPRING of 1948, while Chiang Kai-shek was stealthily moving the Kuomintang to Taiwan, the Ministry of Justice suddenly declared my father innocent of all charges. After two years of incarceration, he was freed. My parents and Zhang returned to Beijing. After more legal wrangling, the government unfroze Father's bank accounts. All but one had been emptied. The government refused to return my father's houses and land, however, instead offering him a diplomatic post, which he declined. Finally, through Mr. Shi's persistence, the government returned a few family heirlooms as a gesture of goodwill. One heirloom – a bronze stirrup that belonged to an ancestor in the second century A.D.– I still have today. Our house in the former Legation Quarter, looted by the KMT, remained sealed until the Red Guard torched it in the late 1960s.

Zhang stayed with my parents to the last. Father offered to take him to Hong Kong, but Zhang was getting old and did not want to leave his native city. He disappeared shortly after the Communists came to power in 1949.

My parents and I were reunited in Hong Kong in the summer of 1948. A year and a half in boarding school had wrought a change in me. I had turned into an awkward teen, reaching for manhood but not quite ready to put aside childish things. Once more Father, Mother, and I circled one another, trying to become a family again. As if by mutual consent, none of us spoke of the immediate past. It was not difficult to avoid the subject. The present was fraught with enough problems to keep us all occupied.

Father devoted the rest of his life to teaching and helping families separated by war. In this latter endeavour, he worked closely with Mr. Shi, who had settled in the United States.

Father had promised to reunite Mother with her sister in Australia. Australia had a whites-only immigration policy, however, and Mother wouldn't go without him. It was not until British and Australian laws were changed in the 1960s that they finally moved. They settled near Sydney, where Father died in 1964.

Albert and his family arrived in Hong Kong from Shanghai about the same time as my parents. Though he and Father reconciled, I had little to do with him. After our encounter in Shanghai, neither of us could bear to be in the same room together. For the rest of his life, Albert dreamed of finding Father's secret fortune. He died disappointed in 1997, two years after Tim.

Tim had been my guardian until my parents came to Hong Kong. The age gap and the lack of common interests militated against any closeness between us. I was in my forties before we were able to talk as equals.

Shortly before Tim died, he asked if I remembered having had drinks with him in the lobby of the Peninsula Hotel in Hong Kong, a long time ago. I recalled the occasion vividly. We had a table at the edge of the central aisle which, like the Bosphorus, divided the lobby into unmarked but nevertheless distinct halves. We were on the Asian side. I wondered what was on Tim's mind, since he had never invited me for drinks before (and never did so again).

Tim finally explained why we'd gone to the hotel that day. While we talked trivialities, a woman had been observing me from across the aisle. Marianne had been corresponding with Mother over the years, mainly about me. She was passing through Hong Kong, from nowhere to nowhere, and had written to Mother asking to see me. Mother refused at first, but was finally persuaded to allow Marianne see me in a public place. I had to be in the company of someone else, and there was to be no contact.

When I asked Tim what Marianne was like, his face fell. He could tell me nothing. After all those years, Father's injunction still stood. And so, as we had early in my life, Marianne and I passed each other like ships in the night.

Mother stayed on in Australia after Father's death, surviving him by more than thirty years. She was the kindest person imaginable, but distant. I think I went out of her life the day I left Qingdao. Though I tried to bridge the chasm between us, particularly after Father died, I could not. On my last trip to visit her in Australia, something her sister said made me twig. In the way very old people talk about the distant past, as though it had happened only yesterday, her sister said, "Ellen was always afraid of being left behind."

In that light, I began to understand why Mother never spoke of the Findlay-Wus after they left China, never answered Maria Contini's many letters, never mentioned Father after he died, and seldom wrote to me. To her, leaving was a personal affront. All of us, including Father, had committed that sin. I don't think she forgave any of us.

Mother's Day, 1997, was the sort of squally day that Australia experiences in late autumn. Fierce lashing storms alternated with splashes of brilliant sunshine. Mother and I were having a leisurely lunch at a restaurant overlooking a charming river in one of Sydney's sprawling suburbs. She was just short of ninety, very frail, but sharp as a tack. Her health was rapidly failing – both of us knew she was dying – but she was in fine fettle that day. We had lobster, her favourite, washed down with a bottle of Pouilly-Fuissé.

Mother was never easy to talk to, but that day our conversation rambled pleasantly. China had ceased to exist for her after she left it, but for some reason at lunch she talked about China – not about the place, but about people she had known.

With a trembling heart I asked, "What was Marianne like?"

She looked at me blankly. "I don't know who you mean," she said.

I felt as though a door had been slammed in my face. A little later, out of nowhere, Mother said, as though to herself, "I found my one true love in that awful place."

At that moment her eyes looked beyond me, perhaps beyond time itself. She smiled, not the sad half-smile I knew so well but a smile that lit up her whole being. She was beautiful.

"There's nothing more to say," she murmured, brushing her lips against my cheek. "Get on with your life."

We both knew we would not be together again. There was no sadness or regret. We had reached a fork in the road. It was time to let go, to move on. She died two months later.